The Warrior Queens
Boadicea's Chariot

~

ANTONIA FRASER

Volume Two

PHOENIX

This edition produced for The Book People Ltd,
Hall Wood Avenue, Haydock, St Helens WA11 9UL

First published in Great Britain in 1988
as *Boadicea's Chariot*
by George Weidenfeld & Nicolson Ltd
First published in paperback in 1993
by Mandarin Paperbacks

Paperback edition published in 2002
by Phoenix,
an imprint of Orion Books Ltd,
Orion House, 5 Upper St Martin's Lane,
London WC2H 9EA

A CIP catalogue record for this book is available from the British Library.

ISBN 978 1 4072 1527 3

Printed and bound in Great Britain by
Clays Ltd, St Ives plc

The Orion Publishing Group's policy is to use papers that are natural, renewable
and recyclable products and made from wood grown in sustainable forests. The
logging and manufacturing processed are expected to conform to the environmental
regulations of the country of origin.

www.orionbooks.co.uk

Contents

Part Two

CHAPTER NINE

Matilda, Daughter of Peter

~

The daughter of Peter and the faithful hand-maid of
Christ.

POPE GREGORY VII, to Matilda Countess of Tuscany

'To you, my most beloved and loving daughter, I do not
hesitate to disclose any of these thoughts, for even you
yourself can hardly imagine how greatly I may count
upon your zeal and discretion.' The writer of this letter in late
1074 was Pope Gregory VII. The 'most beloved and loving'
daughter in question was Matilda Countess of Tuscany, a woman
now in her late thirties, who had inherited vast dominions in
northern Italy from her father some twenty years back. As she
moved towards independence from the various tutelages of
mother and stepfather, increasingly she was acting as the 'faithful
hand-maid' of St Peter – a hand-maid with a sharp sword in her
hand and an army at her back.¹

The combination of Countess Matilda's prolonged military
endeavours with her own sense of a holy mission is what made
her egregious among her contemporaries: 'For St Peter and
Matilda!' her men shouted as they stormed the fortresses of the
Apennines while she termed herself 'Matilda by the Grace of
God'. It also inspired their admiration – if they were on the same
side.

The approval which Matilda received from her allies and subordinates, based on her gender, not despite it, clearly related to
the apparently 'holy' nature of her chosen role. The pious
Christian Matilda would not have relished a comparison to
pagan Boadicea, with her invocation to Andraste on the eve of
battle a thousand years earlier. As a matter of interest, she would

not even have recognized the allusion. Penthesilea was not forgotten and Matilda would receive the usual ration of such comparisons to the Amazonian Queen. However, not only had Boadicea vanished into her unknown grave but her very name had been forgotten, awaiting the rediscovery of Tacitus' manuscripts in a monastery library in the fourteenth century.[2] Yet Matilda's role represents an important aspect of the subject of the Warrior Queen, that of Holy (Armed) Figurehead. Just as Boadicea must have gained strength from the image of the Celtic goddess in her people's minds, so Matilda received practical support from the notion of the halo round her head – and the sword in her hand.

Not surprisingly, it was just this shining white garment of virtue which Matilda's (political) enemies sought to defile. Calumnies included the suggestion of a carnal relationship with the Pope, and the suggestion that the 'chaste' Matilda actually had one of her husbands killed, and possibly her children as well. This was a deliberate attempt to counteract the undoubted propaganda value – to the papal side – of the image of Countess Matilda, both pure and powerful, encouraging her troops to the rescue of the Holy Father. The scandals as well as the paeans of praise bear witness to the successful possibilities inherent in the idea of the Armed (Female) Saint.

The Pope, assisted by his loving daughter, was involved for most of the years of his reign in an incessant power struggle with the German Emperor Henry IV. From the point of view of Countess Matilda, it was an armed struggle which over thirty years would have enabled her to have claimed, with Schiller's Wallenstein, 'our life was but a battle and a march'. So in a sense the Countess Matilda did lay down her life for the papal cause – the cause of Christ, as she firmly believed.

The life she dedicated to the cause was that of a wealthy, high-minded and extremely religious aristocratic woman, who might otherwise have ruled her dominions and endowed her pious foundations with the suitable expectation of peace in this life and further peace to come 'in the heavenly country'. This was the life she finally led as a very old lady, when these papal–imperial troubles were in any case subsiding, helmet and mail finally, as it were, put away. Yet as the devout and filial language of the 'handmaid' Matilda towards the Pope indicates, fully reciprocating his own intimacy, the sacrifice, if sacrifice it was, was one that she herself felt called by God to make. At one point she borrowed the words of the Apostle to say that neither tribulations nor anguish, nor hunger, nor peril, nor persecution, nor swords, nor death, nor life, nor angels, nor principalities, nor virtues, nor the present could ever separate her from the love of Peter.[3]

Matilda of Tuscany – Matilda of Canossa as she is sometimes known – was born in about 1046 somewhere in northern Italy.[4] Her father was the Margrave Boniface II, head of a family based on the mighty Apennine fortress of Canossa, and invested with the office of Margrave by the Roman Emperor-cum-German King, Conrad II, in 1027. Boniface's lands stretched roughly speaking from the Apennines to the Alps, sweeping across the wide plain of Lombardy; but he held many of them in feudal tenure to Conrad II since in a revival of the idea of the 'Roman Empire' of Charlemagne, the elected German King was in his capacity of 'Roman Emperor' currently exercising lordship over northern Italy.

Charlemagne's 'Roman Empire' had been conferred on him in 800 by the Pope and brought back for the German kings in the middle of the tenth century. Officially, therefore, Conrad, like other German kings of this period, owed his position in Germany to election by the German princes; while he had to be crowned by the Pope as Roman Emperor. That at any rate was the theory of the thing.

Matilda's mother was Boniface's second wife Beatrice, daughter of the Duke of Upper Lorraine. Hereditarily speaking, Matilda must have owed at least as much to her clever, capable mother as to her rough warlord of a father; while in terms of environment Beatrice's influence must certainly have been paramount since the Margrave Boniface was killed when Matilda was six.

It was to be a turbulent childhood, a presage of Matilda's adult life. The death of her father and the deaths of her brothers – their precise number is in question but the relevant point to Matilda's story is that they did not survive – left Matilda theoretical heiress of Boniface's extensive lands. But the rules of inheritance, given the vital imperial exercise of Italian overlordship, were not at this date quite so simple. The Emperor Henry III, for example, who had succeeded Conrad II in 1039, claimed the right to invest a male child with those of Boniface's Tuscan territories which he had held in feudal tenure, although this still left Matilda as heiress to the Canossa family heartlands. Moreover Henry III was in an increasingly strong position to enforce his wishes since the fortunes of the German-ruled 'Roman Empire' were waxing. Burgundy had fallen to Conrad II by inheritance; Henry III himself had extended his sway over Bohemia, Bavaria and Hungary, as well as over the Normans in the south of Italy.

In any case the question of female inheritance in this age dominated by force turned more on practicalities than on theories. Where an heiress was concerned, her husband would tend to exercise her military obligations because he was judged physically capable of doing so, although she herself might literally inherit (and later transmit possession of her lands to her children). Similarly, where kingdoms, duchies and counties were at stake, a female's ability to inherit in fact rather than theory often depended on what masculine support she could muster. This is illustrated by the story of the fight for the English crown between Stephen and his cousin Matilda (or the Empress Maud) to be considered in the next chapter: by modern rules of descent, Maud, the King's daughter, had a better claim than her first cousin, Stephen, son of the King's sister. But, as will be seen, such a claim was not necessarily upheld if it could not be enforced. The need for strength or at least protection, and marriage for the sake of protection – these were the elements which dominated the lives of women (and little girls) in high positions, as the need for strength and powerful allies dominated the lives of their menfolk.

Under these circumstances, the swift remarriage of Matilda's mother Beatrice to her cousin Duke Godfrey of Upper Lorraine a year after Boniface's death is easily understood; although by choosing a husband who was at the time in open revolt against the German Emperor, she was hardly likely to achieve a reconciliation in that direction. At one point Beatrice and Matilda were taken hostage. It was not until after the death of Henry III in 1056 that some kind of political calm was temporarily established. The new Emperor Henry IV was another child (at six years old, he was four years younger than Matilda) and the regency was left in the hands of his mother, the Empress Agnes. The conditions of Matilda's own life became less perilous: Duke Godfrey, no longer considered a rebel vassal, was allowed together with her mother Beatrice to govern Matilda's estates during her minority.

Where the chroniclers of her education are concerned, naturally the Tomboy Syndrome is found to be at work.[5] Matilda, like Zenobia, was said to have been eager to learn martial accomplishments to the detriment of traditionally female arts like embroidery: 'Disdaining with a virile spirit the art of Arachne she seized the spear of Pallas', wrote Vedriani in 1666; Arduino della Paluda, later a general, was said to have taught her to ride like a lancer, spear in hand, to bear a pike like a footsoldier and to wield both battleaxe and sword. Fortunately for these activities, Matilda grew up under this treatment tall and strong, if slender. According to later tradition, she was certainly accustomed to the weight of armour: in his lifetime Vedriani declared that he knew of a suit of her armour sold for a song in the Reggio market in 1622.

Whether or not Matilda actually wore armour, which is doubtful, she did, as a matter of fact, embroider: she embroidered well and she sent presents of her work (an embroidered standard) to male contemporaries such as William the Conqueror.[6] The stereotype of the tomboy has to disdain 'the art of Arachne' (spinning) if she dares to pick up the spear, but the real woman had no intention of sacrificing a possible advantage by disdaining those pursuits common to her sex and rank which signalled femininity and gentleness.

Furthermore, Matilda's education left her accomplished in four languages – the four languages concerned, German, French, Italian and Latin, expressing the polyglot nature of her future responsibilities – and, in an age when most Northern rulers usually signed documents with a mere cross, this female would in adulthood be able to write letters herself unaided by a clerk. One should not ignore the effect of this excellent education in giving her confidence to rule her estates. (Queen Elizabeth I had the same kind of education and exhibited the same kind of intellectual confidence towards her male contemporaries.)

At some point during her youth Matilda was married. Like her mother's second marriage, this was another inevitable and practical step, although myth, wishful thinking and the fact that it had taken place beyond the Alps combined to allow a lot of nonsense to be written on the subject later on. The chosen bridegroom was the son of Duke Godfrey by an earlier marriage, a boy known – all too accurately, alas, since he was severely deformed – as Godfrey the Hunchback. Three facts can be extracted for certain out of the various fantasies surrounding this, the first of Matilda's two marriages: that she did marry, that the marriage was consummated because at least one child, who died in infancy, was born of the union, and that the marriage itself was a failure.

The various elaborate legends on the subject divide into those intended to bolster up Matilda's 'holy' image (that the marriage if indeed it took place was never consummated, or, if consummated, only reluctantly in the line of duty) and those intended to denigrate her by making of her some kind of insatiable witch-like creature. It is significant that exactly the same kind of legends – the Chaste Syndrome versus the Voracity Syndrome – attached themselves to Matilda's second marriage at the age of forty-three to Welf of Bavaria. According to the scurrilous accounts, both Godfrey and Welf were supposed to have been impotent in face of Matilda's treatment – in the case of Welf, Matilda was alleged to have boxed his ears with disappointment and sent him home; Godfrey was supposed to have been killed, as were Matilda's two children by Godfrey, both hunchbacks.[7]

On the other hand, a pious story has Matilda cropping her hair deliberately short on her wedding night, adopting a hair shirt and then starkly inviting her husband to a joyless but dutiful coupling for the sake of the dynasty: 'Come, let us to our union.'[8] It is possible of course that the two versions, lubricious and pious, actually bear some relation to each other: one cannot help observing that Matilda's wedding-night tactics required a delicate balance to be struck between performance (desirable) and pleasure (undesirable) in which there may have been an unfortunate degree of miscalculation on her part.

On the subject of Matilda's chastity, two important sources for her life unite in following a more moderate course. The *Vita Mathildis* is a long biographical poem in Latin by the Countess's chaplain Donizo which he intended to present to her personally; her death intervened and the poem was published later. For all its flourishes, it preserves details which would otherwise be lost, and the fact that it was designed for Matilda's own perusal suggests that wild inaccuracies would not have been permitted. Donizo stresses Matilda's personal holiness, while not actually claiming her celibacy. Rangerius, biographer of Anselm of Lucca, Matilda's spiritual adviser, takes the same line: Matilda, he wrote, was not keen on the carnal aspects of matrimony, nevertheless 'her mother's exhortations prevented her from committing herself to the deep religious desire for a chastity which was, in her case, no longer permissible in view of the obligations she had assumed'.[9]

Donizo and Rangerius between them put forward a plausible picture; it is certainly more plausible if less exciting than that of an eighteenth-century Italian work, for example, with the full wind of myth in its sails: 'Matilda, embellished with all the virtues, had the rare destiny of causing lilies to bloom among her martial laurels, and these she bore ever unharmed to her tomb; wife and widow to be sure, but always a virgin too.'[10] Matilda's marriage, for which she had not felt much enthusiasm in the first place given the unprepossessing nature of her husband, petered out with her return to Tuscany from beyond the Alps and her enthusiastic adoption of the papal cause. It ended technically with Godfrey the Hunchback's death in 1076 but before that politics, far more than physical disinclination, had driven the couple apart.

The politics which transformed Matilda from a dissatisfied but dutiful wife into the right-hand woman warrior of Pope Gregory VII were painted in theory on a broad canvas of noble aspect. The eleventh century witnessed that great battle between Pope and Emperor to exercise jurisdiction over each other – and each other's subjects – which had at its heart the relative importance of Church and state in directing men's lives.

Two and a half centuries later, Dante would suggest in *De Monarchia* that the divine plan for the government of the world consisted of a universal emperor acting in harmony with a universal pope; man had 'a twofold end', both spiritual and temporal, and thus needed 'a twofold directive power' to achieve it: 'to wit, the supreme pontiff to lead the human race, in accordance with things revealed, to eternal life; and the Emperor to direct the human race to temporal felicity, in accordance with the teachings of philosophy . . .'[11] Nothing like this ideal was however established in the lifetime of Matilda. And there were some murky details in the corners of the broad canvas of Church and state. As emperors deposed popes to set up rival popes in holy Rome and popes interfered with German affairs by declaring emperors excommunicated (which might result in their own deposition) their motives might be construed as spiritual (the preservation and purification of the Church of Christ) or they might be seen as the less sympathetic ones of power-seeking and power-broking.

It is probable that Matilda's first appearance on the public scene was at just such an ambivalent occasion. In 1059, when she would have been about thirteen, she was present with her mother and stepfather Godfrey of Lorraine at the Council held at Sutri, in the mountains between Rome and Viterbo. The death of Pope Stephen IX, Godfrey's brother, in March 1058 had been a blow to the family interests when the Roman nobles took the opportunity to elect their own candidate. He was however deposed at Sutri in favour of the Bishop of Florence, backed by Godfrey's faction, who took the title of Nicholas II. The death of Nicholas II in 1061 produced yet another crisis. While Anselm of Lucca – a worthy incumbent of the office – was duly elected as Pope Alexander II, a sense of the imperial interests in Italy, somewhat dormant during the childhood of Henry IV, began reviving in Germany. Thus an anti-pope was put forward in the shape of Caladus of Parma, a prelate of notoriously evil character (according to his enemies) who took the title of Honorius II; what was more the lax bishops of Lombardy preferred his cause to that of Alexander II, fearing the upheavals in the name of Church discipline which the latter had promised.

The circumstances surrounding the Council of Sutri of 1059, the election of Alexander II and the years of fighting which followed it give an indication of the background, turbulent, complicated, ever-changing and contentious, against which Matilda grew up. If it were true to say that 'mere anarchy' was 'loosed upon the world' in which she lived, her devotion to the papal cause in the shape of the Pope she principally served, Gregory VII, was the natural reaction of a singularly unanarchic character to such a situation. It was however to be over a decade before the Papacy was so vigorously incarnated. In the meantime Matilda was learning the arts of battle.

So far as one can piece together her story, she made her first foray on the battlefield at the side of her mother, defending the interests of Alexander II against those of the schismatics in 1061 shortly after his election. The seventeenth-century account is eloquent: 'Now there appeared in Lombardy at the head of her numerous squadrons the young maid Matilda, armed like a warrior, and with such bravery, that she made known to the world that courage and valour in mankind is not indeed a matter of sex, but of heart and spirit.'[12] Matilda was also probably present in 1066 when her stepfather finally put an end to the Roman and Norman support for the anti-Pope Honorius II: at the battle of Aquino, at which Godfrey of Lorraine defeated the Normans, she is even said to have shared the command of four hundred archers with the General Arduino, although this is surely an exaggeration.

According to Vedriani, Matilda was by now generally seen as 'the new Bellona among the armed companies'.[13] But although there are later reports to establish Matilda's presence at various military engagements in the 1060s in the cause of Alexander II, it seems unlikely that she had carried out any kind of real military command before the death of Duke Godfrey in 1069.[*] This was the effective moment in Matilda's life when, aided by her mother, she began to exercise proper authority in Italy – in the absence of any male figure able to stop her. Her husband, Godfrey the Hunchback, battled on in Lorraine (physical disability did not prevent him being a doughty fighter) but increasingly failed to support Matilda in Italy with reinforcements.[14] The fact was that Lorraine was beginning to turn away from the Papacy back towards the imperial cause, just as Matilda's own commitment became yet further strengthened by the election of a new pope.

In the summer of 1073 the great reformer and former monk Hildebrand was consecrated as Pope Gregory VII. A strong character, believing in the centralization of the Church as a means to this reform, Hildebrand had already acted as the power behind the throne during the pontificate of Alexander II. In particular he was dedicated to rooting out that practice of lay investiture, by which the symbols of their office were granted to ecclesiastics by laymen. The new Pope Gregory was convinced that the Church would never be purified so long as laymen had in effect an

---

[*] The metaphors of strife and battle used by commentators on both sides at the time make it difficult (except in the case of Sorbara) to be certain when Matilda actually led her men, as opposed to commanded them.

opportunity to buy and sell Church offices, although he would initially have preferred to work through rather than against the Emperor. (In the previous reign, Henry III had been a noted supporter of Church reform.)

In 1075 Pope Gregory prohibited lay investiture under pain of excommunication, and later that year carried out that sentence against various offenders: these included favourites of Henry IV who had been appointed to the vacant sees of Milan, Fermo and Spoleto. At Mass in Rome on Christmas Eve 1075, however, as part of the rough internal politics of the city, the Pope was first violently assaulted and then abducted. The intention was to take him as prisoner to Germany. Only the furious uprising of the Roman people (to whom he had endeared himself) rescued him.

The incident, shocking in its brutality, may well have put the finishing touches to the unofficial break-up of Matilda's marriage. Although there is some evidence that Godfrey the Hunchback suggested a reconciliation about this point, Matilda did not take up the offer: the fact that Godfrey's sympathies were increasingly towards the imperial cause was hardly likely to endear him to her, in view of the Holy Father's beleaguered state. For was not Matilda, wife of Godfrey, by now happily transformed into Pope Gregory's hand-maid, and one 'distinguished by her excellence' (*egregia indolis puella*) in his own words?[15]

The Pope's excellent hand-maid was recommended to throw herself at the feet of the Blessed Virgin whom she would find more attentive than any human mother; frequent Holy Communion was suggested in order that Christ himself might nourish her. Matilda for her part declared herself as devoted to Gregory as Paul had been to Christ. While nothing in Gregory and Matilda's language – or indeed their respective characters – gives any credence whatsoever to the calumnies of their opponents concerning their carnal relationship, the intensity of the mission which they shared cannot be doubted. Matilda, a deeply religious woman, victim of an unhappy marriage, had found a far more satisfying role as the Pope's 'daughter Matilda'. Unlike anything more sinister, the paternal role which Pope Gregory played in Matilda's life – he was twenty-six years older than the Countess – does emerge very strongly through their correspondence.[16]

It was Matilda's good fortune that the love which she undoubtedly bore for Gregory, a love compounded of veneration and affection, was an emotion actually sanctified by the Church since it was the prescribed attitude of any pious Christian 'daughter' towards the 'Holy Father'. Writing of a period many many centuries before the emergence of psychoanalysis, it is fruitless and anachronistic to probe further into the sexual elements which may have lurked into this 'daughter's' passionate devotion to her 'father', since if they existed Matilda herself would have been quite unconscious of them. To make a more pagan allusion, however, Matilda's reporting of her military victories to Pope Gregory sometimes reminds one of Wagner's Brünnhilde reporting her triumphs to her godly father Wotan.

It was Anselm of Lucca, her spiritual adviser, who commented that Matilda combined the will and energy of a soldier with the mystic and solitary spirit of a hermit.[17] Fighting for the head of the Church gave an opportunity to fulfil both sides to her nature; marriage to Godfrey the Hunchback, on the contrary, not even solid in his support of the Papacy, gave her an opportunity to fulfil neither.

At all events 1076 was to be a dramatic year in Matilda's life, as well as in the fortunes of the Papacy. Matilda found a new independence: Godfrey was killed in Antwerp in February and her mother Beatrice died in April. Ironically enough the facet that Matilda's child (or children) by Godfrey had died in infancy added to this independence since Matilda had no male heir to challenge her position. At the same time the Emperor Henry moved against the Pontiff: at the Council of Worms in January 1076 he had renounced obedience to 'Hildebrand, now not Pope but false monk' and declared him deposed. Lastly, and most dramatically of all, Gregory employed the most powerful weapon at his own command in retaliation, a mighty one indeed, that of excommunication.

The terms worked out at Canossa were as follows: an excommunicated monarch – even an emperor – had twelve months in which to make penance; otherwise his subjects were absolved from all obedience to him and he himself forfeited all civil rights and stood to be deposed from every civil and political office (which meant that the Pope was in effect interfering with the political affairs of Germany, much as the Emperor's practice of lay investiture was now seen as interfering in Church affairs). Of course the practical consequences of such a ban depended very much upon the behaviour of those in a position to benefit from the possibilities of independence if offered: that is to say, the Emperor's vassals. When Henry's Saxon subjects used the excuse to rise up in revolt again – for they had rebelled earlier – they made it unpleasantly clear what the consequences were likely to be, including the most hideous possibility of all, the election of another king of Germany. So, as Henry's other vassals began to fall away from him, the scene was set for that celebrated scene of political (and politic) repentance: at Canossa, Matilda's Apennine fortress, in January 1077.

The Pope was already on his way to Germany, for a consultation with the German princes, including bishops, at Augsburg, when the dramatic news of the Emperor's dash towards Italy across the Alps reached him. Such a journey from Rome to Germany – as the brutal events at Christmas 1075 will have made clear – could not have been made by the Pontiff without suitable armed escort, since Piedmont and Lombardy supported the Emperor. This escort was already provided by the troops of Matilda. The Emperor's action demanded a new schedule. The Countess probably came to join the Pope at Florence on about 28 December in order to ride with him personally to Canossa. The choice of this virtually impregnable fortress, lying in the heartland of Matilda's territory, was doubly significant. It symbolized not only security, essential in view of the still unknown intention of the Emperor, but also the powerful protection which Matilda herself was exerting, had exerted and would continue to exert towards the Holy Father.

Canossa stood – and its ruins still stand[*] – on a spur of the Apennines about twenty-five kilometres south-west of Reggio. On a clear day there you could see if not forever at least the rising cities of the Italian plain: Modena, Parma and even Mantua, as well as Reggio. Only one side of the fortress was remotely accessible and that was guarded by three walls; the rest was guarded by the terrain itself. The chaplain Donizo romantically referred to Canossa as a 'new Rome'; if an excess of praise, the description did at least convey that a proper little town existed within the fortress itself: domestics, animals, shopkeepers and men-at-arms jostling with the influx of mighty visitors.

'Lo, I possess at once the Pope, the King [Henry], Matilda, princes of Italy, of France and of those beyond the mountains. Those also of Rome, prelates, sages, venerables . . .' In his biographical poem, Donizo had the fortress of Canossa itself chant this proud refrain.[18] Among the prelates present, to be listed also among the notables, was Hugh, the celebrated Abbot of Cluny, that Benedictine monastery in Burgundy which was one of the sources of the movement for the spiritual reform of the Church; he was accompanied by his secretary Odo, later as Pope Urban II to be Matilda's second guiding 'Holy Father'. Then there were the unhappy German clergy who by participating in the Council of Worms had risked anathema themselves; the Emperor's relations came also to ask for mercy.

Henry IV probably made his first stop at Matilda's outlying sentinel fortress of Bianello; there the Countess visited him, accompanied by Abbot Hugh. From his point of view, a quick absolution was essential if he was to shore up his political situation in Germany. The Emperor besought the intervention of both (Abbot Hugh had been made his godfather by Henry III) in order that he might be relieved at once of his excommunica-

---

[*] But only the foundations of Countess Matilda's fortress remain; the ruins above ground date at earliest from the thirteenth century.

tion. According to Donizo, the Emperor believed, and Abbot Hugh confirmed his belief, that Matilda's intercession was the best hope of melting the hard papal heart: 'Plead for me, cousin,[*] plead for my forgiveness with the Holy Father . . . Go therefore to him, Oh! Most valiant cousin and make him bless me again. Go! I beseech you!' (One notes that Matilda was not thought to have sacrificed the traditional intercessionary powers of a woman.)

There is some evidence that Matilda did intercede and also a suggestion that the Pope became irritated at her persistent efforts. No doubt, he preferred her practical exertions as the Pope's armed hand-maid to her enactment of the more traditional female role of mediator. An illustration to Donizo's *Vita Mathildis* shown an enormous Abbot Hugh (in a monk's robe and carrying a crozier) with a tiny Henry kneeling beneath him. The Emperor's supplication is clearly addressed to Matilda, shown medium-sized, and extending her own hand pleadingly on his behalf. Gregory did not in any case grant the Emperor the speedy relief he desired, sending messages instead regarding the forthcoming Council of Augsburg. So the Emperor's situation was not shored up, or not for the time being.

Instead, in the freezing weather – the winter of 1076/7 was exceptionally severe – the Emperor was obliged to stand barefoot in a coarse woollen penitential garb outside the gates of Canossa itself. Fasting for three days, from 25 to 27 January, there he stood during the hours of daylight, a visible symbol of imperial penitence. From time to time he knocked on the doors of the fortress and still he was not admitted. Inside Canossa the Pope, silent and as it seemed remorseless, remained in the imagination of the world as the invincible symbol of papal determination. To some he stood for more than that. The whole matter of the excommunication with its concomitant of interference in German affairs was to many minds dubious in canon law. 'This was not apostolic severity but rather the cruelty of a tyrant!' Gregory

[*] Matilda was second cousin to Henry IV through her mother Beatrice of Lorraine.

himself admitted in his subsequent account of the episode to the princes and bishops of Germany: 'he did not cease to implore with many tears the apostolic clemency' so that all present were found 'marvelling at our unusual hardness of heart'.[19] But outside Canossa, while still under ban, Henry for the time being had no choice but to persevere.

Finally on the fourth day, the shivering Emperor was allowed to throw himself at the Pope's feet and receive mercy. Even so, his absolution was in theory granted to him only as a man, not as a king: that would still have to wait for a conference at Augsburg. (Although the conference never took place, and Gregory did refer to Henry as king after Canossa.) It was undoubtedly at first sight a sensational victory for Gregory. For all that Henry did not keep his word regarding the notorious investitures – strife between Pope and Emperor persisted well into the next century – he had at least been obliged to bow his neck to the Pope's authority on this single most celebrated occasion. The Emperor had in short 'come to Canossa' and so that famous phrase signifying the recantation of a previous proudly held position, for humbling oneself on a grand scale, was born.

Furthermore, Canossa, where it all happened, was the stronghold not of a prince or bishop, but of a woman. (No wonder that Canossa with its infinite possibilities of defence was the favourite residence of Matilda.) This extra bit of symbolism concerning Canossa's female ownership is however generally missing from the catchphrase which has come down to us.

The practical triumph of Pope Gregory was short-lived. The last years of his life were spent in an unenviable series of confrontations with the Emperor, ending with Gregory's death in exile at Salerno while an anti-pope, Clement III, Henry's nominee, occupied St Peter's. Civil war in Germany – where the princes persisted in electing a new king in Rudolf of Swabia despite the lifting of the ban on Henry – occupied the Emperor until 1080. After that Rudolf's death in battle freed him to return across the Alps to Italy and, after ravaging the north, besiege Rome itself.

Here, with William I of England and Philip of France carefully neutral, Matilda was, as Donizo put it, the only soldier of St Peter left.[20]

Nor had her own affairs prospered since Canossa. The rising Tuscan cities, in particular Lucca, were beginning to desert her cause – since the townsmen, wanting independence, regarded the hereditary ruler of Tuscany as their natural foe. On his return Henry marched on Lucca, had Matilda judged guilty of high treason for refusing feudal allegiance to him, and placed her under the ban of empire which meant that all her goods were confiscated. On the papal side there was nothing but praise for the sturdiness with which Matilda met the fate which her loyalties to the Holy Father had brought about. Anselm of Lucca, the Pope's Vicar in Lombardy, praised the heroic Countess for amassing 'eternal treasure in heaven' by her efforts, confident that she would 'fight with her blood' until God delivered over his enemy (Henry) 'into the hands of a woman'. But the fact was that Matilda's earthly treasure was fast diminishing as a result of her ceaseless campaigns, a fact recognized by Pope Gregory when he pleaded for assistance for 'our daughter Matilda . . . otherwise she will be forced to make peace with Henry or lose all her possessions'. By the spring of 1082, Matilda's finances were in ruins, and much of the gold and silver in the treasury at Canossa had to be melted down to remedy them. Yet still, according to Rangerius, Matilda feared neither dark nor cold and nothing separated her from her soldiers. Nor did she retreat into neutrality.[21]

Matilda's military triumph at Sorbara in July 1084 was a bright spark in the increasing gloom of the papal fortunes. At Easter the anti-Pope Clement III had crowned Henry at Rome, with Pope Gregory held in the Holy City. Subsequently the Norman leader Robert Guiscard liberated Gregory and took him back with him to Salerno where he died the next year; Robert Guiscard also sacked the Holy City, causing the Emperor to flee. North of Rome however Henry's allies continued to harry Matilda's possessions: her castle of Sorbara, on the plain about fifteen kilometres north-east of Modena, seemed an ideal target to invest because of its accessibility compared to, for example, Canossa. Matilda retaliated with a surprise attack late at night when the enemy soldiers were asleep; the celebrated war-cry 'For St Peter and Matilda!' rang out as Matilda personally led her small force to victory. According to tradition, she carried the 'terrible sword of Boniface' (i.e. her father's sword) as she massacred the enemy, standing in her stirrups before her troops.[22] Militarily, one Sorbara did not make a summer, however satisfying to Matilda. The Emperor Henry continued to ravage her possessions.

It is indeed the stoical resistance of Matilda to the idea of making peace with Henry, because it necessitated recognizing the anti-Pope Clement III, which compels admiration over the next fifteen years of her life. As the champion of St Peter, she tried in vain to persuade Gregory's short-lived successor Pope Victor to take up residence in Rome; then the succession of Odo, the former prior of Cluny, as Urban II in 1088 brought about the second great partnership of Holy Father and armed daughter.

It was Pope Urban who, in the need for allies, recognized that Matilda's theoretical marriageability must be employed once more in the cause of Christ. In 1089 the forty-three-year-old Matilda was married to the seventeen-year-old Welf V of Bavaria, thus introducing Bavaria into the papal alliance. The fury with which Henry IV greeted the match demonstrates the success of the move on the political level. In the case of the participants, Matilda's personal reluctance was probably equalled by that of the youthful Welf: some six years later he separated from his masterful bride, his senior by a whole generation, tired of her dominance in the cause of papal politics. As for Matilda, various suitors had been mentioned for her hand over the years since Godfrey the Hunchback's death, without conclusion; it was significant that her second marriage was not only arranged by the Pope, but arranged for the benefit of his cause. To that kind of marriage, Matilda could agree.

There was a moment after Henry had taken Mantua in 1091, followed by Ferrara and other important Italian cities, when peace was once more proposed with Tuscany's *gran Contessa*: if only she would acknowledge Guibert of Ravenna as Pope Clement III. There were by now many who begged her to accede. 'You have struggled long enough, oh! most valiant lady, you and your serene consort, to uphold the dignity of the Pontificate.' Matilda's reaction can however be most closely gauged by an outburst at the same council of war, held in the Apennines, by one Hermit John: 'Are you not that Matilda who glories in the title of daughter of Peter? . . . What sort of peace can be made with the impious?'²³ No peace was made.

It took a series of deaths, marking the passing of a whole generation who had lived most of their lives entrenched in conflict, to pave the way for Matilda's comparatively serene old age. Pope Urban II died in 1099 and the anti-Pope Clement III in 1100. Lastly the death of Matilda's old enemy Henry IV in 1106 ushered in a new era. The Concordat of Worms of 1122 – a compromise by which a clear distinction was made between a prelate's position as a landed vassal of the crown and his spiritual office – was hammered out towards the end of the reign of his son and successor Henry V.

A new age was dawning in more senses than one. Matilda continued to regard the struggles of the Italian cities for independence as part of her own struggle to establish a free Papacy. She had been born too soon or had spent too much of her life in conflict to understand that as the commercial importance of Pisa and Lucca developed, this was a phenomenon in its own right.²⁴ And yet as a governor she was far from being naturally despotic: she patronized jurists such as Ubaldo da Carpineti and Irnerius. One has the sad impression that Matilda's long fights with the Empire, while granting her her reputation in the pantheon of Warrior Queens, actually robbed Tuscany of the possibility of strong, intelligent and benevolent female rule over thirty years.

The new Emperor Henry treated Matilda, towards the end of her life, courteously. He called upon her at Bianello, the sentinel fortress of Canossa, where once his father had set off to shiver in the snow, 'swearing in the whole earth there could not be found a Princess her equal'. But Matilda, as her health failed, spent more and more time at Polirone, a Benedictine monastery near Mantua founded by her grandfather. (Although when there was an uprising in the city of Mantua in 1114, this gallant old lady still threatened to command an army against the unruly townsfolk.) Polirone had been the first northern Italian monastery to accept the reformed Cluniac rule: both Anselm of Lucca and Matilda's second spiritual adviser Bernard of Vallombrosa had been monks at Polirone. The illuminated so-called Matildine Gospels presented by the Countess to Polirone (now in New York, in the Pierpont Morgan Library) commemorate not only her generosity towards the monastery, but also, in the nature of their illustrations, those spiritual sympathies which Pope Gregory and Pope Urban had inculcated.[25]

It was at Polirone that Matilda died on 15 July 1115, in her seventieth year, leaving Donizo (his biographical poem unpresented) to repine, 'Now that thou art dead, oh great Matilda, the honour and dignity of Italy will decline.' It is however a curious postscript to the life of Matilda that her testamentary dispositions brought about considerable trouble – for the Emperor Henry V and also for the Pope. The Countess, childless if not virgin, left no direct heir since with her own death her family died out. Thus in two separate wills of 1077 and 1102 Matilda had transferred all her allodial property – that is, the Canossa inheritance, not within the feudal structure of the Empire – to the chair of St Peter. After peace was made with Henry V, Matilda willed her feudally held possessions back to him, although Henry seized the opportunity to claim the whole of her territories. This left the Pope, at the next moment of strength, to claim Matilda's allodial property in his turn. Ironically enough, even in death Matilda, the Warrior Queen in the course of peace, had not brought about that tranquillity between Emperor and Pope which she so ardently desired for the sake of the Holy Father.

Countess Matilda was originally buried at the monastery but in the seventeenth century her body was transported to St Peter's, surely the appropriate resting-place for her who had been the Pope's 'hand-maid'. Certainly the 'daughter of Peter' would have been a more comforting title in death to the Countess herself than that allusion to Penthesilea inscribed on her original tomb. The first of the three Latin inscriptions contained this passage: 'This warrior–woman disposed her troops as the Amazonian Penthesilea is accustomed to do. Thanks to her – through so many contests of horrid war – man was never able to conquer the rights of God.'[26] And yet, whatever the pious Matilda's reactions, there remained the need to compare one Warrior Queen to another, for verification as it were, however far-fetched the comparison.

Anselm of Lucca himself, in her lifetime, compared Matilda to the Amazonian Queen; he also compared her to the Queen of Sheba.[27] Where Matilda was concerned, however, Anselm was careful to add that 'the garb of a Penthesilea' hid 'the messenger of mercy'. That is, on the judgement seat, God would see in Matilda not the stern avenger of crime but rather the compassionate mother of the feeble and oppressed. For another perceived need was to prevent Matilda losing her proper femininity due to her military command. Matilda's latter-day reputation includes a possible tribute from Dante in the *Purgatorio*: the 'Lady Beautiful' encountered beside the waters of Lethe, who draws him through its drenching waves to the blessed shore, is named Matilda (although there are other more likely claimants for the poet's inspiration). A more valiant and thus more verisimilitudinous picture emerges from Tasso in *Jerusalem Delivered*:

> With manlike vigour shone her noble look,
> And more than manlike wrath her face o'erspread . . .
> Henry the Fourth she beat, and from him took
> His standard, and in Church it offered
> Which done, the Pope back to the Vatican
> She brought, and placed in Peter's chair again.[28]

In general, however, the many tributes to Matilda both in her lifetime and afterwards, down to the twentieth-century

23

biographies of the Countess, are careful to stress the compassionate side of her nature. Like Boadicea, she is excused the final responsibilities for her actions and their consequences by her sex. At Sorbara, for example, the warrior maid with the 'terrible sword of Boniface' raised above her head was also depicted as begging a halt to the slaughter once the fortress was surprised: slaughter, it could be plausibly argued, that she herself had initiated. 'Her heart did not grow hard – she cared for the sick, nursed the wounded, made bandages and dressings, prepared and distributed food, and nourished and clothed the destitute, dispossessed by the German scourge.' So runs a hagiographical modern life of Matilda, published in Italy in 1937.[29]

The judgement delivered by Leone Tondelli in his classic modern biography of Matilda, which has run through many revised editions since its first publication in 1915, is on firmer ground; for throughout it stresses the religious inspiration which not only supported Matilda in her 'so many contests of horrid war', but also justified her participation in them to her contemporaries.[30] The Countess Matilda, wrote Tondelli, was 'a heroine of Christian Italy'. Her whole life constituted 'luminous proof' that if a Christian upbringing tends, with 'modest self-effacement, self-reflection and a mystical union with God, to elevate and refine the spirit', it nevertheless does not take away vigour in action. Most significantly of all, it is to Matilda's 'Christian upbringing' that Tondelli ascribes that martial ability so uncharacteristic of her sex. In moments of need, Tondelli continues, such an upbringing can suggest 'even to a woman's heart the heroism of chivalry and it can mould the female soul – usually rich in generosity but little resistant to long-lasting tests' – shades here of Gibbon and Mommsen on the subject of Zenobia – 'into an indomitable constancy'. One feels that that is a judgement with which the *gran Contessa* herself – 'Matilda by the Grace of God or she is nothing' – would have agreed.

CHAPTER TEN

England's Domina

On bier lay King Henry
On bier beyond the sea,
And no man might rightly know
Who his heir should be.

PIERS OF LANGTOFT, on the death of Henry I (1135)

In 1114, the year before the death of the *gran Contessa* Matilda of Tuscany, there took place the May-and-December marriage of an English princess to the German Emperor Henry V. The girl herself, who was variously known as Matilda or Maud (but owing to the plethora of Matildas in this period, will be here generally described as Maud), was a mere twelve years old, having been betrothed and sent to Germany four years before.[1] Her bridegroom, nearly twenty years older, was a veteran of many a military campaign and military struggle. He had taken part in the prolonged investiture arguments with the Pope, and had actually enforced the abdication of his father Henry IV, scourge of the Countess Matilda, before his death in 1106.

At the time it hardly seemed likely that the young Empress Maud, or Matilda Augusta, daughter of King Henry I of England, would be called upon to take to the field of battle; but perhaps the unlikely nature of their destiny is one of the few things that all the Warrior Queens outside the antique days have in common. Her married life with the Emperor Henry V was, as it turned out, comparatively brief in a long and eventful life: he died in 1125. Nevertheless Maud's youth at the moment of her transference from the royal English court of her powerful Norman father to the imperial court of Germany ensured that these were formative years. The Emperor sent away her English attendants – there were to be no Scottish Maries, as would escort the infant Mary Queen of Scots to France – and he had Maud carefully instructed in the German language and customs.

Some of the apparent haughtiness of which, as we shall see, the Empress Maud was to be later accused must have sprung from these early experiences, working upon a naturally strong character. (It is noteworthy indeed how many of the female descendants of William the Conqueror show a vigour and even guts worthy of their great progenitor, starting with his strong-minded and intelligent daughter Adela of Blois.) Here was a girl who was crowned in Germany before she was in her teens and whose official title was 'Queen of the Romans'. Yet at the time, Maud, having a natural outlet for her energies by contemporary standards for females, in her position as consort to the Emperor, secured nothing but golden opinions. To her German subjects, she was 'the good Matilda'; a description which would have had an ironic ring to many of those English upon whom she attempted to lay her rule, in the course of her prolonged martial dispute for the crown with her cousin Stephen during that English period known as the Anarchy.

It was the death of Maud's brother William in 1120, drowned in the tragedy of the White Ship, which brought about the first stage in her transformation. The Empress Maud was now the only surviving legitimate child of Henry I since Henry's second marriage to Adeliza of Louvain was to be childless (although he was to have more than twenty bastards). The death of Maud's husband, the Emperor Henry, leaving her also childless and thus without stake in Germany, brought about the second stage. The Empress now returned to the court of her father, and Henry now set about making Maud his heiress with all the considerable energies still at the forceful old King's command.

Maud had been well fitted to her imperial role, not only by her dignity and her benevolence but also by her beauty, to which all contemporary chroniclers, English and French as well as German, bear witness.[2] But as to her new role as heiress to the throne, no one knew what the qualities were which might fit her for that, since there had been no queen regnant in England within historical memory – or at least not indisputably so.

What precedents were there for a female ruler? There were some but Boadicea was not among them. It has been mentioned in the previous chapter that the name of Boadicea had vanished from the written records in England and would not reappear for several hundred years (we cannot of course know about folklore). It is true that Gildas, the sixth-century monk who defended Roman Britain, in order to excoriate against the degraded rulers of his own day offered his own version of the events of the British revolt five hundred years earlier.[3] It was not a flattering one. He did not name the war leader of the Iceni, but termed her 'that deceitful lioness, who put to death the rulers they [the Romans] had left in Britain, to unfold more fully and to complete the enterprise of the Romans'. Nor did Gildas allow those 'crafty foxes', the Britons, any credit for the courage of their attack, or for their bravery against the Roman counterattack; on the contrary he described them as having 'offered their necks to the sword and stretched out their hands, like women, to be bound'. This double insult both to the Britons and to the sex which had produced Boadicea was, as we have seen, also historically quite inaccurate. Bede and Nennius both referred briefly to the revolt without mentioning Boadicea or indeed any ruler of either sex.[4]

Negative evidence of the disappearance of Boadicea is indeed provided by the fact that Geoffrey of Monmouth, who discusses the claims of Maud to her father's throne at length, does not mention the British Queen; while he does produce numerous historical instances of reigning women. For although knowledge of Boadicea might have disappeared on a literary level, history pointed to the fact that the instinct for bellicosity in the female sex had not: where there was a need or, as some might say, an opportunity for 'severe womanhood' to exercise its powers.

The phrase is that of Ruskin, gazing in excited awe at Botticelli's portrait of the biblical Judith in the nineteenth century, and calling her 'not merely the Jewish Dalilah to the Assyrian Samson, but the mightiest, purest, brightest type of high passion' into the bargain, displaying 'the purity . . . and severity of a guardian angel'.[5] A thousand years earlier, the militant character of contemporary Judiths had caused no revulsion. The best-known example of a female exercising power before the time of Maud was King Alfred's eldest daughter Aethelflaed (or Ethelfleda), whose marriage to Aethelred, earlderman of the Mercians, led to the completion of the union of Wessex and Mercia under the West Saxon kings.

Aethelflaed, born about 870 and dying in 918, was generally known as the Lady of the Mercians rather than Queen (although the *Annales Cambriae* referred to her as *Regina* at her death). Whatever her title Aethelflaed seems to have held joint authority with her husband during his lifetime, profiting from his illness and subsequent death to assume sole control; her numerous campaigns against the Danes and the Norse included leading her troops personally to victory at Derby. In an interesting variant of the Chaste Syndrome – carrying the alleged policy of Zenobia one stage further – Aethelflaed was said by William of Malmesbury to have abandoned marital relations altogether after the birth of her only child, a girl. The risk of childbirth was too great, and, she declared, 'it was unbecoming the daughter of a king to give way to a delight, which after a time produced such painful consequences'.[6] It is this Lady of the Mercians who probably inspired the tenth-century Old English poem *Judith*.[7]

In this poem, Judith's 'severe womanhood' is treated with a respect worthy of Ruskin: Judith herself is 'white and shining', 'noble and courageous'. The poem also quite ignores the fact that the biblical Judith was actually a widow (of Manasses) in order to concentrate throughout on her virginity: 'wise Judith' is 'the noble Maid', 'the holy virgin' who has been led to the pavilion of Holofernes. Here, where Holofernes 'thought to stain the radiant woman with pollution and foulness', Judith was in principle saved by her belief and her trust in God. In practice 'the creator's handmaiden with curling tresses', the 'valorous virgin' was equipped with a gleaming sword with which she struck off the head of the hostile foe: 'Judith ascribed the glory of all that to the Lord of Hosts'.[8]

As with the life of the Countess Matilda of Tuscany in the following century, there is a perceived connection between the 'purity' of Judith and her severity: the former makes the latter admirable. But it is finally religion, Christianity in the case of Countess Matilda (or some other cause holy to its advocates, that of the goddess Andraste for example), which exercises a benediction over what might otherwise be deemed unsuitable female activity. This becomes relevant in the case of the Empress Maud, who in her claim to the English throne was the recipient of no such healing benediction. No 'holy' war-cry as, for example, 'For St Peter and Matilda!' was appropriate to the lips of her followers: Maud's cause was that of a royal person, who happened to be a woman, asserting a superior right to the throne by force. Being part of the Appendage Syndrome did not save her at a time when she needed in fact to pose as a Holy (Armed) Figurehead. The result was a charge of overweening arrogance on the part of the daughter of Henry I, which the Pope's 'daughter Matilda' never had to sustain.

The ten years between the death of Maud's husband and that of her father were stamped by the energy with which Henry I, now in his late fifties, prosecuted her cause as his heiress. This vigorous campaign was necessary, not only in view of the questionable status – at best – of a female ruler, but also because of the threat posed by an alternative male heir. At this point one must bear in mind the ramifications of the Norman dynasty founded by the Conqueror. Countess Matilda of Tuscany had inherited the lands of the Margrave Boniface as a girl after the deaths of her siblings with the aid of a powerful stepfather to uphold her rights; it was also important that there were no immediate rivals in her family circle (as we have seen, the line came to an end with her own childless death). Maud's situation was very different.

A number of elements went into the making of a king at this

period and it could be argued that the most important of all was the king's demonstrable ability to occupy the throne:[9] forcible seizure of it being one good way of demonstrating this ability. Certainly male primogeniture itself – the right of the heir male to succeed in all circumstances – did not apply. Henry 1 himself was the third son of William the Conqueror and had succeeded the Conqueror's second son, William Rufus, as King of England; he then wrested the other part of the inheritance, Normandy, from the Conqueror's eldest son Robert Curthose. The heir male to the Conqueror's line was undoubtedly Robert Curthose's son William Clito; but Henry 1 did not acknowledge his claims any more than he had respected those of his father.

If male primogeniture, strictly speaking, did not apply, blood itself was not to be ignored, otherwise Maud – 'Matilda the Empress, daughter of King Henry' as she liked to term herself, a neat exposition of the Appendage Syndrome – would not have entered the picture in the first place. Henry's own marriage to the daughter of Malcolm Canmore, King of Scotland, had been an acknowledgement of the power of blood. For his wife's mother, St Margaret, a great-niece of Edward the Confessor, had been herself a member of the English (Wessex) royal house, 'the true royal family of England' in the words of the *Anglo-Saxon Chronicle*.[10]

There was however a veil – almost literally so – around this 'true royal' marriage since as a girl the Scottish Princess had been brought up in a convent. A seventeenth-century biography of St Margaret phrased it most romantically: the saint's daughter came 'out of the Monastery' to marry Henry 'as a fair star, dispelling by her rays the cloud that had obscured, and hid her for some time from the eyes of man.'[11] But if the Scottish Princess had actually taken vows as a nun, then these vows, less romantically, would have rendered her subsequent marriage vows void. It does not seem that this was so; nevertheless it was an argument which the enemies of her daughter Maud would use against the latter's legitimacy.[12]

Meanwhile there was another strong candidate for the English throne: Stephen of Blois, son of Henry's sister Adela, who had been brought up at his uncle's English court. (But again, like his royal uncle, he was not the eldest son of the family.) In the five years between the deaths of Henry's son and Maud's husband, it may have occurred to Henry to make Stephen his heir; at all events he arranged a significant marriage for him to the heiress Matilda of Boulogne. This Matilda could also claim descent from 'the true royal family of England', her mother being Mary of Scotland, another daughter to St Margaret and Malcolm Canmore.*

Now the widowhood of the Empress Maud meant that, in one of those swift dynastic transformations Henry's only daughter became instantly marriageable; the joyful possibility of the continuance of his own line loomed before him. The King's first step was to impose an oath of fealty on his *Curia Regis* – his council of nobles and ecclesiastics. On Christmas Day 1125 they swore to acknowledge Maud – Matilda Augusta – as 'lady of England and Normandy'. The oath emphasized the double nature of her claim; both Norman and English. To her alone 'the legitimate succession belonged from her grandfather, uncle and father who were kings as well as from her maternal descent for many ages back'. The question of Maud's next match was clearly crucial. In his turn, according to William of Malmesbury, the King promised not to give her away outside England, except by the counsel of the magnates.[13] In the event neither promise was kept, King Henry being the first to break his word. A second oath of fealty was sworn at Northampton in 1127. But then to her own great reluctance, and to the disgust of the young gentleman concerned, Maud was despatched to Anjou to wed the Count's teenage son, Geoffrey.

Part of the importance of Anjou to Henry was geographical: it lay next door to Normandy and the King feared its counts; so

---

* Thus Matilda of Boulogne and her husband Stephen were both first cousins to the Empress Maud (but not to each other); Matilda through Maud's mother and Stephen through Maud's father.

coolly Henry bought off Angevin pressure with his daughter's hand. At the same time, the King may also have had his eyes on his son-in-law as his successor, an effective co-ruler with Maud. But from her point of view, to be Countess of Anjou was hardly a distinguished position for one who had been Empress of Germany, and was born a Princess of England. Nor was the ten-year gap between the ages of the bride and bridegroom a good omen for this marriage of state. Maud, having been married to a veteran statesman as a child, was now linked to a boy. Understandably she resented her altered status, life in this petty countdom; there was an initial separation. The couple were however reunited, and reunited most successfully in dynastic terms; for Maud produced two sons before her father's death in 1135 (and one more in 1136). Whatever Henry's intentions towards Geoffrey, the ultimate prospect of a male succession obviously bolstered Maud's position as heiress: the eldest of these sons – the future Henry II, known then as 'Henry FitzEmpress' – was included in the third oath of fealty sworn to Maud. But Maud was not present at her father's deathbed in Normandy; although he had in fact renewed his disposition of his crown to his daughter, her absence gave her enemies the opportunity to pretend afterwards that he had disinherited her.[14]

The immediate situation of Henry I's death was summed up by a rhyme of Piers of Langtoft:

> On bier lay King Henry
> On bier beyond the sea,
> And no man might rightly know
> Who his heir should be.[15]

Then a *coup d'état* by Stephen, resulting in his coronation in Westminster Abbey at the end of 1135, made it clear who that heir might rightly be – at least for the time being. As for the Archbishop of Canterbury, who crowned him, he absolved the nobles from their oaths of fealty to Maud on grounds of duress.

In the contest for the succession which followed, personalities as well as rights became of importance, particularly in view of the nebulous aura surrounding those of the female. The husband was very likely to exercise those rights, as Stephen ruled Boulogne in right of his heiress wife Matilda. Henry I had not allowed Geoffrey of Anjou and Maud to build up what has been described as 'some kind of power base' in either England or Normandy, despite his wish for his daughter's succession.[16] One possible solution to the English succession was to make the infant Henry FitzEmpress king; but this had the disadvantage, from the point of view of the English and Norman baronage, of making Geoffrey as well as Maud regent.

Stephen of Blois on the other hand, five years older than his cousin Maud, was not only reputedly the handsomest man in Europe, but also 'unassuming, generous and courteous' in the words of the *Gesta Stephani*, 'a thing acknowledged to be very uncommon among the rich of the present day'. Maud's supporter William of Malmesbury gave the same picture: 'by his good nature and the way that he sat and ate in the company of even the humblest', he wrote, Stephen 'earned an affection that can hardly be imagined'. Events would show a lack of iron in this agreeable soul: Stephen was 'kind as far as promise went, but sure to disappoint in its truth and execution'.[17] At the date of his *coup d'état*, however, Stephen could well be regarded, in contrast to unsuitable female Maud, as the ideal of the (male) monarch.

As time went on, a further comparison would be made between Stephen's wife, Queen Matilda, and her first cousin, the Empress Maud. Queen Matilda was another of those public women, intelligent and capable, with whom this early mediaeval period abounds. (Queen Matilda, like her cousin Maud, was also beautiful.) In Norman England, female capability was not infrequently tested when ladies had to hold castles against siege in their husbands' absence, as the Countess of Norfolk had held Norwich in 1075. During the long battling years of the Anarchy, other women would come forward and perform a similar service, as the situation demanded it. Matilda of Ramsbury for example, mistress of Bishop Roger of Salisbury and mother of his children, commanded the Bishop's castle of Devizes. [18]

Like the Empress Maud, Queen Matilda conducted sieges and defended castles. She first appeared in the field in 1136 and received the surrender of Derby. But there was one obvious difference between the respective images which the two women presented to the world. Queen Matilda was acting on behalf of her husband and her young son Eustace, Stephen's heir; the Empress Maud – 'Matilda daughter of Henry' – was basing her right on her father, but claiming it for herself. Just as Countess Matilda of Tuscany had a perfectly valid excuse to ride to battle, so did Queen Matilda of England; she could conduct herself as a Warrior Queen, unlike the Empress, without losing her notional femininity or being exposed to accusations of arrogance.

The comparison between Maud and Matilda reached its apogee in the nineteenth century in the reign of Queen Victoria with Agnes Strickland's well-researched *Lives of the Queens of England*, which built on the presence of another queen upon the throne. The author dedicated this massive work by permission to Queen Victoria, quoting those words of Tacitus concerning Boadicea's leadership, 'they do not discriminate against women in matters of military command', and adding a phrase from Boadicea's own speech: 'We British are used to women commanders in war.' Agnes Strickland hereby explained that Queen Victoria ruled 'not only by rightful inheritance and the consent of the people, but also in full accordance with the ancient British custom'. But a few chapters further on, Agnes Strickland is praising 'the good Queen Matilda whose feminine virtues, endearing qualities and conjugal devotion . . . created the most powerful interest in her favour' compared to 'reports of the pride and hardness of heart of her stern relative and namesake' (Maud). Above all, with a sublime unawareness of any possible irony involved, Agnes Strickland commended Queen Matilda for avoiding 'all Amazonian display by acting under the name of her son'. [19] (It was not an example that Queen Victoria inclined to follow with the future Edward VII.)

*

In his *Historia Regum Britanniae* Geoffrey of Monmouth was (as has been noted) concerned to dredge forth numerous examples of female sovereignty in Britain's remote past. In his version of the story of King Lear, for example, the King's youngest daughter Cordelia reigned in Britain after the death of her father and husband: 'And Cordelia, now mistress of the helm of State in Britain . . . governed the kingdom in peace . . .' That is, until her sisters' sons rose up and 'took it in high dudgeon that Britain should be subject to the rule of a woman'. (He may have based the story on the adventures of an actual queen of Central Gaul.)[20] But as a matter of fact a queen regnant was not literally unknown in Europe at this period.

Queen Urraca of Aragon, who belonged to the generation older than Maud (she was born about 1080 and died in 1126), managed to maintain her sway successfully over an enormous tract of territory in Spain (as did her half-sister Teresa later in Portugal). Urraca was a twenty-seven-year-old widow, with two infant sons, when the death of her father resulted in her succession to his kingdom of León-Castile. Thirteen of her seventeen years as queen were in fact to be spent campaigning against her boorish second husband, a king of Aragon with the discouraging name (to an estranged wife) of Alfonso the Battler.

Among Urraca's qualities however was an ability to manage the system in which she found herself. It used to be thought that Urraca's policy decisions were the result of the advice of her supporter Bernard Archbishop of Toledo or of her lover the Count of Lara (Urraca's reputation as a Warrior Queen formed part of the Voracity Syndrome: she too was no Holy Figurehead). A recent study has however suggested that it was the Queen herself, on the available evidence, who was very much in control.[21] In particular she showed herself adept at managing the question of her son's – and heir's – rights, calling him to her aid by having him crowned with her at exactly the right psychological moment.

With Geoffrey of Anjou as a husband, this was not a solution which could immediately present itself to the Empress Maud. Significantly, it was in King Stephen's acknowledgement of Henry FitzEmpress as his heir (following the fortuitous death of his own son Eustace in 1153) that the whole grisly matter of the Anarchy and the English succession was to be finally settled. That, however, in September 1139 when the Empress Maud landed on the south coast of England in pursuit of her claim, was more than a decade and many a battle away.

Joining forces with her stepmother, Henry 1's widowed Queen Adeliza, Maud first held Arundel Castle against Stephen's besieging forces. At this point, in one of those odd twists in the lives of Warrior Queens, as when Zenobia managed to avoid execution on grounds of feminine irresponsibility, Maud's sex told in her favour. For Stephen, reluctant to be seen besieging two high-born and presumably gentle ladies, allowed Maud to depart in order to join her loyal ally and half-brother (one of her father's numerous bastards) Robert of Gloucester in the west. The Empress herself on the other hand displayed no such 'female' clemency when shortly afterwards the tide turned in her favour with the aid of the western barons. In February 1141 Stephen was captured. Maud, unmoved by the pleas of Queen Matilda and her son, sent him in chains to Bristol Castle.

The Empress now made a triumphant entry into Winchester, having assured its bishop Henry of Blois (one of Stephen's brothers) that if he would join her she would make him chief among her counsellors, otherwise she would 'lead all the host of England against him at once'. Bishop Henry accepted this offer that he could hardly refuse. At Winchester, Maud was duly acknowledged 'Lady of the English' (*Domina Anglorum*). The new Domina was not at this point additionally claiming the title of queen: or not generally so. *Domina Anglorum* was her style on the charters and of the two charters extant in which she is termed *Regina Anglorum*, one is described as 'probably spurious'.[22]

It was not customary to employ the style of queen before coronation: it may be however that Maud did anticipate the style in an occasional charter out of impatience and a need to underline her authority. If so, this merely emphasized the fact that Maud's coronation was of particular consequence both to her and to her supporters since her rival Stephen had of course already been crowned more than five years before. He thus enjoyed the sacramental benefit of an anointed king. At midsummer 1141 Maud, Domina as well as Empress, moved on to London, took up residence at Westminster and prepared to be crowned at its Abbey in her turn.

Unfortunately for Maud's cause, Domina never was to be transformed officially into Regina. For the rest of the years of her conflict with Stephen, Maud had to endure the fact that, unlike herself, Stephen had received his crown at the hands of the Archbishop of Canterbury. This was no small advantage in this period when an ill-defined notion of kingship jostled with respect for the Church, a respect that the Church for one was keen to see maintained. (Repeated appeals to the Pope to ratify their claims were to be made by both contestants for the throne.) As it was, an uprising by the Londoners, incensed by Maud's new financial exactions, caused her to flee precipitately to Oxford. Significantly in the context of the Warrior Queen, criticisms were uttered of the very voice in which these exactions were set out: 'she sent for the richest men and demanded from them a huge sum of money, not with unassuming gentleness, but with a voice of authority'. And at the richest men's refusal 'her forehead wrinkled with a frown, every trace of a woman's gentleness removed'. With hindsight, one may wonder whether the most dulcet and submissive tone would actually have persuaded the citizens to part with their wealth – and whether Maud's lack of 'a woman's gentleness' did not merely provide an excellent additional excuse for not doing so. Nevertheless the check to her fortunes was severe. Maud now ran from the very banquet – 'a well-cooked feast' – arranged on the eve of her coronation, as the enraged Londoners poured forth 'like thronging swarms from beehives'.[23]

At the same time Maud no less than Stephen was showing herself incapable of handling the restlessly self-seeking baronage of England, who took advantage of the prevalent Anarchy to demand grants of land and other favours from each side in turn. It is to this period that the many accusations of Maud's arrogance and intractable temper belong: 'arbitrary and headstrong in all she did . . . mightily puffed up and exalted in spirit' are some of the phrases used. Certainly it was foolish – to say the least of it – for Maud to cancel the grants made by Stephen; by confiscations on an even greater scale than his, including the lands of the Church (which had hoped for better things), Maud hardly endeared herself.

It is notable that if Maud the woman was accused of being too harsh, Stephen the man was accused of being too soft. Both reproaches may well have been justified, but of course both reproaches were also in truth politically useful to batter away at the central royal authority, whoever was deemed to hold it. As for Maud, it could be argued that she was in an impossible position. On the one hand the fighting blood of the Conqueror and of the Saxon kings was said to flow in her veins, justifying her original claim to the throne despite her sex. On the other hand, if she tried to display herself as the strong monarch the situation demanded – for which this fighting blood certainly had equipped her – she was immediately accused of being proud and domineering. Any signs of royal strong-mindedness in Maud had a propaganda value for her enemies, just because she was a woman.

As it was one may doubt that either Maud or Stephen or indeed any other monarch alive in this period threatened by a disputed succession, possessed the requisite qualities to bring peace to a land now so beset by horrifying violence of all sorts. In the words of the *Anglo-Saxon Chronicle*, it 'was said openly that Christ and his saints were asleep'.[24]

Thereafter the cause of the imprisoned Stephen began to wax again in the hands of his wife, the 'good' Queen Matilda. In September Maud found herself blockaded within Winchester, once the scene of her triumph, by 'the King's Queen', as Stephen's Matilda was known in a contemporary attempt at clarity, 'with all her strength'.[25] Maud broke out with her vanguard, but after heavy losses, had to flee as far as Devizes with only one follower. Here Maud resorted to an even more desperate expedient to escape. Still in terror of pursuit and rightly recognizing the all-importance of her personal safety to her own side (remembering the blow which Stephen's imprisonment had dealt to his) Maud embarked on a macabre masquerade. It was dressed as a corpse, in 'grave clothes' and roped to a bier, that Maud, once Empress of Germany, was finally carried into the secure town of Gloucester.

Despite Maud's daring escape, the deathblow to her hopes in England had probably been dealt on this same occasion of the break-out from Winchester. This was because her ever-loyal half-brother Robert of Gloucester, while covering for her escape, fell captive to the Queen. A bargain was now possible to secure Stephen's liberty. One prominent prisoner being exchanged for the other, King Stephen was finally set free on 1 November. Naturally his re-emergence gave a new impetus to his supporters. An appeal by Maud to Geoffrey of Anjou for help had to be made in person by Robert of Gloucester – at Geoffrey's insistence. And then, busy with his Norman invasion, the Count of Anjou merely sent his eldest son Henry as a pledge of support. Maud herself was once more blockaded and besieged, this time by Stephen, and within her own headquarters of Oxford.

As the autumn of 1142 passed, Maud and her supporters were brought to the brink of starvation; high hopes were raised of the Empress's capture. But just before Christmas, in another daring coup, Maud once more eluded her would-be captors. Thick snow blanketed the city and its environs; the surrounding river was frozen. Dressed all in white, with similarly white-clad attendants, Maud stole out of a small postern gate of Oxford Castle on to the surface of the icebound Thames. Noiselessly and in their white garments virtually invisible, Maud's party were able to pass through Stephen's pickets, which were 'everywhere . . . breaking the silence of the night with the blaring of trumpets or the cries of men shouting loudly', like so many ghosts. No sentinel challenged them. The royal party then made its way on foot across the snowy wastes to Abingdon, some six miles away, before riding onwards – Maud 'in the male fashion', that is astride. By daybreak, Maud and her attendants had reached Wallingford and safety.

Agnes Strickland ascribes this escape with an air of covert disapproval to 'female ingenuity'. Whosoever the ingenuity was (quite possibly Maud's) it was certainly a remarkable feat and has been rightly celebrated both in myth (where Maud is supposed to have let herself down by a rope from a tower) and in more accurate annal. William of Malmesbury on the one hand called it 'one of God's manifest miracles' and on the other hand praised Maud herself: 'necessity sometimes . . . discovers means and ministers courage'.[26] Maud's reward was to be reunited with her nine-year-old son Henry and her half-brother Robert. For all that courage Maud's cause was still lost, if Stephen's was not exactly won.

Maud lingered in England for several years, mainly in the west, before returning to the safety of Normandy. In any case pressure was now upon the next generation to solve the state of anarchy by arms or treaty. With the agreement of Geoffrey, Maud increasingly allowed her eldest son to exercise her own rights of succession. The death of Stephen, followed by the undisputed accession of this son as Henry II in 1154, left Maud free to complete her life in peace.

As for the whole question of a queen regnant in England, nothing had been proved either way. The fact that Henry II was manifestly ruling in the lifetime of his own mother, and yet his blood claim must have come through her, meant that the matter was left in abeyance. There it remained for the next four hundred years until the death of Edward VI, only son of Henry VIII, leaving only two Tudor sisters Mary and Elizabeth to succeed him, brought it sharply into question again.

Now Queen Dowager, Maud found herself again in a role both highly respected and properly conventional, as she had been in her youth. Maud became to the Normans, as she had been to the Germans twenty years before, 'the good Matilda'. Once more she displayed all those qualities of piety and grace which had made her so beloved; age had brought with it an appropriate wisdom as well. The Dowager Queen and Empress now occupied herself chiefly making a series of pious foundations; but she also dispensed some excellent advice along the lines of moderation and practicality to her son on the throne of England. She persuaded Henry for example not to invade Ireland in 1155. And it was Maud who urged the King not to appoint Thomas à Becket as Archbishop of Canterbury (an unparalleled piece of good advice as it turned out, but, like most really good pieces of advice, it was ignored by its recipient). Subsequently Maud acted as mediatrix between King and Archbishop, as well as endeavouring to bring about peace with the Pope after Becket's death.

The golden opinions won by the Empress Maud in the first and third stages of her life are in such marked contrast to the accusations of pride, temper and intractability which surrounded her in her middle years that it has been suggested that these faults might have had a physical cause. The Earl of Onslow, one of Maud's male biographers, suggested (in 1939) that her change of attitude was due literally to a change of life: 'Maud was now in her thirty-ninth year (on arrival in England) . . . she may have attained that time of life when physical conditions are apt to react on the nervous system'. This suggestion was however firmly refuted by her (female) biographer Nesta Pain in 1978; leaving aside the fact that thirty-eight was early for the menopause even in the twelfth century, she pointed out sensibly enough that 'Not many women are seized with sheer folly at such times.'[27]

It is surely closer to the truth to suppose that Maud, first the child-wife to an older man, then the reluctant wife of a boy (for all the formidable character that Geoffrey of Anjou would later develop), saw, on arrival in England, an opportunity to exert that independence for which as 'Matilda the Empress, daughter of King Henry' she may have long secretly yearned. The other side to this independence was a tenacity and sheer steadfastness which must compel admiration – think of her two remarkable escapes – from the disinterested observer. But of course none of the observers of twelfth-century England was disinterested. Her character and indeed her whole intervention earned her universal abuse from those for whom it was politically awkward. It is true that Bishop Arnulf of Lisieux, her supporter, referred admiringly to Maud's 'intrepid spirit' which had 'nothing of the woman in it'. Far more characteristic was the reaction of a contemporary chronicler (and opponent): at the moment of her greatest triumph at Winchester he referred to her 'scornful and arrogant air' instead of 'the modest and gentle demeanour proper to her sex'.[28]

Maud died in Normandy in 1167. Her epitaph referred to the three men sharing the same name who had dominated the passage of her life, two English kings and a German emperor. 'Here lies Henry's daughter, wife and mother; great by birth – greater by marriage – but greatest by motherhood.'[29] (It was of course an epitaph composed in the lifetime of Maud's son.) Unlike the monument to Countess Matilda of Tuscany which recorded her martial achievements, there was no mention in Maud's epitaph of that period when she had battled her way across England in her own right as a Warrior Queen, or been acclaimed as Domina – 'the Lady of the English'.

CHAPTER ELEVEN

Lion of the Caucasus

A lion's cubs are lions all, male and female alike.

RUSTAVELI, The Knight in Panther's Skin, c. 1200

To pass from the Anarchy of mid-twelfth-century England to late-twelfth-century Georgia is to pass from mire to mountain. Under its great Queen Tamara (or Thamar), a character both wise and splendid, powerful and beloved, the Caucasian kingdom of Georgia flourished as never before – and indeed never since. Memories of its golden age dominate both Georgian history and myth, and these memories are intricately connected to the story of Tamara. Alone of all the Warrior Queens considered in this book, Queen Tamara succeeded lawfully to her father to the acclaim of her people, added to both the prestige and the dominions of her country, and died leaving a legally begotten male heir to succeed peacefully in his turn. In actual fact, her gender, so far from detracting from all this glory, seems to have added to it.

Yet, even here, there has to be some canker on the rose. To the leading Georgian historian of today, Tamara is 'the symbol of Georgia's political might and cultural progress'; but in Georgian folklore and myth her reputation, in addition to this fame and as though provoked by it, is that of a woman of voracious sexual appetite. This Tamara was crystallized in Lermontov's famous ballad *The Demon*, 'with scant regard for history', in the words of his biographer Laurence Kelly, as having the face of an angel but with a heart 'like sprites from hell'.[1]

She dwells in a tower on a gloomy crag, the sight of whose golden firelight 'promising warmth and rest' lures the unwary traveller out of his way. Within the tower, Tamara's strange magnetic voice 'brimming with passion o'er', urges her suitors to enter. Then:

> Warm arms with arms wound eagerly,
> And lips to hot lips flew,
> And sounds of strange wild revelry
> Echoed the long night through . . .

But in the morning, Tamara's wild passion slaked, each suitor would be hurled to death over the precipice.

> Lo! A lifeless corpse is carried,
> Sounds of moaning voices swell,
> From the tower a white gleam shimmers,
> Comes a distant cry, 'Farewell'.[2]

Today in Georgia, part of the former Soviet Union, legends concerning Tamara abound. (And since the name was a common one in the Georgian royal family, the existence of other less famous and less austere Tamaras, such as the Queen's grand-daughter, contributes to the myth). There are also the familiar modern developments of a legend: there are statues to her, to say nothing of Tamara cigarettes, restaurants and comic-strips. The Lermontov tale of the man-destroying Princess loses nothing in the telling. Since the real Tamara was very different, a woman subsequently canonized by the Georgian Church, certainly more of a matriarch than an erotic heroine, her story provides peculiar evidence of the almost wilful connection of a Warrior Queen with sexuality in the (male) imagination.[3] The two syndromes are ready to claim her: if holy chastity happens not to be the desired image, then extreme voracity replaces it. These are two sides after all of the same coin: as though the one thing that a Warrior Queen cannot be is a 'normal' woman; an oddity in political terms, she is also assumed to go to one sexual extreme or the other.

The Georgian kingdom to which Tamara formally succeeded

in 1184 has been compared to the Norman kingdom of Sicily in its cultural importance, as the royal house of Bagrationi, to which she belonged, has been compared to that of the Angevins; her great-grandfather David the Restorer in particular resembling in his vigour and intelligence a Norman king.[4] Certainly both Bagrationis and Angevins had to deal with a troublesome warrior nobility. But there were obvious differences between the Norman world and that of the Caucasus. One of these differences is indeed indicated by the very different fate of Queen Tamara to that of the Empress Maud as heiress to her father: both being only surviving children at their royal father's death and succeeding – or attempting to succeed – according to similar claims.

'A lion's cubs are lions all, male and female alike': so ran a significant line in Rustaveli's epic poem *The Knight in Panther's Skin*, thought to allude to the accession of Tamara; with her father King Giorgi III as the lion.[5] It was a sentiment to which Henry I of England, unlike his baronage, might well have acceded. This notion of the inherited might of the female via her father was not, however, such a bizarre one to the twelfth-century Georgian as it might be to the English or Norman baron.

Queen Tamara's royal position fitted into certain primitive conceptions supported by embedded memories, as it has been argued that Boadicea's own regality derived from the richness of Celtic legend. But in England much of Celtic culture, including gods, goddesses and religious traditions, had been transmogrified into that of the Romans; Boadicea herself was preserved in Tacitus' (Roman) narrative. When Rome itself fell and Roman history vanished, Boadicea vanished with it; England – and Europe – awoke to a Christian culture where a Warrior Queen must incarnate the 'severe womanhood' of Judith in the Bible.

For all the tales of Geoffrey of Monmouth, with his optimistic interpretation of Lear's story – the happy personal rule of Queen Cordelia – the English point of view in the twelfth century was better expressed by the Archbishop of Canterbury releasing the nobles from their oaths of fealty to Maud as having been taken under duress. Queen Tamara on the other hand was nourished in the popular imagination by lurking memories of those goddesses of ancient Georgia – Itrujani, Ainina and Danana – whose cult looked back to the Great Mother; and given Georgia's geographical situation there were later influences of Eastern goddesses. Even with the Christianization of Georgia in the fourth century, these folk memories of the mother goddess did not entirely die away, as reverence continued to be given to mother saints (as opposed to virgin ones) while Lermontov himself may derive his pejorative if exciting picture of Tamara from the kind of orgiastic rites which celebrated the cult of the Eastern goddess Astarte.[6]

The position of women in Georgian tradition and myth was then an honoured one: and as a matter of fact the coming of Christianity supplied yet another legend, honouring the female sex. Where England was proselytized by a man – St Augustine – the Georgian kingdom of Kartli, according to a variety of sources, owed its conversion to St Nino, a slave-woman from Cappadocia possessed of miraculous powers who healed its Queen Nana.

In other ways than that of matriarchal folk memory, geography, both internal and external, is crucial to an understanding of the mediaeval kingdom of Georgia. The fertile trough in which the country lay was bounded by the Black Sea in the west, reaching towards the Caspian in the east; beyond the Caspian but accessible from its shores were Persia, India and Central Asia. To the north the great mountain range of the Caucasus acted as a barricade against southern Russia; to the south the mountainous plateau of Armenia exercised another kind of barricade against the empire of the Seljuk Turks.

On the one hand therefore Georgia occupied a strategic position on the borders of Christianity and Islam from which, under favourable circumstances – if the kingdom itself was strong – it could aspire towards conquest and overlordship of many different empires. On the other hand the fact that the country was diagonally split by its own mountain range meant that the inhabitants of West Georgia (ancient Colchis, Lazica or Egrisi) were historically inclined to be in conflict with those of East

Georgia, including part of Daghestan and Caucasian Albani (modern Azerbaijan). If the kingdom was weak, Georgia obviously lay in an exceptionally vulnerable position, accessible in its turn to numerous conquerors.

The people who inhabited this debatable land shared many of the striking qualities of the Celts to which attention has been drawn in Chapter Four; although possessed since ancient times of their own written and spoken language, they did not share that aspect of Celtic civilization – its lack of written record – which makes it so elusive. Unlike that of the Celts, the Georgian love of the arts could be attested, other than orally and visually. But in other ways the feasting, the splendour of personal adornment and above all the fighting recall those singing, drinking, gold-bedecked Celts, ancestors of the Iceni, who migrated across the English Channel to East Anglia. When the Patriarch of Jerusalem wanted to describe the Georgians in 1225, he called them 'very warlike and valiant in battle . . . much dreaded by the Saracens with their long hair, beards and hats': words which recall those of Strabo concerning the Celts, a whole race high-spirited and war-mad. Here too were chieftains and aristocrats, and by the twelfth century a society which could be described as feudal in Norman terms, that is with a strong tradition of kingship balanced by a strong tradition of warrior independence. (It has been said that in Georgia every peasant is a prince, or behaves like one.)[7] Above all the Georgians enjoyed their roistering if feudacious lives – as, given the slightest opportunity, they have continued to do ever since.

The ancient history of Georgia stretches back to that fabulous time when the Argonauts, some fifteen centuries before Christ, set out for Colchis to recover the golden fleece.[8] (Medea, tragic prototype of the woman scorned, was the daughter of the Colchian King.) But the whole legend may reflect the actual journeys of the Greek adventurers from Miletus to benefit from the mineral wealth of the Caucasus. The kingdom of Colchis was certainly flourishing about the sixth century BC and the powerful kingdom of Kartli at the beginning of the Christian era, itself falling under the sway of the miracle-making St Nino in about AD 330. The partial Arab conquest of the seventh century brought Georgia into the oriental world: at the same time it was subject to the territorial ambitions of other aggressive neighbours, the Byzantine Empire to the west and the Armenian monarchy to the south. It was not until the late tenth century that the unification of East and West Georgia into an independent feudal monarchy was made possible by the collapse of Muslim power in the Caucasus, and the waning imperialism of both Byzantium and Armenia.

The ruling family of Bagrationi were the beneficiaries. Originally hailing from the marchlands of Georgia and Armenia, the Bagrationis had travelled northwards and, by a mixture of dynastic luck and political energy, garnered to themselves a number of princely patrimonies including Kartli. Bagrat Bagrationi was crowned in AD 975. It was a taste of things to come – as well as underlining the honour paid to women – that a woman regent in the shape of the intelligent Queen Dowager Mariam Artsruni should rule most successfully in the early part of the eleventh century. It was however the Bagrationi King David II, known for his achievements in raising his country from its state of collapse as the Restorer (or Builder), who was responsible for the most memorable epoch of Georgian history before the age of Tamara.

David the Restorer was crowned at the age of sixteen in 1089, that is, some twenty years before Henry I ascended the throne of England, and died ten years before the English King, in 1125. In his celebrated will, David the Restorer bequeathed to his royal heir a state 'from Nikopsia [on the Black Sea] to Derbend [on the Caspian] and from Ossetia to Arragat'.[9] It was not an idle boast. As his ancestors had benefited from the collapse of Muslim power and the decline of the Byzantine empire, David the Restorer in his turn benefited from the effects of the First Crusade of 1096, and the Norman–French campaigns against the Seljuk Turks. The Turkish victory of Manzikert in 1071 had brought their menacing presence close to the very borders of Georgia; in the 1080s hordes of Turkish nomads began to roam the Georgian heartlands of Kartli. After years of campaigning, it was the achievement of David the Restorer to push them back successfully: after the victory of Didgori in 1121, in which some Crusaders participated, Georgia was increasingly seen as a Christian bulwark.

Finally, in the climax of his reign, David the Restorer recovered Tiflis (Tbilisi), the ancient Georgian capital, which from the Georgian point of view had languished as an Islamic city for nearly four hundred years. The fortress of Rustavi built to the south of Tiflis signified a new security. And in his last years David the Restorer, as a Christian, was even able to exert overlordship over Muslim Shirvan. It was a hegemony made easier to endure by the essentially constructive nature of David's sovereignty (as his sobriquet indicates): his newly acquired Muslim subjects within Tiflis, for example, were granted an amnesty. 'He soothed their hearts', wrote a Muslim contemporary of this act of grace, 'and left them alone in all goodness'.[10]

With such a progenitor (who also patronized scholarship and building) it might seem that the reign of Tamara, great-great-granddaughter to David the Restorer, was assured of glory: not so. In the intervening years – nearly sixty of them[*] – before Tamara's assumption of sole rulership, Georgia, that bold ship surrounded by so many troubled and troubling seas, ran into rough weather once more.

The twenty-five-year reign of David's successor, Dimitri, has probably been treated too curiously by the annalists writing in the reign of his younger son (and Tamara's father) Giorgi III.[11] This was because Giorgi III succeeded (somewhat as did Richard III of England) in place of his own great-nephew Demna, heir to

---

[*] It gives some indication of the time scale involved to point out that Queen Tamara stood in the same relationship to David the Restorer as Queen Elizabeth II of Great Britain to King Edward VII; although Elizabeth II acceded only forty-two years after her great-grandfather's death, as opposed to fifty-nine in the case of Tamara.

Dimitri's elder son, David III, who reigned a mere six months. Propagandists wisely did not care to emphasize the virtues of the father at the expense of those of the son. Nevertheless it is undubitable that King Dimitri failed to hold on to the signal conquests of David the Restorer, as the Muslims began to recover strength and the Crusader kingdoms of Syria and Palestine in turn began to fail.

If one overlooks the coarseness and cruelty of Giorgi III, it has to be admitted that he kept the thrusting nobles in check: on the other hand he indulged freely in favourites. Nor is the cruelty easy to overlook. When Demna attempted to regain his rightful throne in 1174, with much support from the princely houses of the kingdom, he was defeated in battle at Hereti. After that, cornered at Lori, in a scene which once again needs Shakespeare's pen, Demna, the rightful heir, was first blinded and then castrated.

Thus it was that Tamara, last of the direct line of the Bagrationis, thanks to the careful atrocities of her father, came to inherit.

The accession of Queen Tamara had not been without careful preparation on the part of the previous monarch. Where King Henry I of England attempted to bond his nobles to his heiress with oaths of fealty (but did not associate her with his rule) King Giorgi had his daughter actually crowned as co-ruler in 1178, six years before his own death. Declaring Tamara to be the 'bright light of his eyes', he hailed her as queen with the assent of the patriarchs, bishops, nobles, viziers and generals. The new Queen sat on her father's right dressed in purple ornamented with gold and silver fringes. Giorgi gave her the official title of 'Mountain of God' and placed on her head a crown richly encrusted with rubies and diamonds.[12]

At the death of Giorgi in 1184, Tamara became sole ruler, and was consecrated queen once more by the Archbishop of Kutaisi. She was also proclaimed 'King of Kartli', by that interesting expedient by which the royal title magically transforms the sex of its bearer rather than the other way round. (The Georgian word was *Mepe*, there being at this date no word for queen in the language.)

Queen Tamara was in her late twenties at the time of her accession.[13] Even so, she was put under the official guardianship of her father's sister Rusudani. It is suggested that she felt some impatience at the 'domination of women', but as an unmarried queen regnant there was of course another domination to which she must sooner or later subject herself – that of a husband who would, if nothing else, generate those heirs of which the house of Bagrationi stood in urgent need. The first husband chosen on the insistence of her aunt was George Bogolyubski, son of the Grand Prince Andrew of Suzdal from the adjacent south Russian kingdom of Kiev, who had been exiled as a child. They were married in 1187.

It proved to be an ill-fated union, not least because it was the union of an ill-matched pair. Tamara's natural austerity of temperament, even puritanism, has already been mentioned. No such restraints troubled Prince George Bogolyubski. A series of military expeditions against the Muslims in the south brought him some popularity among a fighting people; the man of war did not easily adapt to the manners of Tamara's court. The couple's rare moments of happiness together were experienced out hunting: Tamara, like many another Warrior Queen, enjoyed the mimic battle charge of the chase. Otherwise it was a disaster. The Queen might have dealt with his overbearing and truculent demeanour or even his drunkenness, as indeed for two years she endured the excesses of his debauchery with numerous slaves and concubines. But the fact that Tamara remained childless – something for which her husband reproached her personally in public, a notable affront – meant that there was no practical motive for shoring up the marriage. She had no real need to overlook his gross sexual misconduct further.

The Queen however refused to have her husband punished, a sentence which in that age and in that country might have been harshly carried out (witness Giorgi III's handling of his great-nephew). She allowed him simply to go into exile; furthermore she sweetened his dismissal with opulent gifts. There is no evidence that Tamara regretted her leniency, despite the subsequent attempts of her first husband to raise the standard of revolt against her in her own country: the ghost of her father might have pointed out that dead (or imprisoned and blinded) husbands were in no position to foment rebellion.

All this lay ahead. In the meantime Tamara was married – with renewed celebrations to signify renewed hope – to David Sosland. This Ossetian prince came from an especially suitable background in that he was descended from the half-brother of a former Bagrationi monarch: he was also an excellent horseman, something to appeal to the Georgians (as it would have appealed to the horse-mad Iceni). In other ways he proved suitable: a son Giorgi was born in 1194 and a daughter Rusudani the following year. The succession was secure. This second marriage freed Tamara to pursue those policies of military expansion which, if they did nothing else, would engage her nobles in their favourite pursuit of war, thus taking them away from their other favourite pursuit, jockeying for power and position.

Certainly from the start Queen Tamara, with the assistance of her aunt Rusudani, showed in dealing with the various factions in her nobility a delicate appreciation of the need for tact which the Empress Maud, for example, signally lacked. The possible unrest at the prospect of female rule was assuaged by giving a noted general command of the province of Lori; other commands were given to sons of prominent nobles to bind them to her side. The promotion of upstart favourites of her father's reign had aroused indignation then and was liable to arouse something more than mere indignation now that Giorgi was no longer there to support them. But Tamara, by honouring former supporters of her wretched royal cousin Demna on the one hand and drawing in Sargis Mkhargrdzeli, one of Giorgi's Kurdish minions, on the other, managed to tread the tightrope. A move to limit the powers of the sovereign by setting up what has been described as 'a kind of House of Lords' – to be compared with the trial of strength between the baronage and King John in England at roughly the same date – did not succeed.[14] There was to be no Georgian Magna Carta.

Instead there were to be Georgian military triumphs. But before Tamara could seek to bring these about wholesale, she had to deal with the problem of the dispossessed – in every sense – George Bogolyubski. In 1191 with the probable assistance of the Seljuk Sultan of Erzerum, the Russian Prince attempted to seize the kingdom, aiming at the support of those disaffected nobles still resentful of the power of the central monarchy at the expense of their own. Although the rebellion failed – following two pitched battles won by the Queen – such a failure was by no means a foregone conclusion since originally only the eastern sector of Georgia remained solidly loyal to the Queen.

The errant Prince was finally captured and brought before the Queen. Once more she treated him with a clemency which it might seem appropriate at this point (since it was done twice) to describe as characteristic: George Bogolyubski was permitted to withdraw to Byzantium.

This was not the last internal revolt which faced Tamara, nor the last attempt by George Bogolyubski to recover by force that position which his own violence had sacrificed in the first place. The mountain lords of Samtzkhe rebelled against the Queen a few years later and in 1200 George Bogolyubski, at the head of Turkish troops, had to be driven off once more. Indeed, the fact that for twenty years after the first revolt of 1191 Tamara pursued policies of extreme military aggression – virtually until her death in 1212 – must in part be seen as an eloquent commentary on the internal problems which faced her.

War, for Queen Tamara, was what compulsory court attendance was to Louis XIV: a method of keeping control over those not naturally prone to be controlled by their sovereign. As a matter of fact, when campaigning was in abeyance Queen Tamara employed Louis XIV's plan of insisting on personal court attendance as well. Sport – the hunting which enabled her too to 'ride to battle' – was another method of ensuring that Satan did not find conspiratorial work for these idle hands.[15]

Of course the actual conduct of a campaign always presented problems for a Warrior Queen unless she literally took part in it all the grim way: control in time of war (as Queen Elizabeth I was to be gloomily aware) tending to pass from the woman on the throne to the man on the spot. Each successful Warrior Queen had to find her own solution to this dilemma. There were two possible approaches. One was to inspire from on high as if in the guise of a goddess – or as a Holy (Armed) Figurehead. The other artifice – rather more physically testing – was to provide from time to time, as Zenobia had done, the spectacle of a fragile female sharing the military rigours: such a display of courage in the notoriously timorous sex being equally calculated to inspire.

Queen Tamara practised both arts, presenting herself now as the presiding goddess or figurehead, now as the Queen–general by the side of her men. At home she made plans and plotted battles, displaying a flair for military strategy. On the field she made speeches: before the battle of Cambetch in 1196 she spurred on her men with a rousing address, ending 'God be with you'. 'To our *king* Tamara!' her men shouted in reply.[16]

At the famous battle of Basiani in 1205 in which Tamara's troops routed the Turkish army under the Seljuk Sultan of Rum, the Queen began in one incarnation and ended as the other. On the eve of the conflict Tamara (who was now in her forties) marched with the vanguard of her army to the encampment – traditionally, the Queen went barefoot. She then harangued her men, receiving once again the loud huzza: 'To our king!'

The following day it was the Queen – or should one say the King? – who gave the command to mount. But at this point the Queen, the goddess and the ikon, became too precious to trust to the clash of battle: Tamara the referee took up a presiding position from which she could watch the event. In no way, however, should the hardihood which Tamara showed in following her men, if not actually fighting, be underestimated: as her chronicler commented on the course of her last illness (when she was in her late fifties), a woman's constitution was bound to suffer from the hardships of continual campaigning.[17]

The conquests for which this exhaustion was the price were extensive indeed: on the map the breadth and depth of the early-thirteenth-century Georgian territory astound, as does the dimension of Zenobia's enormous if short-lived empire a thousand years before. After the capture of Byzantium in 1204 by the promulgators of the so-called Fourth Crusade, Tamara sent troops to Trebizond and Kerasund, as a result of which her relative Alexios Comnenos was established as emperor. But this new empire was in effect a Georgian Christian protectorate. There were to be other Muslim semi-protectorates, over which Tamara exerted a loose sway; while beyond the great range of the Caucasus to the north, some of the south Russian peoples paid her tribute.

Where a protectoral relationship did not follow, there could still be substantial rewards for military raids. The Emir of Ardabil, crossing the Arak mountains, indulged in a colossal slaughter of the Georgians in 1209 – twelve thousand killed and others taken into slavery. The next year Queen Tamara ordered Ardabil to be taken by surprise: in revenge an equivalent number of its inhabitants were killed including the Emir himself; and this time the Christians captured the slaves. Daring raids on Marand in Azerbaijan, Tabriz and Kazvin took the Georgian troops deep into north Persia; on their return they brought a good proportion of its treasure back with them. The victory of Basiani had resulted in the surrender of Kars by the Sultan, to which Tamara's son Giorgi was eventually appointed governor.

With Tiflis, the capital, a city of some hundred thousand people, with Georgia trading not only with its neighbours but far afield, with Russians, Armenians, Persians and Turks among others bowing to her command, Queen Tamara had by the time of her death fulfilled the wildest dreams of her great-grandfather David the Restorer. 'One knows a lion by its claws and Tamara by her actions': so ran a contemporary saying.[18]

Queen Tamara's mercy towards her first husband has been mentioned; it is further to the credit of this Warrior Queen that her administration was generally marked by benevolence. The appalling punishments inflicted by her father found no place in her scheme of government.[19] This in itself contradicts the suggestion that Shakespeare in *Titus Andronicus* legitimately founded the character of the Queen of the Goths – 'that heinous tiger Tamora' whose life was 'beast-like and devoid of pity' – upon that of the Georgian Queen. According to this theory, the Byzantine Emperor Andronicus 1, who reigned from 1184 to 1185, would have supplied some of the inspiration. One may remark in passing that the dreadful vengeance on Titus Andronicus' daughter Lavinia for which Gothic Tamora is remembered with a shudder was set off, rather like Boadicea's bloody rampage, by the cold-blooded murder of her own two sons 'for valiant doings in their country's cause'. But in any case it is generally thought that the sources of the play lie quite elsewhere and Georgian Tamara is acquitted.[20]

She has her own literary monument. For it is finally in the great Georgian renaissance of letters and arts that Tamara's glory lies, as much as in her conquests, and above all in the inspiration given by her – and her court and culture – to Georgia's national poet Shota Rustaveli. (Georgian brides still regard his poetry as an essential part of their trousseau, so as to teach it to their children.)[21]

Rustaveli's exact date of birth is unknown although his birthplace is presumed to be, from his name, the town of Rustavi, south of Tiflis, founded by David the Restorer.[22] Tradition declares that he was educated in Athens and travelled in Asia – hence the Eastern influences in his work; most importantly tradition declares that he loved Queen Tamara. As a result, he was said to have retreated to the Monastery of the Cross at Jerusalem where he became a monk (there is no suggestion that the love was requited). Whatever the truth of this romantic legend, Rustaveli's passion for the Queen would not have been that of a languishing poet for some unseen *princesse lointaine*. He was a court official, possibly the Royal Treasurer and even perhaps the Queen's chronicler who thus described her 'sevenfold brilliance': God 'who in six days brought forth out of nothingness all that is, rested the seventh day in the sweet and gentle spirit of Tamara'.[23]

The Knight in Panther's Skin, Rustaveli's great epic poem (of about sixteen hundred quatrains) concerns the long and various adventures of Avtandil and his brother-in-arms Tariel (he of the panther's skin), in the style of an Eastern romance. It has been described as 'a hymn to friendship, loyalty and high endeavour' as well as giving an allegorical portrait of Georgia's golden age.[24] If Rustaveli's poem is also 'the Odyssey of Georgia', it is unfortunate that because of the closed nature of the Georgian language to most foreigners (unlike classical Greek taught for so long in English-speaking schools) *The Knight in Panther's Skin* has never enjoyed the same lyrical appreciation outside its country of origin. An eloquent tribute paid to it by Sir Maurice Bowra in *Inspiration and Poetry* (1955) gives however some indication of the riches in store even in translation: 'It is notoriously dangerous to write about the poetry of a language which one does not know . . . Yet sometimes [i.e. in the case of Rustaveli] the temptation is too strong.'[25]

The poem* is dedicated to Queen Tamara, 'the jet-haired and ruby-cheeked', and it is believed that the description of the Princess Tinatin, beloved of the knight Avtandil, stands at Rustaveli's tribute to his queen. As in a fairy story, Tinatin is 'radiant as the rising sun, born to illuminate the world around her, so fair that the very sight of her would make a man lose his wits. It would need ten thousand leagues and the wisdom of the sages to utter the praise of the king's daughter.'

Beautiful as Tinatin may be, the story has to begin with the decision whether she – the only child of the King, but female – may reign after him. The verdict of the viziers, leading to Tinatin's coronation, is a deliberate echo of the circumstances

---

* Here quoted from Katharine Vivian's prose translation for the Folio Society 1977. A 'poetic recreation' in English by Venera Urushadze was also published in Georgia, 1979.

of Tamara's own accession: 'Woman though she is, God had created her to be a sovereign. We may say without flattery that she knows how to rule, as indeed we have often remarked among ourselves.' In short: 'A lion's cubs are lions all, male and female alike.'

In spite of this, one notes that Tinatin's father is still sad at his lack of a son, which means that he has no knight who is his equal. Yet Avtandil, sent out into the world by Tinatin, describes her to strangers in formidable terms: she is 'the sovereign of Arabia whom her hosts of strong-armed vassals regard as king'. Nor is Tinatin the only powerful female character in the story. Quite apart from Avtandil's own valorous travels, *The Knight in Panther's Skin* gives a fascinating picture of a world where men and women mix as equals. There is no hint here, in what the author himself described as 'a Persian tale' found in Georgia, of the restrictions of the Islamic world; women receive men freely in their chambers, for example, clearly knowing nothing of the harem or purdah.

Dularkukht is another princess who succeeds to the rule of a kingdom, in this case on the death of her brother: moreover she is described as a Warrior Queen: 'though she is a woman, [she] is hard as rock – even her fighting men cannot excel her in feats of arms'. Another princess, Asmat, is made ruler of a seventh part of India, and instructed to 'take the man of your choice for consort'. It is indeed with marriage that the poem ends: Avtandil marries Tinatin and ascends the throne as 'lord and sovereign of Arabia'.

Queen Tamara died on 18 January 1212, having reigned for twenty-four years, and was buried at Gelati, the tomb of her ancestors. Her son Giorgi, then eighteen, succeeded her. But with her death the golden age of Georgia was fast fading away, even as the adventures of the knight Avtandil had drawn to a close. Giorgi gave himself over to base favourites and died leaving only an illegitimate child. His sister Rusudani was then proclaimed 'King of Kartli'; her lusts too were in stark contrast to the pious austerity of her mother. On the horizon the drumming hordes of Genghis Khan promised a threat to Georgia in the future far greater than these unfortunate dissipations on the part of her royal family.

In 1236, little more than fifty years after Queen Tamara's accession, her daughter Rusudani fled Tiflis from the Mongolian invasion, leaving her lands, once the great empire of Tamara, to be ravished. The golden age of Georgia had become a memory. In the words of the Epilogue to *The Knight in Panther's Skin*:[26] 'Their tale is ended like a dream of the night. They are passed away, gone beyond the world. Behold the treachery of time; to him who thinks it long, even for him it is a moment . . .'.

CHAPTER TWELVE

Isabella with her Prayers

~

She with her prayers
He with many armed men.
JUAN DEL ENCINA on Ferdinand and Isabella of Spain

I t was in April 1492, at Santa Fe, an encampment outside the
recently conquered Moorish town of Granada, that Christo-
pher Columbus received the final agreement to explore the
new world. He set off a few months later. Columbus was granted
the vital backing by a woman as well as by a man: by Isabella
of Castile as well as Ferdinand of Aragon. For the two were
independent monarchs and had been so since the inception of
their reigns. Their extraordinary partnership had lasted twenty-
odd years so far. Instead of confirming Isabella as a typically
devout and secluded Spanish princess, leaving the sphere of
action to her dominant warrior husband, the passage of time
had actually transformed her. To the Pope himself, Ferdinand
and Isabella were jointly the 'Catholic kings' and in a phrase
euphonious to modern ears, 'the athletes of Christ'.[1]

In the forging of this partnership, both destiny and the laws
of inheritance played their role: and so did the necessity for
armed conflict which preoccupied the royal pair from the earliest
moment of their joint reign in Castile. A contemporary, Juan del
Encina, described the relative contribution of Ferdinand and
Isabella to their conquests in these conventional terms: they
fought, 'She with her prayers, He with many armed men'.[2] But
while in no way deriding the efficacy of Isabella's prayers (a
subject about which no positive information can be garnered)
one must also note that she made a public contribution to their
victories which puts her in a unique category in this book:

the Warrior Queen as partner. Moreover the Queen's military fervour in the cause of right both nurtured her marriage to Ferdinand and was in turn nurtured by it. Her crusades, jointly carried out with her husband, took on some of the sacramental nature of marriage itself in the eyes of a deeply religious woman. As for her contemporary reputation, the decorous wifeliness with which she conducted herself within this partnership earned general approval. At the end of the chapter this approval will be contrasted with the disapproval shown to Caterina Sforza – a would-be Warrior Queen who was neither decorous nor wifely.

Queen Isabella was a woman of forty-one – with twelve more years to live – when Columbus was authorized to return to the Indies 'and supervise the preserving and peopling of them, because thereby our Lord God is served, His Holy Faith extended and our own realms increased'.[3] She was in fact born in the same year as Columbus himself (King Ferdinand was a year younger). With hindsight, this patronage of Columbus resulting in the European discovery of America can be seen as the Spanish 'Kings'' most resonant achievement; but the endless sound waves which would flow from this decision were hardly foreseen at the time. Ferdinand and Isabella had already presided over one dazzlingly successful crusade: to restore the Moorish kingdom to Catholic Spain after eight centuries. At the instance of their religious advisers, they would promulgate a further internal crusade, less dazzling because less practically beneficial: to expel the Jews along with the Muslims.

The relative importance – and approval – which history would give to these respective crusades would have been incomprehensible to Queen Isabella, the denizens of one age rarely comprehending the apparently weird standards of another. To modern appraisers, the protective attitude of Ferdinand and Isabella towards their new Indian subjects – 'What does he [Columbus] think he is doing with my vassals?' Isabella is supposed to have asked – contrasts most favourably with their chilling attitude to the Jews who had been citizens of Spain for centuries.

After 1492 the latter, if they failed to convert, were cast out. According to the priest–chronicler Bernáldez:

> They [the Jews] went out from the land of their birth boys and adults, old men and children, on foot, and riding on donkeys and other beasts and in wagons . . . They went by the roads and fields with much labour and ill-fortune, some collapsing, others getting up, some dying, others giving birth, others falling ill, so that there was no Christian who was not sorry for them . . . the rabbis were encouraging them and making the women and boys sing and beat drums and tambourines, to enliven the people. And so they went out of Castile.[4]

Similarly, the Moors who were originally granted generous terms after the fall of Granada in the same year, including their own laws, their own religion and their own dress, ended by being expelled in their turn if they did not accept conversion. In 1487 during the series of campaigns known as the Reconquista Queen Isabella had given money for the Moors to be reclothed in the Castilian fashion as a propaganda exercise; in 1508, four years after her death, Moorish dress, in a final insult suggesting the total suppression of a culture, was prohibited altogether.

To Isabella herself, however, the need for religious unity in Spain put these expulsions on quite a different level from the protection a sovereign must accord to distant subjects.* Furthermore the expulsions were recommended by her rigorous confessors, including the formidably bigoted Cardinal known as Ximenes (or Francisco de Cisneros). This was a woman who stepped out of the role expected of her sex in one direction – she had become a public crusader expressing such (male) sentiments as 'Glory is not to be won without danger'. One can understand

---

* 'Religious unity cannot easily be criticized as an objective by those who live in a world of mutually repellent secular orthodoxies, quite as compelling and all-inclusive in their claims', wrote J. N. Hillgarth in 1978.[5] It is an apt comment. Nevertheless many manage to do so.

how she might compensate for this in another direction by extreme spiritual humility in private, and devotion to the will of her (male) religious advisers.

In the earlier years of her reign, such complications were not evident. Other perils had to be faced. And Isabella's personal crusading impulse, the product of faith and determination, was not only approved by her contemporaries, but also seen as a holy destiny which might be implicit in the union of the crowns of Aragon and Castile. 'With this conjuncture of two royal sceptres,' wrote Bernáldez, 'Our Lord Jesus Christ took vengeance on his enemies and destroyed him who slays and curses.'[6] First, before that destiny could be accomplished, Ferdinand and Isabella had to destroy those who threatened to slay them – or at least rebelled vigorously against Isabella's succession to the throne of Castile.

It was the death of Isabella's half-brother, Henry IV, son of John II of Castile by his first marriage, in 1474 which provoked this crisis. Although he had acknowledged Isabella as his heir, Henry IV did have a daughter of his own. This girl however was reputedly illegitimate (either the King was impotent or his wife was wanton or both), her nickname Juana la Beltraneja making scornful reference to her supposed conception by Don Beltrán de la Cueva. Whatever the truth of Juana's legitimacy,[7] there were plenty of potentates to seize the opportunity of backing her in their own interests; particularly since she was unmarried, her hand bringing with it the possibility of the Spanish throne.

Isabella's own husband, Ferdinand, whom she had married five years earlier, also had a claim to the throne, since he too had his place in the Castilian succession (Isabella and Ferdinand were second cousins). It is true that the royal house of Aragon was only a minor branch of that of Castile; but then he was a man. This was more relevant in Aragon where the Salic Law operated – that law originating in France in the early fourteenth century which precluded females from the royal succession – than in neighbouring Castile where it did not. Nor had Ferdinand, in his marriage treaty of 1469, pressed his public claims unduly; at that date securing marriage to the heiress Isabella, from his own lesser position, had been the prime consideration.[8]

As it happened, Isabella was in Segovia when her brother died, while Ferdinand was away campaigning for his father, the King of Aragon. It was in order to cope with the threat of Juana's pretensions – she being temporarily captive to a Castilian noble – that Isabella immediately had herself proclaimed *Reina Proprietaria* (Queen Proprietress). She also had herself crowned, still in Ferdinand's absence; and she had the unsheathed sword of justice carried before her at the ceremony, a revival of an ancient practice it is true, but one that had never been performed for a female monarch before. Ferdinand, when he heard the news, is said to have cried out publicly: 'Tell me, you may have read so many histories, did you ever hear of carrying the symbol of life and death before queens? I have known it only of kings.'[9]

All this was however directed by Isabella rather against Juana and her supporters than against Ferdinand her husband. In addition, the proud Castilian nobility would not welcome subjection to an Aragonese. Isabella's personal 'proprietorship' of the crown, regardless of her sex, also carried an important point of principle with it for the future, as she pointed out to Ferdinand. Supposing their own surviving child or children were also female? (This was the actual case during the early years of Isabella's reign and would also incidentally be the case at her death.) If Isabella's personal hereditary right in Castile was not acknowledged, then the 'Princess our daughter's' right would be similarly endangered at her mother's death.

In effect, Ferdinand did always act as co-ruler with Isabella. Proclamations in Castile were probably from the very first in their joint names; both their effigies were displayed on Castilian coins; whereas when Ferdinand succeeded to his father's throne of Aragon in 1479 (where the Salic Law ran) Isabella was merely in title his Queen Consort. Gradually as the years passed and the marriage – the partnership of state – flourished, rights and titles in both countries were ignored in favour of the delights of joint rule. The deliberate impression was given of Ferdinand and

Isabella's 'sharing a single mind'. The fact that the Castilian castles and the Castilian crown revenues were reserved in theory to Isabella personally – 'at the Queen's will alone' – faded in importance compared to Ferdinand's free exercise of power in Castile; similarly Isabella, despite her technical position as a consort, was allowed to administer justice in Aragon.[10] The monarchs came to resemble two great oaks whose roots were inextricably entwined somewhere below the surface.

In 1474, however, the determination which this young woman of twenty-three displayed, far from her husband's side, was crucial in holding on to that throne of which she judged herself to be Queen Proprietress. She showed herself from the first a remarkable character as well as a redoubtable one. It was not as if Isabella had been educated in any way to handle matters of state; she had been raised in virtual seclusion by her mother, after her father's death when she was three years old, having another elder (full) brother who before his premature death was regarded as heir presumptive to Henry IV. The rigorous intellectual training granted to the young Elizabeth Tudor for example – whatever the constraints of her situation – was quite absent from the upbringing of the Castilian Princess. As a result, Queen Isabella set herself much later to learn Latin, the language of diplomacy and statecraft, in order to talk to foreign dignitaries – a decision which will earn the sympathy of all those deprived of necessary languages in resilient youth, and condemned to learn them in far less elastic middle age. (In urging on the production of a Castilian–Latin dictionary, she would observe that it was necessary because women too often learned their Latin from men.)[11] Her own daughters – including Catherine of Aragon – were notably well instructed by the great Spanish educationalist Vives; the obsessive education of daughters is often the sign of a mother who has regretted her own deprivation in that sphere.

Nor was there any sign of the Tomboy Syndrome here in childhood, no tales of a childish Isabella riding freely in the forests, no comparison to Camilla of the Volsci. Once again it was in later years that Isabella had herself instructed in those martial arts and exercises that she would have learned in childhood had she been born a prince rather than a princess. Yet in another way Isabella's enclosed upbringing, coupled with the subsequent scandals centred round the name of Henry IV's queen, and the disputed birth of Juana la Beltraneja, had left a deep mark upon her.

The pious austerity for which she was renowned must surely be ascribed not only to a natural inclination in that direction but also to an awareness of the dangers brought to a queen, expected to be the bearer of a royal family, by incontinent sexuality. Isabella's nineteenth-century biographer W. H. Prescott (whose great work can never be entirely superseded, if only for the incomparable style in which it is written) suggested that like The Lady in Milton's *Comus*, Isabella enjoyed divine protection at the court, thanks to her own virtue:

> So dear to heaven is saintly chastity . . .
> A thousand liveried angels lackey her
> Driving far off each thing of sin and guilt.[12]

In the forging of this virtue, however, childhood influences must also have played their part.

Austerity in private even extended to her own personal adornment. Isabella understood perfectly well the need for public ceremonial, the jewels, the gorgeous brocades and richly embroidered velvets which must be draped heavily around the woman who wore the crown for Castile. Off-duty as it were, her tastes were very different: she once related to her confessor as a matter for self-congratulation how she had worn 'only a simple dress of silk with three gold hem-bands'.[13] (That was not a boast which would have dropped easily from the lips of Queen Elizabeth I.)

It was appropriate, given her religious temperament, that Isabella should remain devoted to her wedded husband from the moment when, according to tradition, she instinctively picked him out from among a group of other young men crying: 'That is he! That is he!'[14] With less virtue and more human feeling she also remained jealous of Ferdinand's numerous *amours*. Adopting the obviously feminine role beloved of some Warrior Queens – like Matilda of Tuscany – she occupied herself in embroidering Ferdinand's shirts, as though the flashing needle might weave him closer to her side. It was not to be. Unfortunately for Isabella, Ferdinand's own natural inclinations were very far from lying in the same chaste direction.

Isabella's portraits show her with a long nose and a down-turned mouth, characteristics not likely to inspire fidelity in one predisposed to philander. (Portraits of Isabella's daughter Catherine of Aragon, in a time of youth and hope, show a certain similarity although the expression is much softer and the mouth turns upwards; Catherine's unhappy daughter Queen Mary Tudor, on the other hand, displays quite a marked resemblance to her grandmother, including the same glum expression.) According to the evidence of their respective suits of armour, Isabella was also taller than Ferdinand by as much as an inch: a superiority not always welcome even in a royal wife.

Yet in real life, whatever her physical imperfections, Isabella must have been endowed with charm as well as authority; for goodness does radiate its own kind of charm. Her famous virtue, the key to the generally pure tone of her court (never mind the Aragonese King's very different attitudes) was much praised. The chronicler Bernáldez called her 'a fine example of a good wife'. Isabella, like another virtuous sovereign, Tamara of Georgia, also had her bards protesting their respectful passion. The famous chastity did not preclude such ardent literary offerings as this, probably by Alvaro Bazán, which made of the Queen the object of a cavalier's unrequited adoration:[15]

> When we part
> Departs my heart
> Glory hides
> Sorrow abides.

Victory vanishes
Memory languishes
And grievous smart.

Even more significant were the comparisons literary and otherwise which made of Queen Isabella some kind of mystical figure, akin to the luminous pictures of the Blessed Virgin by Isabella's favourite Flemish artists. The poet Montoro for example went as far as to declare the Queen worthy to have given birth to the son of God. He was not alone in the comparison. After the restoration of southern Spain to Christianity by her agency, Isabella was frequently pictured as a second Virgin Mary, repairing the 'sin of Eve', in the words of Fray Inigo de Mendoza. Following her death, there would be moves to canonize Isabella, moves not limited to distant times, but recurring in the twentieth century.[16]

This latter-day history illustrates how close the halo always hovers above the head of the Warrior Queen, who has presided over a war of avowedly religious purpose: the Holy (Armed) Figurehead. At the time, it was more relevant that with her authority threatened, her pretensions questioned, these comparisons undoubtedly stood Isabella herself in good practical stead.

Civil war between Isabella's supporters and those of Juana la Beltraneja followed shortly after the death of the King of Castile. Juana, not lost for suitors under the circumstances, became affianced to King Alfonso v of Portugal; the conflict which ensued was thus in a sense as much a tug-of-war as a civil war, since the outcome would decide whether Castile in the future leaned west to Portugal or east towards Aragon.

It was Ferdinand, naturally, who was in charge of the prolonged military campaigning. As an Aragonese, he brought knowledge of new military techniques, as well as the possibility of northern alliances.[17] But Isabella, as the official co-ruler – and the Castilian – also had to play a figurehead's visible role as the inspiration of her party. She did more than that. She participated personally and effectively. It may be impossible to assess the precise military achievement of Queen Isabella, due to the general rule obtaining that any female presence or initiative upon the battlefield is greeted with a special enthusiasm born out of surprise at the successful upsetting of the natural order: as when the Venetian minister, Viaggio, wrote that 'Queen Isabel by her singular genius, masculine strength of mind and other virtues, most unusual in our own sex as well as hers, was not merely of great assistance in but the chief cause of the conquest of Granada'.[18] Nevertheless there is sufficient contemporary evidence to support the picture of a genuine contribution beyond those 'prayers' which the poet juxtaposed with Ferdinand's 'many armed men'. For one thing, it was in these first five years of that civil war that Isabella discovered in herself a vital capability for the organization of supplies which complemented the gifts of her husband.

Is is true that Isabella deferred to her husband publicly, almost ostentatiously, on all military matters in her official guise of Only-a-Weak-Woman: 'May your lordship pardon me for speaking of things which I do not understand', she began one intervention. At the same time, she was not above employing the useful Shame Syndrome when necessary to secure her own way. During the reconquest of Granada, some younger nobles were trying to persuade Ferdinand to retreat, against Isabella's advice. Isabella succeeded in gaining the day: 'The grandees, mortified at being suspended in zeal for the holy war by a woman, eagerly collected their forces.'[19]

Over the organization of supplies, and above all in the founding of the first military hospital in Europe, the Queen had less need of these tricks and ploys, since supply, possibly, and nursing, certainly, were of course traditional female concerns. Isabella had been described as 'a great general but an even greater quartermaster-general'.[20] Pioneers in thousands were recruited by the Queen (as Bernáldez attests) to build roads for the passage of the guns, while it was the King who concentrated on their disposal once they arrived. It was Isabella at the beginning of the

Reconquista who engaged Don Francisco Ramirez, known as El Artillero; he saw to it that the Castilian army was equipped with expert smiths and gunners. She approved the sending for seasoned troops in the shape of Swiss mercenaries, a very practical step. As for nursing, the equipment of 'The Queen's Hospital', six vast tents trundling from siege to siege equipped with beds and medicines and bandages, anticipated Napoleon's ambulances by more than two hundred years.

Not that the soul was ignored in all this concern to heal the body. One notes that chaplains were an essential part of Isabella's hospital force, just as Mass was always celebrated in the centre of the camp with prayers for victory, the altar plate being provided by the Chapel Royal. Even where the mercenary Swiss were concerned, Isabella convinced herself that they were good people who only 'took part in wars that they believe just'.[21]

From the first in the Civil War, the Queen did not spare herself. She rode hundreds of miles, often across the bleak Castilian mountain lands, pleading for support, invoking loyalty. Her early history of miscarriages must be attributed to these ordeals; this was especially unfortunate since the birth of a son would as ever in the case of a queen regnant have bolstered up her cause (as the birth of the future Henry II had improved the chances of the Empress Maud). In any case a daughter could not succeed in Aragon. It was not until 1476 that Isabella's only son, Prince John, was born.

One of these miscarriages occurred in the summer of 1475 after the Queen herself had taken command at Toledo, riding among her men dressed in full armour, Ferdinand being absent. Her presence — whether or not because she was careful to end each exhortation with a prayer invoking 'the aid of Thine arm' — was said to inspire exceptional confidence. But the welcome respite which the Queen's illness gave to her enemy Alfonso of Portugal illustrates all too neatly the unenviable fate of the Warrior Queen as would-be mother (a complication to which the story of Louise of Prussia will also bear testimony).

The encouraging victory by which the Castilian troops

recaptured the northern castle of Burgos in January 1476 was celebrated in the presence of the Queen. The Castilians now needed to repossess Toro and Zamora, two fortresses on the River Douro which controlled the route into their country from Portugal. Ferdinand however failed to take Zamora and the Portuguese retreated to Toro, an apparently unassailable stronghold. Since Isabella's new baby was to be born in June, she must once more have been pregnant. Nevertheless it is said that Isabella herself gave the courageous advice to pursue them, into what might well have proved a Portuguese trap. When Toro was taken, boldness paid results: Zamora itself fell shortly afterwards. Then the baby was born and it was a boy.

The child, symbol of hope, was displayed to his people in the presence of his mother, who abandoned her preferred simplicity for such an important public occasion: 'The Queen went capering on a white palfrey in a very richly gilt saddle and a very rich harness of gold and silver and she for her dress [wore] . . . brocade with many pearls of different kinds.'[22] Nor was the hope disappointed. The birth of the boy, named John after both his grandfathers, kings of Aragon and Castile respectively, did indeed signal the decline of the Portuguese cause; Juana, the loser, ended by being locked up in a nunnery, abandoned by the rapacious King Alfonso. When Ferdinand succeeded in his turn to the throne of Aragon in 1479, the stage was set for that momentous crusade, the reconquest of the last Moorish kingdom of Spain.

Ferdinand and Isabella gave their own version of the motives behind the Reconquista: it was not undertaken in order to 'lay up treasure', for they could have stayed at home 'with far less peril, travail and expense'. But 'the desire which we have to serve God and our zeal for the holy Catholic faith has induced us to set aside our own interests and ignore the continual hardships and dangers to which this cause commits us'.[23]

It is true that at one level this explanation (given incidentally to the Pope) is evidently too simple. In the words of J. H. Elliott, 'The Reconquista was not one but many things. It was at once a crusade against the infidel, a succession of military expeditions in search of plunder, and a popular migration.' This southwards migration suited the Queen of Castile, whereas the King of Aragon for obvious geographical reasons remained preoccupied with his northern French neighbour. Then there was the question of the restless Castilian nobles: as Queen Tamara had discovered in Georgia, repeated conflicts against foreign neighbours constituted one good way of occupying them and maintaining perforce their loyalty to the crown.[24]

But given the millenarian atmosphere of fifteenth-century Europe following the capture of Constantinople in 1453, and given the devout character of Isabella herself (Prescott called her 'the soul of this war'), the statement of the 'Catholic Kings' should never be dismissed by a later age as in itself insincere. 'It is very true that your war is a just one,' wrote Isabella to Ferdinand of his French involvements, 'but my war is not only a just one but a holy one.'[25] She made much of the distinction.

In 1482 the Christians captured Alhama, south-west of Granada, and from that date onwards there was a series of campaigns, as the Moors were stalked through their once proud kingdom by the predatory Spanish tigers. These were stirring days for Christians, particularly those who had long been held as prisoners of the Moors. When Ronda was recaptured, the filthy and emaciated prisoners who emerged from its dungeons were comforted by the Queen herself. The royal entry into recaptured Moclin was marked by a solemn Te Deum sung in the royal chapel; as the words were being intoned, those present heard faint underground echoes and it was gradually realized that the dungeons lay somewhere beneath the chapel. In a scene reminiscent of the prisoners' emergence in *Fidelio*, the Christian captives, long incarcerated in darkness, were led forth.

It was helpful however that the Moors were disunited by this date. A feud within the family of the aged Nasrid King Mulay Hassan meant that the realm itself was split. When Mulay Hassan's son Boabdil was captured in April 1483, he thought it worth his while to bow as a secret vassal in order to combat his father, just as Ferdinand, in those negotiations at which he was expert, thought it worth his while to accept the notion of a two-year truce. Boabdil was a faltering ally at best – at the final siege of Granada in late 1491 it was once again Boabdil who would defy the Spaniards after various changes of side in between. But his vacillations, besides giving strength to his enemies, enraged his family. His father's brother, the champion known as El Zagal ('the Valiant') preferred in his turn to surrender to the Christians after the fall of Baza in 1480, rather than to Boabdil.

This is not however to denigrate the staunchness of the Spaniards. They were obliged to mountaineer as much as fight in stark and inhospitable country, at least in the early stages of the campaign. And if Boabdil was no great general, El Zagal on the contrary justified his name by inflicting a crushing defeat on the Christians in 1483.

Isabella's own efforts divided, like those of Queen Tamara, into her private strategic contributions and her public 'Figurehead' appearances. The latter included the ceremonial occasions, such as that at Seville, when the militia were reviewed in full battle array, with successive battalions lowering their standards as the Queen passed. Isabella was seated in a saddle-chair embossed in gold and silver, borne by a chestnut mule whose bridle was of crimson satin covered in gold embroidery. At this review Isabella formally raised her hat to her husband (which meant that her head was still covered by her coif) and the 'kings' bowed to each other thrice.

But there are also numerous glimpses of her, splendidly serene and courageous before sieges: it was lucky for her, perhaps, in terms of public display of her person, that the Reconquista was predominantly a war of sieges. The latter created their own mythology by which the arrival of the Queen was said to spur on the Castilian troops, to the extent that victory, previously in doubt, became certain. Her visit to Málaga for example, in the summer of 1487, came as it turned out at the end of three months' arduous siege: for on 18 August Málaga finally surrendered, a turning-point in the Reconquista, after which it was doubtful that the Moors could long preserve their kingdom. The arrival of the Spanish mascot – or rather Holy Figurehead – came to spell doom to the Moors. It was the arrival of Isabella before the walls of Baza late in 1488 which broke the gloomy news to the inhabitants (led by El Zagal) that the siege was to be prosecuted with renewed vigour.

We hear of the Moors craning their necks over the walls of the city in order to catch a glimpse of the legendary Queen. They must have felt shock as well as curiosity. Certainly Isabella in her mail ('No bad personification of chivalry' in this attire, Prescott called her) constituted a very different feminine image to that of the bewitching Sultana Soraya, Boabdil's mother. Although originally a Christian captive, Soraya had accepted the rich opportunities for intrigue and influence – but not for overt warfare – presented by the world of the royal harem. 'Weep for it like a woman, since you have failed to defend it like a man', Boabdil was told by the Sultana when he finally left Granada and turned back for one last melancholy look towards the lost Paradise.[26] But the woman at whom the Moors gaped from the walls of Baza did not weep; on the contrary, she passed her whole army in review mounted on a spirited Andalusian horse with a flowing mane. The cry which sprang from the lips of her soldiers will come as no surprise to those who have followed the fortunes of Tamara, King of Kartli: 'Castile, Castile, for our King Isabella!'[27]

And so the Christian campaign moved forward inexorably to the final siege of the city of Granada late in 1491. For this siege that celebrated camp – as it was then – of Santa Fe, to which Columbus would repair, was specifically created. To the last Isabella maintained the traditionally double role of a Warrior Queen: on the one hand she continued to plot the final strategy to secure Granada with Ferdinand, and has sometimes been credited with the idea of encirclement which proved so successful. On the other hand she maintained her figurehead's role: the chivalrous 'Queen's Skirmish' took place when Isabella was spied aloft with her children, out to view the exotic palace of the

Alhambra (curiosity was not all on the Moorish side). A javelin with an insulting message 'for the Queen of Castile' affixed to it had been hurled in the direction of her quarters; single combat between the Moorish champion Yarfe and the Christian Garcilaso de la Vega, which the Christian won, was held to settle the matter.

Boabdil formally surrendered on 2 January 1492. Four days later, on the feast of the Epiphany, Ferdinand and Isabella entered the city of Granada in triumph. By this time – in a gesture which was both symbolic and practical – the principal mosque had been reconsecrated as a church; here Mass could be celebrated and thanks for the great victory could be given. After that the two 'kings' processed to the Alhambra and in the *Mexuar* or presence chamber in another symbolic gesture possessed themselves of the seats of the Moorish rulers of Granada. Soon the flag of St James, Christian patron of the crusade, would fly above the town: and the traditional cry of 'Santiago! Santiago!' would join the universal acclamation: 'Granada, Granada, for the illustrious kings of Castile!' An eye-witness termed it 'the most distinguished and blessed day there has ever been in Spain'.[28]

The imperialist energies of the 'Catholic kings' (the Pope gave them the title following the Reconquista) were naturally released by the end of the military engagements which had preoccupied them for the last eighteen years. On the one hand Columbus was sponsored in his western venture. On the other hand Ferdinand began to look elsewhere in Europe; not only towards neighbouring Navarre, but to the south of Italy. Here he desired to establish the kingdom of Naples as an appurtenance to that of Aragon, much as Isabella had added Granada to Castile. In so doing, he introduced the influence of Spain into that mess of duchies, despotisms, cardinals and *condottieri* which constituted late-fifteenth-century Italy. One of the duchies was the Sforza duchy of Milan. When Ludovico Sforza invoked the aid of the French King to bolster up his doubtful claim to rule it, he did more than merely add to that general central Italian turmoil. For France – the House of Anjou – as well as Spain, had its pretensions towards the debatable kingdom of Naples.

The story of Ludovico's niece, Caterina Sforza, bold and tragic, both virago and victim, provides a melancholy footnote to these Spanish endeavours, which were ultimately successful and went towards establishing the vast Habsburg Empire, including Spain, Spanish America and Naples, which was ruled over by Isabella's grandson Charles v.* In a sense the fortunes of Isabella the Catholic and Caterina Sforza are as much a counterpoint to each other as were those of Matilda of Tuscany and the Empress Maud. Unlike the latter pair, Isabella and Caterina were in effect contemporaries. But Caterina, subject throughout her life to convenient scorn on the ground of her sex by her political enemies, ended by being violated at the hands of her conqueror. Isabella, as has been noted, was not only a possible early candidate for canonization soon after her death but remained one.

As with Matilda and the Empress Maud, it was religious purpose which was the apparent difference. To Isabella in August 1492 the Borgia Pope Alexander vi could write: 'Your serenity, as greatly befits a monarch, from whom others must copy the example of virtuous living, desires to protect and defend the Catholic faith . . .'[30] This was not the language which the Pope felt inclined to use towards Caterina Sforza, who ruled Forlì and Imola, part of the territory stretching from Ravenna through the Romagna over which the Pope claimed overlordship. Caterina was on the contrary in one papal bull 'the daughter of iniquity' and in another communication 'the daughter of perdition'. But it was not in fact the relative morality of the two ladies (far apart as that might be) which was at issue. The truth was more cynical, or perhaps one should say more political.

* Although if, as has been suggested, Caterina Sforza was the 'cultural model' for the queen in the game of chess, which attained its present power as a piece in the late fifteenth century, then she has achieved another kind of immortality.[29]

Alexander VI (by birth from Valencia and thus a subject of Ferdinand) passionately needed the support of the 'Catholic kings' in his papal campaigns and intrigues: Spain was finally part of the Holy League including the Pope and the Emperor which would drive the French out of Naples and establish Ferdinand's claim to southern Italy. On the other hand Alexander's son, Cesare Borgia, needed those lands ruled over by Caterina on behalf of her young son in order to form a powerful central Italian bloc. The sexual freedom of choice which Caterina Sforza determinedly exercised gave useful ammunition to those opposed to her for quite different reasons; here was a Warrior Queen whose lustfulness could be denounced to good effect. For Isabella there was the Warrior Queen's other potential reward of the halo.

Caterina Sforza was born in 1462, the illegitimate daughter of Galeazza Maria Sforza, later Duke of Milan, and his mistress.[31] She was brought up by her grandmother Bianca Visconti-Sforza. Her father was assassinated by the Viscontis in 1474, the year in which Isabella ascended the throne of Castile. Three years later, Caterina was married off by proxy to Girolamo Riario, nephew of the then Pope Sixtus IV.

Caterina was well educated according to the humanist tradition, and even in youth was said to have been fascinated by the deeds of famous men and women. The Tomboy Syndrome is here seen at work. Unlike Isabella, Caterina is said to have excelled at boisterous athletic sports: she was obsessed by hunting and dogs – big dogs such as bloodhounds, setters and greyhounds. (And unlike Isabella, Caterina was beautiful.) Her earliest soldiering was in 1483 when she defended her husband's territory of Forlì from the Venetian threat. From the first Caterina relished such martial activity as she had once relished hunting; she maintained an iron discipline, not always without the aid of cruel punishments. The death of the Pope, her husband's uncle (and the fear of the decline in the Riario cause), found Caterina, riding at the gallop with a cry of 'Duca, duca, Girolamo! Girolamo!', to hold the fortress of Sant' Angelo until it could be handed over to the legal successor of Sixtus. Significantly, Caterina, once inside the fortress, invoked the name of Galeazza Maria Sforza – the nearest strong male figure – to illustrate her defiance. She had as much brains as her father, she shouted to those who wished her to admit a plenipotentiary to negotiate.

Caterina was seven months pregnant at the time and in her gold satin gown with a vast train, a huge velvet hat with long plumes, a contemporary wrote that 'only her belt with the curved sword and bag of gold ducats hanging down from it was masculine'. He might have added: that and the free cursing towards the soldiers in which Caterina on that occasion and many others indulged.

The illness of Girolamo Riario meant that Caterina effectively ruled Forlì; his death in 1488, slaughtered by the Orsi, meant that she ruled it entirely, if nominally for their son. For the next twelve years, she led a life of extreme turbulence as she attempted to maintain her independence in the light of neighbourly oppression, papal claims and finally the arrival of the French forces. Her refusal to surrender the fortress of Ravaldino stands in general for her attitude towards her own rights – theoretically those of her family, but in fact one detects in her a more personal stubborn refusal to be consigned to the female world of submission. (Not that she was above invoking the image of Only-a-Weak-Woman like many other Warrior Queens when it was to her advantage: 'nobody believes me . . . being just a lady and timid too', she wrote to her uncle Ludovico Sforza concerning the Venetian threat to Marradi which she had persistently predicted.)

When Caterina's large family of children were held hostages for the surrender, she is supposed to have shouted – in a famous story related in a series of versions of increasing coarseness: 'Do you think, you fools, that I haven't the stuff to make others?' And so saying, she scornfully lifted up her skirt. (In the version which Caterina Sforza's biographer, Ernst Breisach, thinks the most likely, Caterina pointed out that she was already pregnant with another child when her existing children were threatened, adding that even if she wasn't she could always remarry and have another family.)[32]

As for her bloodthirstiness, Caterina's treatment of the Orsi family who were the assassins of her husband recalls the vengeance of Boadicea against the wreckers of her daughters: in both cases the details justify that primitive fear concerning the virago unloosed as being deadlier than the male. There were public executions and secret stranglings, followed by the frightful death of the eighty-year-old Andrea Orsi. Dressed in a vest, shirt and one sock, with his hands tied, the patriarch was first of all condemned to watch his house being pillaged and demolished. Then he was dragged round a square tied to a board at a horse's tail; finally his heart was cut out and his aged body dismembered, the pieces thrown to the crowd.

'Oh glorious Madonna, be merciful with a miserable sinner', pleaded Simone Fionni, another potential victim. But Caterina replied: 'Let vengeance rule, not pity. I shall let the dogs tear you to pieces.' (In the event he was spared and managed to escape.)

Then there were the lovers, increasingly young, continuously virile: placing Caterina within the Voracity Syndrome may have been politically expedient for her enemies, but it was not exactly unjust. The vengeance which Caterina would take in 1495 upon another family responsible for the death of her beloved castellan Giacomo Feo (he who transported her into 'the heaven of Venus and Mars') would rival that exacted upon the Orsi. The assassin was killed, his wife and sons flung down a well and left to die. But on the other hand Giacomo himself, probably with the connivance of Caterina's legitimate sons, had been speared and then horribly mutilated before he was killed.

The sufferings of the Jews, Muslims and suspect Christians at the hands of the Inquisition in distant Spain were inflicted on the orders of Isabella's religious confessors, not her own; Isabella herself disliked the shedding of blood (including, incidentally, bullfighting). Once again it was easier to be the pious Isabella at her prayers than Caterina, who on certain occasions could hear the sound of the tortures she had ordered in her own chamber.

Yet the Orsi and the murderers of Giacomo had personally bereaved and insulted Caterina; the victims of Isabella the Catholic died for a principle – a principle of religious unity. But in the judgement of history where a Warrior Queen is concerned, it seems to be better to be associated with religious principle than with personal vengeance.

First of the lovers was Mario Ordelaffi, with whom Caterina was probably in love, in an idyll which lasted through the summer of 1489. Then the Pope took the opportunity to announce that because of 'Caterina's disorderly life' he intended to award Forlì to his own son, Francescolotto Gibo, whose life was quite as dissolute. The trap lying in wait for a Warrior Queen (who could not be compared to 'the new Eve', like Isabella the Catholic) becomes apparent.

Caterina's recipe book shows herself obsessed by the preservation of her beauty, in the most traditionally feminine manner: Queen Elizabeth I could not have done more, and in fact where teeth were concerned did less. Lotions of nettle-seed, cinnabar, ivy leaves, saffron and sulphur were applied to maintain the fairness of her celebrated blonde locks. Other lotions removed unwanted hair from her wonderfully white skin. Pearly teeth were guaranteed by daily applications of charcoaled rosemary stems, pulverized marble and coral cuttlebone. There was rose-water to bathe famously blue eyes, and cream for her white breasts. These appurtenances and practices of a Renaissance beauty were all very well; but when Caterina fought a long battle – masculine by the standards of the time – to hang on to her beloved territories of Forlì against the Pope's desire to grant them elsewhere, she found that her very femininity was gleefully turned against her.

In 1497, for example, Venice expressed itself shocked by her 'boundless sensual appetite', when the real problem was that of Florentine aggression, which it was believed that Forlì might encourage. It hardly needs saying that a 'boundless sensual appetite' was if anything the mark of a Renaissance prince. But Caterina was not born a 'prince' – nor had she established herself as such in the minds of her people, once again unlike Queen Isabella.

The accession of Louis XII to the throne of France in 1498 brought with it new turmoil for central Italy. Cesare Borgia went secretly to France, where a deal was struck that Louis would help Cesare to drive the ruling families out of the Romagna in his own interest, while Louis' own claims to Milan and the southern Italian kingdoms of Naples (also claimed by Ferdinand) would be respected. The Treaty of Blois of February 1499 was an especial blow to Caterina by which Venice, her traditional predatory enemy, allied with France. Finally on 9 March Alexander VI promulgated that papal bull which designated Caterina as the 'daughter of iniquity' – and formally invested Cesare Borgia with Imola and Forlì.

By the autumn of 1499 Milan had fallen to the French and Ludovico Sforza had fled. Beset in Forlì, Caterina wrote to Ludovico: 'should I have to perish, I want to perish like a man'. That bold wish was not however to be granted to her.

Imola proved finally impossible to defend against Cesare Borgia. Caterina however clung on to Ravaldino fortress and refused to flee. Some of her plans for defiance were perhaps over-optimistic, such as sending the Borgia Pope Alexander VI letters which had been impregnated with poison or left in a plague chest (it needs a long spoon to poison a Borgia and the plan was bungled). On 12 December she said that she would 'show the Borgia that a woman too can handle artillery'. The town itself capitulated by the end of 1499. Still Caterina maintained her defiance within the stronghold even after the inhabitants of the town had been given short shrift – rape as well as pillage described by Caterina robustly as 'just punishment for a city which had surrendered like a whore'. Caterina continued to refuse such inducements as a safe conduct and a pension (showing herself in this respect more of a Boadicea than a Zenobia).

The final assault took place in January 1500. Cesare asked for '*la bellicosa signora di Imola e Forlì*' dead or alive, and on receiving her alive – despite the fact that she had been captured by a

French officer and was thus officially the captive of the French King – held her incommunicado for forty-eight hours while he treated her as his soldiers had treated the women of Forlì. Bernardi wrote of the 'injustices committed to our unfortunate Madonna Caterina Sforza who had such a beautiful body'. But Cesare quipped to his officers that Caterina had defended her fortress better than she had defended her virtue.

Still Caterina would not sign away her rights to Imola and Forlì. She was not released until June 1501 by which time her beauty, that carefully tended asset, had vanished. She still tried to negotiate the return of some of her rights, but in vain. Her last years were happier, however; she began to train up her young son by Giovanni de' Medici, Giovanni della Banda Nera, born in 1498, to be a solider, a worthy member of the house of Sforza. She died in May 1509.

It could be argued that at least as a mother Caterina died with more hope than had Isabella the Catholic five years earlier. The Castilian Queen's only son, Prince John, whose birth had been attended by such rejoicings, had died in 1497. Of her three surviving daughters, Juana was mad: but she inherited the crown officially since her husband Philip the Fair of Flanders refused to allow Ferdinand more than the regency after his wife's death. (Isabella's defence of female inheritance had born fruit.) Another daughter Maria, who had been married to the King of Portugal, was already dead, as was her son Miguel, who might have united in his person the crowns of Portugal and Spain, as once his grandparents had united those of Aragon and Castile. Isabella's third daughter Catherine of Aragon was already a widow following the death of her first husband Prince Arthur of England; she lingered in that country with a view to marrying – perhaps – his younger brother Henry.

Ferdinand expressed his own reaction to his wife's death: 'there is therefore hope that Our Lord has her in His Glory, which for her is a better and more lasting realm than those she ruled here'. Peter Martyr of Anghiera, on the other hand, the humanist historian, did not forget her martial achievements: the world – not only Spain – had lost its noblest ornament, he wrote, since Isabella had been the mirror of every virtue, the shield of the innocent 'and an avenging sword to the wicked'.[33]

Isabella's own will, however, expressed the matters which had preoccupied her on earth, including the unity of Spain for which she had fought, and just rule for the Indians in the New World.[34] But her instinct for simplicity prevailed at the last: she requested that there should not be an extravagant funeral; instead money should be spent on providing dowries for poor girls (otherwise unable to get married) and ransoms for the Christian captives in the hands of the Moors in Africa. And Isabella, still with her prayers fighting the fight for the Faith, prayed that Ferdinand should continue to expand Spain into Muslim Africa, as he had once expanded Castile into Granada with Isabella at his side: she with her prayers (but in full armour), he with many armed men.

CHAPTER THIRTEEN

Elizabetha Triumphans

~~~

They couch their pikes and bow their ensigns down
When as their sacred royal Queen passed by
In token of their loyal bearèd hearts
To her alone, and none but only she –

ELIZABETHA TRIUMPHANS (1588)

The reign in which the character of chariot-driving Boadicea was destined to be restored to British mythology (or history) did not begin under auspicious circumstances for a woman ruler. The concept was on the contrary generally attacked. 'Murmur ye at mine anointed because she is a woman? Who made man and woman, you, or I? If I made her to live, may I not make her to reign?' These affronted questions were put into the mouth of Almighty God in a pamphlet of 1559: *An Harborowe for Faithfull and Trewe Subjectes against the late blown Blast*. The anointed woman in question was Elizabeth Tudor, who had succeeded to the throne of England in the previous year at the age of twenty-five. The author was John Aylmer, newly restored Protestant Archdeacon of Stow.[1]

Aylmer's intention in quoting God, as it were, was to defend the new Queen from a far noisier piece of propaganda: John Knox's *The First Blast of the Trumpet against the monstrous regiment of Women*. The virulence of Knox's language in attacking the whole concept of female sovereignty can scarcely be exaggerated. Neither the passage of time nor the standards of another age have paled the rich colours of his abuse.[*][3] 'How abominable

---

[*] But the nineteenth-century editor of Knox's works – male – observed that if John Knox had foreseen Queen Victoria ruling over a vast Christian empire, he would have died happy, like Simeon singing the Nunc Dimittis in the temple![2]

before God, is the Empire or Rule of a wicked woman, yea of a traiteresse and bastard . . .' he writes. Again: 'For to promote a woman to bear rule, superiority, dominion or empire above any realm, nation or city, is repugnant to nature, continuously to God, a thing most contrarious to his revealed will and approved ordinance, and finally it is the subversion of good order, of all equity and justice.' As for women in general: 'their sight in civil regiment is but blindness; their strength, weakness; their counsel foolishness and judgment frenzy, if it be rightly considered'.

The fathers of the Church are quoted, including St Paul, Tertullian (the whole sex is 'the port and gate of the devil') and St Augustine ('woman ought to be repressed and bridled betimes, if she aspire to any dominion'). Then nature is brought into play: 'no man ever saw the lion make obedience, and stoop before the lioness . . .' Finally history is invoked: 'For when the males of the kingly stock failed, as oft chanced in Israel and sometimes in Juda, it never entered into the hearts of the people to choose and promote any of the king's daughters . . .' In short: 'where a woman reigneth and papists bear authority . . . there must needs Satan be president of the council'.

The reference to papists is significant. The 'Regiment' or rulership (its contemporary meaning) of females to which Knox so spuriously objected was that of three Catholic queens – Mary of Guise, regent of Scotland in the absence of her daughter Mary Queen of Scots (crowning her was 'to put a saddle upon the back of an unruly cow'),[4] Catherine de' Medici in France, and Mary Tudor in England. It was a classic piece of historical bad timing that no sooner had Knox denounced the female regiment than a Protestant monarch – but one who unfortunately for Knox happened to be a woman – replaced Catholic Mary on the throne of England. Nor was Knox alone in his denunciation. The great Calvin too had joined in deploring such an unnatural development.

Speedy and embarrassed revisionism was the order of the day lest Elizabeth, the hope of the reformers, be fatally offended. It was particularly awkward that both Calvin and Knox, in an extension of that idea attributed to Muhammad that 'a people who place a woman over their affairs do not prosper', had stated that civil wars generally tore apart those kingdoms ruled over by women.⁵ Insecure at the beginning of her reign, Elizabeth would hardly welcome the notion that God himself might foment a rebellion in her own realm, just because she was a woman.

Calvin wrote a mortified letter to Elizabeth's Secretary of State, William Cecil. He admitted that Knox had asked him in a private conversation what he thought of female sovereignty. 'I candidly replied, that as it was a deviation from the original and proper order of nature,' among the punishments Man had to endure since the Fall 'it was to be ranked no less than slavery.' On the other hand, individual women *were* occasionally well endowed to govern, evidently raised up by God's authority, either to condemn the inactivity of the opposite sex or simply to set forth His own glory (as a creator). Calvin instanced the biblical Deborah and Huldah and quoted the prophet Isaiah: 'Queens should be nursing mothers of the church.' (Knox had dismissed both Deborah and Huldah in *The First Blast*.)⁶

Even Knox himself was compelled to backtrack. In July 1559 he wrote with the best air of apology he could muster to the English Queen. 'Nothing in my book conceived is, or can be prejudicial to your grace's just regiment,' he declared, adding characteristically, 'providing that ye be not found ingrate [ungrateful] unto God.' The official line to cope with Elizabeth's presence on the throne was that indicated by Calvin to Cecil: female rule was still unnatural but every now and then God would provide for it for His own good reasons. Knox however added the rider that this put a special burden upon a female (as opposed to a male) sovereign to prove herself worthy of the task. In general the Protestants now fell back on the distinction between Good Queens and Bad Queens: useful in an age which would be marked by the ostensible public rivalry of a Catholic Mary Queen of Scots and Protestant Elizabeth.⁷

Aylmer's defence in *An Harborowe for Faithfull and Trewe Subjectes* leaned heavily on historical precedent.⁸ The stage army of

Warrior Queens was dutifully paraded across his pages, including those who had enjoyed an 'antique glory' such as Artemisia, famous for vanquishing Xerxes. Revisionism was not entirely on the side of the Calvinists: Aylmer pointed out that it had been an obvious error to prefer Stephen to Matilda (the Empress Maud), since England had been punished with prolonged civil war for ignoring the claims of the rightful heir to the kingdom – or in this case heiress. This stood the previous Calvinist argument on its head. But perhaps the most remarkable piece of revisionism was that which introduced the name of Anne Boleyn among celebrated women of the past such as Margaret of Flanders:* for had it not been Anne Boleyn who had brought about the wonders of the Protestant Reformation?

Historical precedent apart, Aylmer's point of view was not really so far from that of Calvin, as revised, or even that of Knox. It was God who had appointed Queen Elizabeth to reign, as part of His divine plan: even, as in the selection of a female governor, working through weakness. When Aylmer wrote that if God made her to live, might He not also 'make her to reign?', he was expressly defending the divine selection of Elizabeth Tudor; in no way did Aylmer, Elizabeth's other defenders, Elizabeth's other critics and above all the Queen herself attempt to defend the right of women in general to rule equally with men.

As it is impossible to exaggerate the virulence of Knox's language in *The First Blast* it is also impossible to exaggerate the general distaste and anxiety felt towards the notion of a female ruler. When Elizabeth's half-sister Mary Tudor ascended the throne in 1553, many questioned whether it was even legal for a woman to inherit: there had been no queen regnant since that doubtful, because unsubstantiated, claim of the Empress Maud four centuries before. The rights of the female in the table of

---

* It was another awkward situation that Henry VIII's Act of Succession of 1536 declaring Elizabeth to be a bastard had never been repealed. Nor was it repealed now.[9] Since Elizabeth was able to succeed under the terms of her father's will, it was thought more tactful to let that sleeping and by now rather embarrassing old dog of King Henry's matrimonial entanglements lie.

royal succession had generally been subsumed into those of her husband, who would often have a lesser claim of his own. Thus in 1485 Elizabeth of York had in fact an infinitely better dynastic claim to the throne than her future husband, Henry VII, *de facto* monarch after the battle of Bosworth. Then their marriage added her right to Henry's might and he was of course the one out of the pair who ruled (Elizabeth being merely Queen Consort). The will of Edward VI had concentrated on the *male* heirs to females within the English royal succession such as his Grey cousins, although it was finally disregarded in favour of the superior dynastic claim of his elder half-sister Mary Tudor.[10]

Where might and right did not coalesce, the choice of a husband was always likely to be a problem in the case of a queen regnant. It was not at all clear that the husband of such a queen might not have the actual right to be regarded as the king: when the youthful Mary Tudor was betrothed to her cousin the Emperor, Henry VIII was worried whether he might not thus secure a title to her throne. One Chief Justice advised that although the husband could not call himself king by right, because the crown lay outside the bounds of feudal law (the husband of a feudal heiress automatically assumed her titles, rights and possessions), the Queen Regnant could grant him the title if she chose.[11] In the event Mary Tudor's actual husband, Philip II of Spain, was considered to be King of England as well (a worrying precedent). Mary Queen of Scots' disastrous second husband, Darnley, whom she married in 1565, was always referred to as King Henry.

Under the circumstances it was understandable that Cardinal Reginald Pole should have tried to persuade Queen Mary Tudor to take that course actually adopted by Queen Elizabeth: no marriage, but a single-minded devotion to that role granted her by heaven, and for which through many dangers she had been signally spared.[12] (Where marriage and position were concerned, as the relative fortunes of the unmarried Elizabeth and much-married Mary Queen of Scots demonstrate, queens regnant in the sixteenth century resembled career women in the late twentieth century, in that they experienced regrettable difficulty in 'having it all'.)

The objections to female regiment were not entirely theoretical. As Sir John Neale pointed out in his biography of Elizabeth I, government itself was 'a masculine business, with its world a court constructed for a king'. The idea of protecting a queen from the rigours and difficulties of government was of course implicit in the concentration on the topic of her marriage; Elizabeth's widowed brother-in-law Philip II (and putative suitor at the beginning of her reign) advised her to marry soon, if only that her husband could then relieve her 'of those labours which are only fit for men'.[13]

In vain the coronation tableaux leaned heavily on such stories as that of Deborah, ruling for forty years of peace. The popular mood was better expressed by the fears of the Spanish Ambassador de Feria following Elizabeth's accession: 'what can be expected from a country governed by a Queen, and she a young lass, who though sharp is without prudence?' This was not mere chauvinism – in both senses of the word. There was trouble in the House of Lords over Elizabeth's title as 'Supreme Head of the Church' in view of her inconvenient sex, and Nicholas Heath, Archbishop of York, made what were described as some 'ripe remarks' on the subject. In the end the Queen became the 'Supreme Governor'.[14]

This, then, was to be the triumph of Queen Elizabeth I. She ascended the English throne at a time of outright popular hostility towards female sovereigns, and by a mixture of artfulness, intelligence and instinct survived to rule for forty-five years, her personal prestige – both as a woman and as a monarch – growing with every year.

Such a triumph did not happen overnight. Two years after Elizabeth's accession – in 1560 – when the question of her own successor was being raised, the claim of Henry Hastings, Earl of Huntingdon, the last of the Plantagenets, was advanced over those of a host of females of royal Tudor descent (including Mary

Queen of Scots): 'the cry is that they do not want any women rulers'. How sublimely different was the mood of Leicester's will of August 1587 in which he hoped Queen Elizabeth, now in her fifties, would prove to be 'the eldest [i.e. the longest-living] prince that ever God gave over England'! If Leicester, the favourite, is held to be a prejudiced source, then one might cite the tribute of the Pope Sixtus V, around the same time, against whom the same charge of prejudice can scarcely be laid. The Queen of England might be only a woman, he wrote, and only mistress of half an island, yet she had made herself feared by Spain, by France, by the Empire and 'by all'.[15]

The triumph also remained personal to Elizabeth. Forty years on, when this question of the old Queen's successor had become acute, it was Mary's son, Scottish James, who was the front runner (even though excluded, as an alien, by the will of Henry VIII), not only because he was of commensurate rank, but also because he was a man. The ever-confident French Ambassador – ultimately however no great prophet – wrote that it was 'certain' that the English would never again submit to the rule of a woman.[16] The early years of James's reign were also marked by a warmth on the part of the English towards the new ruler – just because he was a man, and a vigorous one in his prime – which is often overlooked in view of their subsequent disillusionment.

The general estimate of the female sex, never high, not only declined in the seventeenth century, but declined amid percept-ible relief, now that humble lip-service did not have to be paid to She-who-was-on-the-Throne. In a poem printed in 1650 in memory of 'our dread Virago', Elizabeth, Anne Bradstreet called attention to this decline following the Queen's death: 'Now say, have women worth? Or have they none? Or had they some, but with our Queen is't gone?'[17]

The fact was that the 'dread Virago' herself had never made any effort to improve the general appraisal of woman's worth; for cogent reasons, that was the very last of her intentions. An interesting article in *Feminist Review* of 1980 by Allison Heisch considers Queen Elizabeth I at length in terms of those women who are 'honorary males', and thus have no particular impact 'unless indirect and negative' on the status of women of their time.[18] (The same 'negative' argument was often applied by feminists to the presence of Mrs Thatcher as Prime Minister of Great Britain since, as will be seen, Mrs Thatcher explicitly denied any debt to Women's Liberation.) Queen Elizabeth would hardly have approved of the source of these sentiments – a feminist review. Had she been granted a glimpse into the future to witness the rise of feminism, she would, one must believe, have greeted the spectacle with a royal shudder; just as Queen Victoria, another queen regnant, looked on Women's Rights with abhorrence.[19] On the other hand, Queen Elizabeth I would have heartily approved of the verdict of 'honorary male'.

It was customary for her to deride her own sex along stereotyped lines, out of policy. For example, women were popularly supposed to be chatterboxes: when the Queen was congratulated on knowing six languages, she remarked wryly that it was 'no marvel to teach a woman to talk; it were harder to teach her to hold her tongue'.[20] She also believed what she said. For she was different. That was the constantly reiterated message.

The differentness of the Queen from all other female subjects was the cornerstone of her self-presentation, worked out or perhaps simply instinctively felt, by a genius at the art. Her weapons in this self-presentation were two. Firstly, she worked upon her female nature to provide a delicate, exquisite image of the lady who needed to be protected – and the goddess who had to be adored. Secondly, she presented herself as a 'prince': like many successful pieces of composite propaganda, the second part was in direct contradiction of the first.

In all this, there was one real danger and another possible one. The possible danger was of a husband, bringing with him perpetual masculine control. But by maintaining herself as a virgin goddess to the end of her life, despite a farrago of courtships, the Queen avoided that particular peril. Sir James Melville, visiting the English court on behalf of Mary Queen of Scots, observed to Elizabeth when she had been on the throne five years without committing herself to a bridegroom: 'Madam . . . you think if you were married, you would be but Queen of England, and now you are King and Queen both; you may not endure a commander.'[21] He went to the heart of the matter although neither he nor the Queen herself – whose most profound decisions were taken by the highly roundabout method of endless procrastination – can have envisaged that Elizabeth would end her life, still King and Queen, still without suffering a commander.

The real danger to Elizabeth, both as goddess and as 'prince', was war. For in the late sixteenth century Europe was a sphere where control passed inevitably to a man. In his *History of Scotland* George Buchanan, tutor to the young King James of Scotland, digressed in his turn on the unnaturalness of female government, especially in war: ''Tis no less becoming [in] a Woman to pronounce Judgment, to levy Forces, to conduct an Army, to give a Signal to the Battle, than it is for a Man to tease Wool, to handle the Distaff, to Spin or Card, and to perform the other Services of the Weaker Sex.' For that which was reckoned 'Fortitude and Severity' in a man turned to 'Madness and Cruelty' in a woman.[22] This was one challenge to her authority that Elizabeth could not avoid. When and if war broke out, the Queen not only had to suffer a commander, but she also had to go further and appoint one.

Under the circumstances, it is hardly surprising that Queen Elizabeth showed from the beginning of her reign to the end a dislike and fear of war verging on the pathological. Her very jewels – always the emblematic messengers of her true feelings – spoke in favour of peace; as the years passed, she took to wearing jewels in the shape of spring flowers, in order to symbolize the peace which she was proud to have brought to the kingdom.[23] As to her commanders, she was of course extremely careful that they should be seen at all times as the royal representatives. The first need for a military initiative on the government's part came in 1569 when the northern earls revolted. (Eleven peaceful years had passed since Elizabeth's accession: in a poem written to celebrate the suppression of this rebellion, the Queen was to refer – without regret – to 'our rusty sword'.) The revolt was put down by Lord Hunsdon. But when the Queen thanked him officially, it was for being 'by God appointed to be the instrument of *my* glory'.[24]

Then the Queen used every conceivable card in her hand – including that potential ace of trumps (which would never in fact be played), her marriage, in order to avoid military involvement in the Netherlands, where Protestant rebels were locked in conflict with the overlordship of Catholic Spain. When Elizabeth could hold back no longer, and command had gone to Leicester, she enjoined him firmly 'not in any sort to hazard a battle without great advantage'. (There were to be no false heroics about the sheer glory of the contest here.) That zest for conquest which possessed Zenobia and Tamara was quite lacking in Queen Elizabeth I, who made of this deficiency – as some might have rated it – a virtue: 'In my ambition of glory I have never sought to advance the territories of my land . . . I have used my forces to keep the enemy from you.' She added pointedly, 'I have thereby thought your safety the greater and your danger the less.'[25]

War of course brought another kind of bondage, and this bondage applied to monarchs male and female alike: for war was liable to bring the monarch under the control of those who financed it, notably Parliament voting for the necessary taxation. Elizabeth practised an ostentatious parsimony in this respect, regarding war as a 'cancer' which ate up private men and their patrimony, princes and their estates. As Simon Adams has written recently, not only did Elizabeth have 'no martial ambitions' but she had on the contrary 'a healthy suspicion of expensive military adventurism'.[26] This sensible attitude (to those indifferent to the rival claims, so costly in men and money, of national glory) was especially prudent in view of her sex. If she were to exercise any control in the sphere of war, such a control might be considered unsuitable coming from a woman: in or out of her control, a war might bankrupt her.

It was Mary Queen of Scots, not Elizabeth, who referred to

herself in the sad declining years of her captivity as one who would rather pray with Esther than take the sword with Judith; but the English Queen too was no Judith at heart. As a result of avoiding Judith's severe and sword-wielding womanhood, Elizabeth had by 1574 freed herself from debt for the first time. This has been significantly contrasted with the situation in the last years of her reign, when she was no longer able to emulate peace-loving Esther or peacefully ruling Deborah: war now cost her the horrifying sum (then) of three and a half million pounds.[27]

Part of the trouble with the ambitious young Essex in the 1590s was that his hotheaded love of war was inimical to his royal mistress, dote as she might upon his stylish rashness when it was displayed, for example, in a court tournament in her own honour. When Francis Bacon was advising his patron Essex how to secure a reconciliation with the Queen, he suggested that he should not be so warlike in his talk 'for her majesty loveth peace'.[28]

As the young Indian braves in Western films used to be routinely portrayed as eager for war, where their elders were content to smoke the pipe of peace, so Elizabeth and Essex were ranged against each other by their generations, he as a war-loving young man, she as a peace-loving old woman. It proved a recipe for disaster, but thanks to Elizabeth's long practice of what she called the 'wit of the fox', it turned out in the end to be Essex's disaster, not her own. The reference is to the Queen's interview with the historian William Lambarde. In 1601 Lambarde presented her with his *Pandecta*, the various records of the Tower of London during the Middle Ages. A discussion concerning the meaning of certain mediaeval legal terms followed in which the Queen was pleased to demonstrate her own considerable learning. Were *rediseisnes*, for instance, as she supposed, unlawful and forcible throwing of men out of their lawful possessions? Lambarde confirmed that they were. 'In those days', the Queen observed with satisfaction, 'force and arms did prevail: but now the wit of the fox is everywhere . . .'[29]

*

Integral to Queen Elizabeth's creation of herself as a 'prince' were sedulous references to her descent from King Henry VIII – 'Great Harry' – in a rich working of the Appendage Syndrome. Knox had advised the Queen in his somewhat limited apology not to 'brag of your birth' but brag she did, in full measure, and over and over again. ('Well did she show, great Harry was her sire, Whom Europe did for valour most admire', wrote Lady Diana Primrose after the Queen's death.) Elizabeth was also artful in associating herself with contemporary male leaders, in order to underline her possession of 'masculine' courage. It was her recurrent theme (not only in that reverberating speech at Tilbury to which we will return) that she had 'the heart of a man', not of a woman. 'And I am not afraid of anything', she added on one occasion, having made the familiar boast to the Spanish Ambassador, declaring herself in the process to be quite as brave as the kings of Spain, France, Scotland and the whole house of Guise.[30]

The greatest art of all was deployed paradoxically in persistently reminding her audience that she was Only-a-Weak-Woman, in order to evoke the desired reaction of wonder and disbelief: for surely here was the equal of any prince of the past! In 1586 for instance, Queen Elizabeth described her reaction to her accession: 'bethinking myself on those things that fitted a King'. And she listed 'justice, temper, magnanimity, judgement' among them, adding modestly: 'As for the two latter, I will not boast; my sex doth not permit it.' The implication was clear. The Queen kept up these quasi-modest allusions to the end of her life. In almost her last public speech she reminded her audience of her 'sexly weakness', before going on to boast once again that God had given her a heart 'which never yet feared foreign or home enemy'.[31]

Then there were the numerous otherworldly references to Diana, Juno, Astraea, Gloriana, Sweet Cynthia, the Fairy Queen and so on and so forth, as a goddess untouched by the depredations of time. (An ode celebrating her funeral referred to 'this sweet slumbering *maid*' with the air of one on her way to

Parliament, not to her burial.) The extensive researches of Roy Strong in art and history have exposed the workings of this subtle and brilliant campaign – like some huge campaign for re-election lasting forty-five years, except the votes were cast in loyalty, not at the polling booth – by which Queen Elizabeth I secured first the affection, then the adoration of her people.[32] In the apogee of this campaign, the 'Accession' picture of 1600 showing the triumph of Astraea, the Queen had finally been transformed into the first Virgin of Virgil's Fourth Eclogue: Virgo and Venus (at the age of sixty-seven) ever young and ever beautiful.[33]

Nor, happily, did this self-presentation as a virgin goddess prevent the Queen from appearing also in the guise of the mother of her people, as the years passed. When Leicester expressed that hope in his will that Elizabeth would be the longest-reigning 'prince that ever He [God] gave over England' he went on to wish, in a splendid transfer of genders, 'that she may indeed be a blessed mother and nurse to this people and church of England'. Sir John Harrington referred to her as the 'natural mother' of her subjects; Thomas Dekker, in his epitaph, described her as 'having brought up (even under her wing) a nation that was almost begotten and born under her'.[34]

For gradually her femininity, which called for a chivalry and protection denied to a king, became an asset, not a weakness. At the beginning of her reign at a tournament given in honour of the Duc de Montmorency, Queen Elizabeth watched with her ladies at the tiltyard while the earls of Rutland and Essex charged at each other at a signal given by her. But it had to be admitted that for all the prettiness of the torchlit spectacle – the two earls in blue and silver, the young Queen gilded and radiant – it was not thus that Great Harry had conducted himself at the beginning of his reign, he who had tired out eight to ten horses hunting, and then played tennis, and finally jousted himself. Twenty years later when the Queen, still more gilded, yet more radiant, watched a tourney of armed 'Amazons' versus knights, she had become the centre of an astonishing cult, in which even the warlike 'Amazons' had to be played by men, since such games were far too rough for the delicate sex of which she was the most delicate of all.[35]

There is a special piquancy in this respect about Queen Elizabeth's legendary meeting with Grace O'Malley, the Irish pirate captain, who is supposed to have appeared before her at Greenwich in 1593, barefoot, dressed in wild and ragged Irish costume. (One should say that this meeting is legendary only in the sense that it has given rise to many legends: the meeting did take place, as a result of Grace O'Malley's petition to the Queen regarding her family and properties, although unfortunately no other details concerning it are known.) For Grace O'Malley, a woman of about the Queen's own age – that is, sixty – had led exactly the kind of buccaneering life which went to make up an old-style Warrior Queen. 'This was a notorious woman in all the coasts of Ireland', wrote Sir Henry Sidney in 1577 of her numerous piratical ventures. Even if Grace O'Malley was not actually in rags, as the legend has it, the weatherbeaten appearance of this real-life Warrior Queen must have provided a sharp contrast to that of the bedizened and bejewelled English sovereign, pampered by a lifetime at a chivalric court.[36]

Of course the process of incarnating the goddess Diana meant that hunting, that standby occupation of the Warrior Queen, could be vigorously pursued. The Queen, who had had arrows headed with silver and flighted with peacock's feathers when she was a mere princess at Enfield, hunted with enthusiasm till the end of her life. On the other hand her renowned progresses around the country – that art form of self-display which she did not invent but energetically developed – showed her more statically: her purpose was to look, as a contemporary wrote, 'like a goddess such as painters are wont to depict'.[37]

And all the time, the tributes, the sonnets, the literary sighs and the long lyrical eulogistic poems poured forth. It was indeed a measure of the Queen's success that in the last decade of her reign Shakespeare could create in *Henry VI* the savage character of Margaret of Anjou, and be confident that lines such as these following would not be regarded as treason.[38] Here York, smeared by Queen Margaret with his own child's blood, crowned by her in mockery with a paper crown, knows that he is about to die:

> How ill-beseeming is it in thy sex
> To Triumph like an Amazonian trull
> Upon their woes whom fortune captivates! . . .
> O tiger's heart wrapped in a woman's hide!

When Shakespeare had York tell Margaret of Anjou (who was of course French):

> Women are soft, mild, pitiful and flexible
> Thou stern, obdurate, flinty, rough, remorseless

he could not possibly be thought to be addressing Gloriana, Sweet Cynthia, Venus, Virgo, Astraea – or his sovereign. A man's heart was evidently easier to accommodate within 'a woman's hide' than a tiger's.

History, as well as art, was summoned to the aid of Queen Elizabeth. The return of British Boadicea, driving her 'cart' as it was unromantically known in the sixteenth century, contributed most helpfully to the picture of a patriotic female leader. But there was also a fruitful cross-fertilization. For in turn the presence of a queen regnant on the throne ensured that when Boadicea did quite coincidentally re-emerge from the historical mists into which she had vanished, she was accorded respectful treatment. The first English translation of Tacitus was that of Sir Henry Savile in 1591: it was dedicated in flattering terms to Queen Elizabeth herself. Perhaps his own humble efforts might encourage the Queen to share with the world her own 'rare and excellent translations of Histories', wrote Sir Henry, 'if I may call them translations which have so infinitely exceeded the originals'. The printer however issued a different message to the reader, according to that custom of the time by which some pertinent moral lesson was expected to be drawn from a historical work.[39]

This was the moral of Tacitus: 'If thou mislike their wars be thankful for thine own peace; if thou dost abhor their tyrannies, love and reverence thine own wise just and excellent Prince. If thou doest detest their Anarchy, acknowledge our own happy government, and thank God for her, under whom England enjoys as many benefits, as ever Reign did suffer miseries under the greatest Tyrant.' And so we come back, but now in English, to the fortunes of the Britons' previous queen 'Voadica [*sic*], a lady of the blood of kings: for in the matter of governing in chief, they make no distinction of sex.'

The story of Boadicea had already been introduced to readers in Latin through the works of Polydore Vergil, an Italian humanist, who came to England at the beginning of the sixteenth century and became a member of the circle of Sir Thomas More. Polydore Vergil's *Anglica Historica*, written about 1512, with its first printed edition in Basle in 1534, drew on both Tacitus in the original and those epitomes of Dio Cassius, which were the only form in which his works survived.[40] It was Polydore Vergil who divided the protean Warrior Queen into two: in his case named Voadicia and Bonduica, using Tacitus for one and Dio for the other, an error which along with his confused geography was later copied by the Scottish chronicler Hector Boëce.

Boëce, a native of Dundee also writing in Latin, followed Polydore Vergil by placing all the fatal events of Boadicea's rebellion in the north: his Queen Voada, as he calls her, is the widow of Arviragus (Prasutagus), and when she is daily lashed with 'insufferable stakes' while her daughters are deflowered, she appeals to her brother Corbrede, King of Scots, to avenge her. The King does send a message of protest to the Romans, only to receive an 'outrageous answer' loftily dismissing the protests of a mere 'barbarian people', with a reference to the 'majesty' of Rome itself.[41]

It was Boëce's *History of Scotland* which Ralph Holinshed quarried for his own chronicles, first issued in 1577; just as Shakespeare in his turn would work over Holinshed's material.[42]

It must indeed remain one of the minor but titillating What-might-have-beens of literature to speculate what would have happened if Shakespeare's fancy had lighted on the story of Boadicea instead of, say, that of Macbeth, also taken via Holinshed from Boëce. Holinshed's Queen Voada – a woman 'not unworthy to be numbered among doughty chieftains' – strongly resembles that of Boëce except that she has been brought slightly further south. The characters of her two daughters, unnamed by Tacitus or Dio, are also for the first time developed, as they were to be in subsequent seventeenth- and eighteenth-century dramas.

The elder daughter, also named Voada, subsequently marries that 'noble Roman' called Marius 'who had deflowered her before her time'. (This sexual theme of the raped daughter either marrying a Roman or falling in love with him will be developed in the Boadicean plays of the seventeenth and eighteenth centuries.) The younger daughter, Voadicia, having gathered together a crew of soldiers on the Isle of Man, attacks the Romans as her mother had done, and is captured in Galloway by the Roman Petilius: 'Upon her stout answers made unto him as he questioned with her about her bold enterprises, she was presently slain by the soldiers.'

The false distinction created by Polydore Vergil between Voadicia and Bonduica was one which Petruccio Ubaldini, an enterprising Florentine desiring royal patronage, kept alive. After a series of travels, including a visit to Scotland, Ubaldini, born in about 1542, settled down in England under the patronage of the twelfth Earl of Arundel. But he was after bigger game. In 1576 he presented to Queen Elizabeth the manuscript of *Le vite delle Donne illustri del regno d'Inghilterra, e del regno di Scotia*, which was printed still in Italian in 1591 (Italian was of course among the many languages in which the Queen was proficient).[43] There is a long dedicatory epistle 'to the most serene and very wise Elizabeth, most powerful Queen of England . . .' in which Ubaldini manages to blow his own trumpet as a scholar with almost as much vigour as he proclaims the Queen's manifold virtues, which include, incidentally, her 'valour' in defending her peoples from the enemy, as well as her 'clemency'. Among the illustrious ladies considered are Cartimandua, 'a warlike woman', and Matilda Augusta (Maud), praised for playing a manly role (*intervenedo virilmente*), which demonstrates that 'women can be wise, prudent and capable . . .' so long as they eschew all 'softness'.

The next year Ubaldini gave Queen Elizabeth a further volume in manuscript, *Le vite e i fatti di sei Donne illustri*, which was never printed, perhaps because it did not involve British queens. The six ladies included Zenobia who was described as *virile*: 'in that while her husband lived she was his equal in virtue and valour, and after his death she became famous far and wide for her great achievements in peace and in war'. Thanks, presumably, to this historical barrage, the relationship flourished: not only in 1577 but in 1588 the Queen and Ubaldini exchanged New Year gifts.[44]

Both Spenser in the reign of Queen Elizabeth and Ben Jonson in that of James I (for his *Masque of Queenes*) drew upon the *Britannia* of William Camden for their allusions to Boadicea. Camden's is an upbeat picture: 'the Britains under the conduct of Boadicea had unanimously resolved to recover their old liberty'. It is also scholarly: based, as ever with Camden, on a proper study of the available sources, including not only Tacitus but the monk Gildas.[45] And although he hesitates over the name of the Warrior Queen as many have done before and since – Boadicea? Bunduica? *Boo*dicia? – he places the Iceni in roughly their correct geographical position; it is true that Boadicea is described as capturing Maldon in Essex instead of Colchester, but the East Anglian Queen is no longer driving her chariot through the mountain passes of the north.

Spenser's Warrior Queen, 'stout Bunduca', is one of the several 'women valorous' who are celebrated as the ancestresses to his 'fair martial maid', Britomart. It is a sympathetic portrait, with 'stout Bunduca' seen as a patriot, who 'up arose and taking arms the Britons to her drew'; there is no hint of any atrocities being committed. Even her defeat is blamed upon the treachery of her captain, here named as Paulinus, and as for her suicide, that too is seen as glorious:

> And yet, though overcome in happless fight,
> She triumphed on death, in enemies despite.[46]

Britomart herself, who dresses in man's clothes for convenience, has had the classical Tomboy upbringing: as her father's only daughter and his heir, she is taught to upset the most warlike rider with her spear and shield. (She naturally loathes such ladies' pastimes as 'to finger the fine needle and nice thread'.) Britomart's whole delight is in 'feats of arms': the feat to which she is set by Spenser is that of rescuing the knight Artegall from the clutches of the evil Radegunde, Queen of the Amazons.

Nothing illustrates more forcibly the distinction successfully made by the 1590s between one valorous female warrior and the general notion of female rulership than Spenser's treatment of Radegunde and Britomart respectively. Like the other captured knights in the Amazonian stronghold of Radegunde, Artegall is set to spin and sew: nor is there a choice in the matter for this captive househusband, for Artegall has to spin before he is allowed to eat. This behaviour on the part of the Amazons represents an odiously unnatural order to Spenser, as it did to the ancient Greeks. The Amazons are cruel (like Queen Margaret of Anjou) just because 'they have shaken off the shamefast band, With which wise Nature did them strongly bind', which is to obey the orders and laws of men. In short:

> Virtuous women wisely understand
> That they were born to base humility
> Unless the heavens them lift to lawful sovereignty.

Britomart herself, her task of rescue performed, and the 'Tyranesse' Radegunde defeated, removes the helmet which made her look like the war goddess Bellona, and drops her shield. She now becomes 'a gentle courteous Dame'. For a while she remains with the chastened Amazons, to be adored as a goddess; taking the opportunity however to repeal that 'liberty of women . . . which they had long usurped; and them restoring to men's subjection . . .' Her story ends with her happy union with the knight Artegall, the warrior maid symbolizing Chastity – one of the many allegorical figures representing Queen Elizabeth in the poem – united to the knight who symbolizes Justice.

Throughout *The Faerie Queene* there are plenty of other women lifted (like Queen Elizabeth) to 'lawful sovereignty', who exist to be contrasted with those evil or licentious creatures such as Radegunde, Semiramis and Cleopatra.[47] The last named, a figure of lust, is now to be found in the unpleasant House of Pride: in contrast the lawful queens are virgins or at least chaste. There is Belphoebe (one of Elizabeth's favourite allegorical incarnations), the huntress who puts Braggadochio to flight; Mercilla, 'a Maiden Queen of high renown', who wins her duel with the malevolent Duessa, representing Mary Queen of Scots. Most powerfully described of all is Spenser's Gloriana, 'the flower of grace and chastity'. Having been chosen – like Queen Elizabeth herself – to rule by God, Gloriana inspires a 'sacred reverence' in all her subjects, as being 'Th' Idol of her makers [God's] great magnificence'. It was this sacred reverence which Queen Elizabeth I, no Radegunde at the head of an unnatural order of cruel women, had worked so hard to inspire.

Queen Elizabeth's incandescent appearance at Tilbury in August 1588, at a moment of national peril, affirmed in practical terms her theoretical triumph. It was just on thirty years since Elizabeth's tricky accession to the throne of England, when the cry was 'they do not want women rulers'. Now her country was facing, as it was thought, the assault of the Spanish Armada. Here was one challenge from which this reluctant Britomart could not gracefully extricate herself. Instead, how brilliant she made of the challenge the apogee of her glory both as a monarch and as a Warrior Queen!

Leicester described how her appearance 'inflamed the hearts of her poor subjects'. Bishop Goodman spoke for many who would now freely 'adventure our lives to her service'. Camden, as her first historian, summed it up: 'Her presence and words fortified the courage of the captains and soldiers beyond all belief.'[48] Emulating chaste Diana might be her preferred course in public, but in 1588 Bellona too proved to be within Elizabeth's range: at least, her own special version of Bellona.

This was her version and this was her performance. A woman in her mid-fifties, raddled and rather overdressed, mounted on a carefully selected docile horse, reviewed loyal troops on top of a small hill in Essex. Yet that feat on the part of the Queen – if feat it can be called – quickly passed into the romantic annals of our history as a deed of daring to be ranked with the first charges of Boadicea's scythe-wheeled chariot fifteen hundred years before. Boadicea and her daughters were said to have lived again at Tilbury 'through this our Queen, England's happie Queene', in the words of a contemporary poet (James Aske); their bravery no greater 'in those actual deeds . . . than did our sacred Queene, Here signs display of courage wonderful'.[49]

The Earl of Leicester officially invited his sovereign to visit Tilbury on 27 July 1588. He did so in his capacity of the 'Queen's lieutenant' or the 'Lord General' as he was sometimes otherwise known. Tilbury Camp – actually at West Tilbury where a church recently turned to a private dwelling now stands – contained the flower of the Queen's troops and was consequently known as the Camp Royal. Tilbury Fort itself, on the River Thames, some twenty-six miles below London Bridge, had been constructed by Henry VIII in 1539. Some two miles from the river, the site of the camp had been chosen with a view to blocking the Spanish invader from reaching London either by road or river, part of a network of defensive fortifications. Since it lay on a kind of plateau on top of its hill – its sides about one hundred and fifty feet high – the camp provided 'as goodly a prospect as may be seen or found'.[50]

It was on 20 July that the Spanish Armada had been sighted approaching the English Channel; whereupon the English fleet engaged it. Such was the good fortune of the English fireships that by the end of the month the Spanish fleet was compelled to flee northwards, 'driven like a flock of sheep' in the immortal phrase of Sir Francis Drake. At this point however the stately Spanish galleon–sheep vanished from view. It is important to realize that just because they did vanish, the extent of their dispersal and damage was not appreciated for some time. (Some messages concerning the damage were received while the Queen was actually at Tilbury.) Elizabeth's appearance, *dea ex machina*, at Tilbury, should not therefore be understood in terms of an empty exercise. It was an exercise, it is true, but one intended to perform a vital function in rallying the national morale in time of war. 'Ye shall comfort not only these thousands', wrote Leicester of the camp's inhabitants, 'but many more that shall hear of it.'

The Queen set forth for Tilbury by water on 8 August. Silver trumpets blew to mark her progress, or as one of the contemporary eyewitness accounts had it, with a characteristic allusion to her illustrious parentage:

> And to barge upon the water
> Being King Henry's royal daughter
> She did go with trumpet's sounding . . .

But when she landed at about midday (at the present blockhouse of the fort) there was music of a more martial kind: drums, fifes were heard and finally the guns thundered. And so like Boadicea – in the words of the Essex historian Morant like the war goddess Bellona, or like 'a king' in other contemporary accounts – Queen Elizabeth was brought ceremonially into the centre of the Camp Royal.

The method of transport used was a coach: but this bejewelled and spangled affair was indeed different from Boadicea's mythical chariot, and different again from the light wooden structure of the Celts which that forgotten figure Boudica would actually have used. This chariot – never intended to see a battlefield – was chequered with precious stones in patterns of emeralds, diamonds and rubies. According to the poet James Aske (who was present among the soldiers) it reminded observers of nothing so much as 'the heavenly car' of the sun god Phoebus, drawn by his 'foaming steeds'.

One side-effect of Elizabeth's thirty-year propaganda campaign was the frantic desire to protect and cosset the Queen's own person, a desire which of its very nature could never have been applied to the same extent to a male sovereign. (The Earl of Pembroke offered to attend Her Majesty with 300 horses and 500 foot armed at his own cost; a Dorset regiment was said to have offered five hundred pounds to form part of the Queen's Guard.)[51] Now, as she passed, the men actually fell on their knees as though in prayer to her. Aske, whose descriptive poem of the whole wondrous occasion was aptly titled *Elizabetha Triumphans*, described her passage thus:

> They couch their pikes and bow their ensigns down
> When as their sacred royal Queen passed by
> In token of their loyal bearèd hearts
> To her alone, and none but only she . . .

It was ironic that at one point the cries of the kneeling soldiers as they called out blessings upon her name became so enthusiastic that the Protestant Queen sent messengers of reproof. Officially at least Elizabeth frowned upon such 'idolatrous reverence'. However much her subjects might happily sublimate their feelings for the banished Virgin Mary of the old Catholic religion in their adoration of their female sovereign, this was not to be a conscious process. Deafening cries of 'God Save the Queen' were one thing, prayers quite another. The Queen's behaviour looked forward not back: for her particular stance, 'cheerfully her body bending' and 'waving her royal hand', prefigured royal behaviour on ceremonial occasions up to and including the present day.

The Queen spent the night at Saffron Garden.[52] The next day – 9 August – she returned to the camp, and with her princely image cunningly enhanced by the expedient of abandoning her customary female attendants – 'her ladies she did leave behind her', wrote Aske – she reviewed her troops and made that speech which would make of her the female equivalent of King Arthur, a symbol of a nation's proud defiance of danger. Furthermore, for once it is gratifying to relate that mythology has not burnished the event, for Queen Elizabeth I *did* deliver the famous speech – we have the evidence of the Earl of Leicester's chaplain, Leonel Sharp, who was present at Tilbury, was summoned to record it the next day and related her words later to the Duke of Buckingham: 'This I thought would delight your Grace . . .'[53] (It should be further noted that its contents, far from being unusual, were, as we have seen, at the very core of her utterances concerning her 'sexly weakness' from beginning to end of her reign.)

The Queen was dressed in white velvet, with a silver cuirass over her dress, to symbolize once more – to those who might have missed it – the ever-present danger to her person: 'the most dainty and sacred thing we have in this world to care for', as Leicester expressed it.[54] A page walked behind her holding a helmet adorned with white plumes: but this Bellona-like helmet was never actually put on, lest one iota of the contrast between the Queen's fragile femininity of person and the bold masculinity of her demeanour be missed by her audience. Part of the review was conducted on foot. But for the speech itself the Queen was, in Aske's words, 'most bravely mounted on a stately steed': the steed in question being a stout white gelding which could be trusted to behave itself, specially imported for the occasion. Nevertheless the presence of the white horse – which could be a mettlesome charge in the eye of an adoring beholder – was, like the armour and helmet, another piece of careful planning; these were the sumptuous trappings for the message which was to follow.

She had come among them, said Queen Elizabeth, as they could see, 'not for my recreation and disport, but being resolved, in the midst and heat of the battle, to live or die amongst you all, to lay down for my God, and for my kingdom, and for my people, my honour and my blood, even in the dust'. She continued with that deathless declaration, the very watchword of Elizabeth I as a Warrior Queen: 'I know I have the body of a weak and feeble woman, but I have the heart and stomach of a King, and of a King of England too, and think foul scorn that Parma or Spain or any Prince of Europe should invade the borders of my realm . . .' Aske, paraphrasing that section of her speech in his verse tribute, fails, unlike the Queen, at the last fence of inspiration:

> Although she be by Nature weak
> Because her sex no otherwise can be
> Yet wants she not the courage of her sire.

'Rather than any Dishonour shall grow by me,' went on Elizabeth, 'I myself will take up arms . . . In the meantime my Lieutenant General shall be in my stead.' The latter sentiment is almost an afterthought compared to the thrilling – but frightening – possibilities of the former.

How far distant the Queen on her white steed had now removed herself from the rest of the lowly female race! Dazzled by the matchless words, it is difficult even to bear in mind that the so-called weaker sex actually played an important if subservient role in European armies of the time. 'As woman was created to be a helper to man, so women are great helpers to armies, to their husbands, especially those of the lower condition . . .', Sir James Turner would write in the next century. In the army, as outside it, women provided what has been called 'the warp of the social fabric' by giving sexual favours and by childbearing, quite apart from their ceaseless cooking and nursing which was taken for granted. Three years before Tilbury, Leicester himself in the Netherlands had drawn up a list of 'sundry disorders and horrible abuses' among his troops. These included the presence of 'many vagrant idle women in an army'. But he deliberately excluded from their number the many lawful wives 'to tend the sick and serve as launderers'.[55]

Elizabetha Triumphans simply did not belong to the same gender as these inferior but essential workers. Or if she did, it was only to enhance still further the measure of her own kind of military glory, far from the sweaty field of battle, close to the minds and hearts of her people.

CHAPTER FOURTEEN

Jinga at the Gates

Rome for empire far renown'd
Tramples on a thousand states
Soon her pride shall kiss the ground, –
Hark! the Gaul is at her gates.

WILLIAM COWPER, 'Boadicea'

When Queen Christina of Sweden, daughter of the warrior Gustavus Adolphus, expressed a wish to abdicate in 1651, it was to make room for her first cousin Charles Gustavus. She did so, she declared, in the best interests of her country: 'The realm would be granted a man and a champion who when war threatened could ride with his people to battle, while a woman could not.' (As we shall see, this passive estimate of a woman leader's role in wartime was not shared at this date by Warrior Queens in other continents, where the thrilling or menacing practical involvement of the female in her country's cause by one such as Jinga of Angola continued.) Although Christina was persuaded not to abdicate in 1651, three years later the eccentric scholarly creature, a convert to Catholicism, who had worn man's clothing not with martial intent but for the freedom it gave her, departed for Rome. For all the legends which have her wearing Amazonian costume on this occasion, she and her ladies actually wore plain grey gowns to enter the Holy City.[1]

The particular intellectual temperament of Queen Christina – 'You know how it distresses me to lend my time to matters other than studying', she wrote – did not prevent her from taking part in various political intrigues in her new life in the south. But like many European queens regnant, she expressed the notion that participation in war was a masculine business. It is of this period that Joan Kelly has written of the phenomenon of the 'disarmed lady'.[2] Queen Elizabeth I, gamely acting the Warrior Queen at Tilbury despite a prudent natural pacifism, belonged to a vanished age. Then there were still relics of feudalism in the national unconscious, a vague expectation that the chief must personally wave the sword. Now a female ruler had no need to issue the fake if exciting threat that 'I myself will take up arms' in order to shore up her authority. A queen, no longer posing as an honorary male, could give vent to perceived natural feminine dislike of the actual battlefield, leaving the sword to be grasped by the nearest male. Queen Christina, publicly encouraging the trained soldier Charles Gustavus to take the sword away altogether, was merely carrying this trend to the extreme. He did so, incidentally, with alacrity, initiating a series of carnivorous campaigns of conquest.

'Oh Lord, when will all this dreadful bloodshed cease?' Thus with fervour exclaimed Queen Anne, reigning over Great Britain a century after the death of her kinswoman Elizabeth, a Britain in full spate of Marlborough's victories. 'I have no liking for war,' she observed on another occasion, 'and shall end it as soon as possible.' She was indeed improbable even as a symbolic Warrior Queen, as has been noted with regard to her 'Amazonian' display at Bath. 'Though this great Queen had made a very glorious figure in Europe by her arms and fleets abroad,' wrote Sir John Clerk, 'she appeared to me the most despicable mortal I had ever seen in any station.'[3] Yet the time when the sad private spectacle would have fatally negated the glamour of the glorious public figure had passed.

At the battle of Oudenarde in 1708, the young Prince George of Hanover, the Queen's distant cousin and eventual heir (the future King George II), took part. His courage in fighting on when his horse was shot under him was celebrated by Swift:

> Full firmly he stood as became his high blood
> Which runs in his veins so blue

For this gallant young man, being a-kin to Queen Anne,
Did as, were she a man, she would do.[4]

Were the Queen a man . . . the Warrior Queen, no longer pretending to have the heart and stomach of a king, now admits freely to her very different (female) nature. On the other hand, *were* the Queen a man, she would undoubtedly be a very brave one; the behaviour of her gallant young male relation epitomizes this. She might of course under certain circumstances show herself to be a great deal braver than the timorous men surrounding her. This – an aspect of the Shame Syndrome – received its most famous manifestation in the expostulation of Queen Victoria to Disraeli in 1878. 'Oh if the Queen were a man', she wrote furiously, 'she would like to go and give those horrid Russians whose word one cannot trust such a beating.'[5] It is a wonderful expression of unreality; but the Queen's frustrated sentiments are not purely comic. The ageing Queen Victoria (fifty-eight to Queen Elizabeth's fifty-four at Tilbury) has no intention of deserting her bonnet and shawl even for white plumes and silver armour. The limitations of her sex are thoroughly accepted.

Boadicea herself, in English literature, begins to float away from the historic queen of Tacitus and Dio, wronged in her situation and bloodthirsty in her behaviour, the one justifying the other: she enters some other idealized sphere of womanhood. At first her character merely underwent a subtle transformation from the appropriate Elizabethan heroine to someone representing the much lower estimate of women in Jacobean times; 'women's worth', as Anne Bradstreet had it, having departed 'with our Queen'. Fletcher's *Bonduca*, first performed in about 1614, has as its centre a hero not a heroine: the British Caratach (for Caratacus, whose historic involvement was of course with Cartimandua, not Boadicea). Even the goddess Andraste emerges here as a god: Andate, who inspires the British Queen proudly to roll her 'swarty [iniquitous] chariot wheels over the heaps of wounds and carcasses sailing through seas of blood'.[6]

Bonduca herself is a distinctly unheroic figure, for all her chariot wheels and her 'armed cart'. She is for example sharply ticked off by her ally Caratach for being boastful. After her first victory, Bonduca exults: 'A woman beat 'em . . . a weak woman, a woman beat these Romans!' to which Caratach replies sardonically: 'So it seems.' Then he adds: 'A man would shame to talk so.' Throughout the play, indeed, Caratach, the trained soldier, shows more respect for the Romans – professionals like himself – than he does for Bonduca or her daughters. He will not let the Queen deride their 'weight and worth'. As he confesses at one point: 'I love an enemy, I was born a soldier.'

Most powerfully of all, Caratach saves some Roman soldiers from torture at the daughters' hands, since they have been captured by treachery. It matters not to Caratach that these are the soldiers responsible for the British princesses' brutal violation (his language will sound a sombre but not unevocative note to modern ears):

Caratach: A woman's wisdom in our triumphs? Out, out, ye sluts, ye follies, from our swords filch our revenges basely? [To the Romans] Arm again, Gentlemen. [To the Britons] Soldiers, I charge ye help 'em.
Daughter 2: By —— Uncle, we will have vengeance for our rapes.
Caratach: By —— ye should have kept your legs closed then.

Caratach's best advice to his nieces is to 'Learn to spin, and curse your knotted hemp.'

Throughout the play, a Jacobean misogyny prevails. It is Fletcher's Bonduca – unlike Spenser's betrayed heroine – who brings about the defeat of the Britons by a military mistake. This elicits from Caratach the violent condemnation, 'O woman, scurvie woman, beastly woman', before the Queen in her turn is told to go home and spin. For the Romans equally, Bonduca is 'woman, woman, unnatural woman' when she urges her daughters to kill themselves rather than face the Roman depredation (that fate so coarsely dismissed by their uncle) a second time. Only Bonduca's patriotic Britishness – her final refusal to plead for mercy with the noble words 'I am unacquainted with that language' – is still admired; her sex is scorned.

The floating away of Boadicea from this human, if despised, figure into some gauzier sphere is well illustrated by the changes which have taken place to Fletcher's play by the time it emerges in an adaptation, with music by Henry Purcell, performed in 1695.[7] Fletcher's original is referred to in the Prologue to the printed play book as 'so ingenious a Relick' of time past; in this new 'fighting age' – that of William III's continental campaigns against Louis XIV – it is appropriate that 'proud Bunduca', played here by Mrs Frances Knight, should once more tread the British stage. But proud Bonduca is a figure much chastened by the passage of a century, a period in which even the official lustful energy of women has been stripped from them in the public estimation.

Purcell's score has been described as ranking 'among his finest' with the invocation 'Divine Andate, President of War', an exquisite tenor recitative; although *Bonduca* has been generally overshadowed in reputation by *The Indian Queen*, written about the same time.[8] But the drama lacks all the violence which once made it a savage but effective piece. The language has been generally softened with Fletcher's lusty expletives omitted. The daughters' characters have been made tender, languishing, even sentimental, and since they no longer take rebellious action against their unpleasant fate, Caratach is no longer compelled to castigate them. As for Bonduca herself, this is the meek fashion in which she now addresses Caratach:

> My Fortune wound my Female Soul too high
> And lifted me above myself; but thou
> Hast kindly work'd down all my Towering Thoughts . . .

This was an opinion – and language – more calculated to appeal to John Knox than to Queen Elizabeth I.

It was not that scholarly interest in the ancient Britons waned in the course of the seventeenth century: very much to the contrary. The 'discovery' of the North American Indians by the West Europeans led to a happy obsession with the concept of the so-called noble savage. In many cases, antiquarian accounts of the ancient Britons borrowed characteristics observed in the Indians. On her arrival in England as the wife of an Englishman, John Rolfe, in 1616 Pocahontas, daughter of the chief Powhatan, caused a sensation as a member of the Sioux tribe, who were all about six feet tall with 'the cleanest and most exact limbs in the world'. But the 'Nonpareil of Virginia', as she was known, had turned gracefully into 'the Lady Rebecca' on her Christian baptism.[9] Nor was Pocahontas in any sense a Warrior Queen; she was the biblical Ruth, not Judith, a well-treated Madam Butterfly, not a Boadicea. Originally she had twice saved the life of an Englishman, John Smith, preferring his welfare to that of her own tribe; peace not war had followed her marriage to Rolfe.

Among antiquarians destined to feel interest in the ancient Britons, another happy obsession which emerged in the seventeenth century concerning the origins of Stonehenge focused particular interest on Boadicea. As has been mentioned in Chapter Seven, Edmund Bolton in 1624 proposed Stonehenge as her missing tomb (where, according to Dio, she had been given that rich burial by her tribe). Thomas Heywood, in his *Exemplary Lives* of 1640, followed suit. His Boadicea, duly buried at Stonehenge – 'that admirable monument of the stones upon Salisbury Plain' – is illustrated in the plumes and pearls of the day, a Caroline court lady dressing up, one breast tastefully exposed in something which may have been designed to resemble the Amazon's chiton, but certainly does not. She is also described as a 'Mother and nurse of magnanimity', a description which surely fits Pocahontas more closely than the first-century Queen.[10]

Outside history, Boadicea as a name gradually developed into a useful generic term for a heroine. It was employed for example when the making of lists of such became common in the second half of the century, figuring with severe Judith but also with peace-loving Deborah, the prophetess Hannah and the learned Abbess Hilda of Whitby; these lists themselves, generally compiled by women, being a form of protest against the prevalent denigration of their sex's 'worth'. To term someone a Boadicea was to make of her a heroine, but was not even necessarily to connect her to military feats. The petition of the Leveller women for the release of John Lilburne in 1649 pointed to the various 'deliverances' wrought by God by women's 'weak hands', as Boadicea had helped the Britons to defeat the Danes (a well-meant if inaccurate historical comparison).[11] A great lady such as Charlotte, Countess of Derby, who defended her castle against siege in the Civil War, might be compared to the British Queen; but so might the spirited playwright Aphra Behn, the first professional woman writer, whose fortitude was evidently in another sphere than that of the battlefield.

Historians and antiquarians similarly began to make of Boadicea more of a generic figure of patriotic intent, than a rounded female character. Aylett Sammes, in his *Britannia Antiqua Illustrata* of 1676, relies heavily on Tacitus for his account of 'those insufferable Insolences' (towards the royal women) which caused the British revolt. But he discounts the idea that Boadicea's death could have discouraged her people, and salutes her with a laudatory verse beneath her portrait:

> To War, this Queen doth with her Daughters move
> She for her Wisdom, followed, they for Love . . .
> But they being ravisht, made her understand
> 'Tis harder beauty to secure than Land.
> Yet her example teaching them to dye,
> Virtue, the room of Honour did supply.[12]

This 'Thrice Happy' Princess is as stylized, no more real than Purcell's Bonduca. Her portrait (engraved by W. Fairthorne) shows her voluptuous rather than brawny. Here is the character-istic oval face, small curly mouth, dimpled chin and long nose of the late Stuart beauty; her long rippling hair has a tiny little crown set on top of it; the low-cut gown sets off her 'torc', in fact a double-stranded necklace; on her feet are a pair of elegant sandals. With her toy spear and its pretty tassel, she too is a lady in fancy dress, but with the march of time she has become a professional actress rather than a court lady: one of the stately Marshall sisters perhaps, who specialized in tragedy, playing Zempoalla, Dryden's tempestuous Indian queen who fell in love with Montezuma.

Two courtly episodes illustrate this increasingly 'fancy dress' aspect of Boadicea. In 1669 the Honourable Edward Howard printed 'An Heroick Poem', dedicated to his aristocratic friends, including the poet Rochester, in order to elicit their comments.[13] Rochester himself took advantage of this opportunity to designate the poem as 'incomparable' but also 'incomprehensible'; Thomas Hobbes, on the other hand, from the library at Chatsworth, with more reason to appreciate the demands of aristocratic friendship, responded that it was a virtue in any poet 'to advance the honour of his remote Ancestors' while murmuring encouraging names like Homer and Virgil.

After the statutory hesitation over his heroine's name – and finally going for Bonduca[*] – Howard launched himself into a description of a paragon of beauty and virtue. Everyone, it seems, wants to marry this peerless maid, including notably Albanius, son of King Arthur, and the British chieftain Vortiger. Bonduca herself, although courageous – 'she dares, above her blushing Sex's gentle fears' – is hardly a brash Warrior Queen. For one thing her voice – that perennial test – is 'too soft to accent the rough Laws of War', and in any case 'Wars' stern horrors her soft Soul affright'. Seated as she is on a white charger, with auburn

---

[*] Bonduca is the name usually, but not invariably, employed in the seventeenth century, following Dio's Greek; but frequent references to Boadicea, in all its rich variety of spellings, following Tacitus, also continue. (Howard himself cites both Voadicia and Boadicea before plumping for Bonduca.) To John Horsley in his *Britannia Romana* of 1732 has been ascribed the honour of settling the spelling generally in favour of Boadicea.[14]

tresses 'softer than gossamer', in a robe embroidered with the dawn stars, surrounded by fellow virgins compared to Spring and Morning, it is hardly surprising that, after the taking of London, this Boadicea goes about the city tenderly nursing the wounded, Britons and Romans alike.

In the end Bonduca virtually dies of modesty, so far as one can make out. Since in her 'bashful accents' she is unable to choose between Albanius and Vortiger, they fight it out in a tournament at which both perish; Bonduca temporarily dies too or at least faints into death, until Merlin resurrects her:

> The Queen's soft life so far were fled
> His Art must now recall her from the Dead.

One cannot resist observing that the bold Celtic Warrior Queen who led her armies to Colchester, to London, to St Albans and beyond, must have been turning in her grave at this amiable travesty – wherever that grave happened to be.

The Society of Roman Knights, which was formed in 1722 and lasted for three years, was the brainchild of William Stukeley, the first Secretary of the Society of Antiquaries founded in 1718.[15] Stukeley was a man of an unconventional cast of mind, with a passion for Druids which finally overwhelmed his archaeological good sense – he did much valuable fieldwork at Avebury for example. Members of the Society, whose aim was to 'search for and illustrate' Roman monuments in Britain, took their titles from Celtic princes and other notables associated with the Roman Conquest, such as Cingetorix (Lord Winchelsea), Prasutagus and Venutius (Maurice Johnson and Roger Gale, fellow antiquaries) and Agricola (adopted by Sir John Clerk, author of that unflattering portrait of Queen Anne quoted earlier). Stukeley himself was Chyndonax, then believed to be an authentic Druid's name.

The constitution actually allowed for members of both sexes – doubtless part of Stukeley's scorn for the conventions, since this was two hundred years before the Society of Antiquaries admitted its first women fellows. At some point Stukeley's wife

Frances was admitted as Cartimandua, a development which, with members sticking closely to nomenclature in their frequent correspondence, led to laments like this from Cunobelinus (Samuel Gale): 'Having been inform'd since the arrival of Prasutagus . . . of the never enough to be lamented Miscarriage of the incomparable Cartimandua, a Misfortune which not only myself but all Albion must be seriously touch'd with, since without doubt we have lost a second Chyndonax, or at least another Boadicea.'[16]

Boadicea herself was chosen by Frances Thynne, Countess of Hertford (later Duchess of Somerset). In one sense it could be argued that this wealthy and well-born patroness of writers was an admirable incarnation of the British heroine. Lady Hertford, who would have been in her twenties at the time of her induction into the society, acted as Lady of the Bedchamber to Queen Caroline both as Princess of Wales and Queen Consort. It was Lady Hertford who pleaded for Richard Savage, convicted of homicide, and secured his pardon. Other writers upon whom she looked with favour included Watts, Shenstone and James Thomson, author of 'Rule Britannia', who dedicated his 'Spring' to her and in another poem, 'Liberty', written later, featured Boadicea herself 'with her raging troops' – although once Thomson was admitted to her circle, according to naughty Horace Walpole, he took more pleasure in the aristocratic but unintellectual conversation of her husband than in her ladyship's 'poetical operations'.[17]

In another sense, the character of Frances Countess of Hertford, the philanthropic court lady and poetaster, was about as far from the patriotic and partisan Celtic Warrior Queen as it would be possible to imagine. (An equally inappropriate sobriquet was that of 'Veleda, Archdruidess of Kew' – a reference to Tacitus' tower-dwelling prophetess – applied to the Dowager Princess Augusta, mother of George III, by William Stukeley in 1753, when dedicating a book about Druids to her.) The final accolade for misplaced use of the Boadicean myth must however be reserved for William Cowper in his eponymous ode of 1780.[18]

Cowper's 'Boadicea' begins, apparently, in fine historical fettle:

> When the British warrior queen,
>   Bleeding from the Roman rods
> Sought with an indignant mien
>   Counsel of her country's Gods
>
> Sage beneath a spreading oak
>   Sat the Druid, hoary chief,
> Every burning word he spoke
>   Full of rage and full of grief.

Here is a picture both plausible and poetic, without too much licence, one feels, in its details. It is only when one realizes that Cowper, no friend to the American patriots currently engaged in the War of Independence, is actually casting the Americans as the *Romans*, that the full extent of the transference emerges. For Cowper devoutly hoped for the triumph of the British forces. And he uses the story of Boadicea as a test on which to hang the British right to empire; Boadicea herself may be defeated but the future belongs to Britain – not the Romans (or the Americans).

> Regions Caesar never knew
>   Thy posterity shall sway
> Where his eagles never flew
>   None invincible as they.

The ode ends:

> Ruffians! pitiless as proud
>   Heaven awards the vengeance due;
> Empire is on us bestow'd
>   Shame and ruin wait for you.

For Boadicea, the British Warrior Queen who attempted to throw off the Roman yoke, to be regarded as a symbol of

Britain's inalienable right to its own imperialism – towards America – is indeed an audacious use of patriotic legend.

About the time Christina of Sweden was formally granted power as 'king' – only to surrender it voluntarily a few years later – another genuine Warrior Queen was giving the Portuguese in Angola good reason to regret the persistent tradition of African female leadership in war. An eccentric, intellectually inclined female, a woefully insipid princess as Boadicea had become in certain literary works: these would certainly have provided riper targets for the seventeenth-century Portuguese. Instead they faced Jinga Mbandi. This at least was her tribal name, but since the rich variety of its spellings approaches that of Boadicea, including Nzinga, Singa and Zhinga, she will here be described by the name invariably used by the Portuguese then, and dignified by widespread popular usage in the People's Republic of Angola today: Queen Jinga.[19]

Unlike Queen Elizabeth I, for example, with her private pacifism and her artificial creation of a Warrior Queen persona, Queen Jinga followed in the bold tradition of Boadicea as she actually was (so far as we can tell about the British leader). That is, the Angolan Queen, described by a European with much truth as 'a Cunning Virago', led her people in war against the forces of an alien would-be occupying power, failing in the end to throw off their yoke. As a result, there is another parallel with Boadicea. Jinga's story, too, has survived down the centuries in its own emolliated form, to make her a patriotic heroine in her country today.

The Queen as a symbol of national resistance is of course a category into which female rulers can fall without necessarily displaying the sheer belligerence of a Boadicea or a Jinga. As we shall see, both Maria Theresa and Catherine the Great shared Elizabeth I's prudent love of peace not war; a preference which in Europe and its environs was fast becoming the hallmark of an intelligent female leader, and, one might argue, has remained so ever since. On the other hand, there is always a special niche for the Boadicean type of Warrior Queen in her country's pantheon, which does at least suggest a lingering connection in the popular consciousness to the ancient goddesses of war.

Within the confines of this book, the nineteenth-century Rani of Jhansi will also be found to come into that category: but examples are found in many different civilizations throughout the world and straddle history. In AD 39, twenty-odd years before Boadicea led her own uprising, two Vietnamese sisters, Trung Trac and Trung Nhi, led the first rising in their country against the domination of the Chinese.[20] The parallels between the story of Trung Trac and that of Boadicea are even more exact than those of Queen Jinga; Trung Trac was a lady of title, the widow of a man murdered by the Chinese, and she herself was raped by them. Together with her sister, she mustered an army of vassals to avenge her husband's death. Hers was not the only female heroism attached to her cause: of Trung Trac's supporters, Phung Thi Chinh, who was heavily pregnant, did not hesitate to plunge into the middle of the fray and, when she actually gave birth, paused merely to strap her baby on her back before hacking her way out. The kingdom of the battling Trungs, extending south to Hué and north to southern China, lasted only three years: finally defeated by the Chinese, the sisters flung themselves into a river and drowned.

Like the Trungs, Trieu Au in the third century has survived in Vietnamese myth as a female war leader who stood out against Chinese oppression. Trieu Au's story is the stuff of Western fairy tales as well as Vietnamese myth: an orphan who was cruelly treated by her brother and sister-in-law, she killed the latter and escaped to the mountains. A virgin warrior (she is sometimes known as the 'Vietnamese Joan of Arc'), she raised a thousand troops to liberate her country from the Chinese in 248. When her brother tried to remonstrate with her, Trieu Au answered him boldly in words which have become enshrined at the heart of her legend: 'I want to rail against wind and tide, kill the whales in the ocean, sweep the whole country to save people from slavery, and I have no desire to take abuse.' Trieu Au's story too ended in defeat and suicide: but the Vietnamese prints which show her in her golden armour, a sword in either hand, riding upon an elephant, give a better impression of the undying quality of her reputation as a patriotic Vietnamese heroine (a reputation only enhanced in Vietnam today where she is regarded as an early resister against Vietnam's modern enemy: China).

It is the oppression of an imperialist power – the Romans, Portuguese, British and Chinese respectively – which not only links the fortunes of Boadicea, Jinga, the Rani of Jhansi and the Vietnamese heroines, but is also half responsible for their immortality. The other essential element is of course the subsequent resurgence of the defeated people in question, without which their heroines' martial reputations might have perished with them. (A street in Luanda was named after Queen Jinga immediately after Angolan independence.) Cowper's ode was written to justify Britain against America – 'empire is on us bestow'd' – in an age when a queen no longer needed to be overtly militaristic, and Boadicea had become a mere waxwork figure of generalized patriotism. Yet ironically its lines could have been taken as rallying cries for these other far more genuine 'Boadiceas'.

Jinga Mbandi was born in the 1580s and lived until 1663, an extraordinary span for any human being at that time. But then Queen Jinga *was* extraordinary, the mere facts of her career, ungarnished by propaganda, causing wonder. As in the case of Queen Tamara of Georgia, the swirling legends of creation which wreathed so many African societies were not inimical to the idea of a powerful, even all-powerful, woman. These legends included a tradition of female semi-deities, such as the two mighty queens of the Mpororo of central East Africa, priestesses to their people, carried round in baskets by their ministers. In the Hausa lands of northern Nigeria (where creation was said to have begun with a woman going out and founding a kingdom), a queen known as Amina ruled in Katsina in the first half of the fifteenth century; south of Zaria, a woman, Bazao-Turunku, led another warrior tribe. There were feats of arms by the women of the Nilotic Lango.[21]

Nor did this tradition die away with Jinga's own death. Livingstone and Stanley encountered independent queens ruling the Fanti in Ghani; the 'King's Amazons' of Dahomey were not so much notorious in the eyes of their opponents as celebrated. During the course of King Gueso's disastrous war against Abeokuta, they stood their ground while the men fled, or, as Captain Duncan of the Life Guards expressed it, 'On a campaign I would prefer the women of that country, as soldiers, to the men.' *Sarraounia*, a recent film directed by Med Hondo of Mauritius from a novel by Aboulaye Mamani of Niger, was based on real events that occurred in Central Africa at the end of the nineteenth century. It tells the story of an African queen, half-warrior, half-sorceress, who leads her people to victory against the oppressive French colonial power in true Boadicean style, a towering figure of matriarchal strength as she shakes her spear and invokes the tribal gods before battle. Nor have such manifestations died away in the present century: popular uprisings in Uganda in 1987 were headed by a woman, Alice Lakwena, a self-styled high priestess of magic who inspired her Holy Spirit Movement to battle.[22]

Jinga herself operated in central West Africa, where the two principal kingdoms were those of Kongo and Ndongo. She was probably the daughter of the King – the Ngola – of Ndongo, with a mother from a vassal tribe. Until a few years before Jinga's birth, the Portuguese presence in Ndongo had consisted of friendly missionaries; but its geographical situation made it an ideal base for the growing Portuguese slave trade. With that in mind, Luanda was founded in 1576, and given its first Portuguese governor. It is from the century of conflict which followed – ending in the Portuguese victory – that Jinga's name has emerged as a heroic national figure.

We first hear of her, however, as an official negotiator with the Portuguese on behalf of her brother, the new Ngola, in the early 1620s. By the beginning of the seventeenth century, the slave markets based in Angola were rapidly expanding: an enthusiastic official wrote that the huge interior population would provide slaves enough 'until the end of the world'.[23] Ten thousand of them annually were already being exported from Luanda. It was a trade from which the African chiefs (like the Arabs) did not flinch when it suited their local purposes. Their selling members of rival or hostile tribes for a good price was one part of the process which enabled the Portuguese to build up such a gargantuan and horrifying trade, in order to satisfy the greedy labour demands of the Brazilian plantations and mines. But the Africans wanted co-operation to be on their own terms: and they also naturally wished to preserve their independence. Thus the aggressive new Portuguese Governor of Luanda – João Mendes de Vasconcelos – had exiled the Ngola of Ndongo to the Kwanza Islands.

Jinga's task was to negotiate the independence of Ndongo from the Portuguese, and at the same time to enlist their help in expelling the Imbangalas from the Ndongo kingdom. It is generally agreed that Jinga conducted these negotiations skilfully although certainly not as one raising her voice 'for suppliant humanity' (as that watered-down Zenobia was purported to do in the eighteenth century: the real Zenobia had much more in common with Queen Jinga). Perceiving for example, in the desire of the Portuguese to baptize her, a possible entry into their favour, she allowed herself to add to her armoury of names with that of Anna de Sousa (in honour of the incoming Governor Correira de Sousa). Her sisters, who would show themselves, like Jinga, wily and intelligent characters, became the Ladies Grace and Barbara respectively.

In 1624 Jinga's brother the Ngola died under mysterious circumstances: possibly he committed suicide, but possibly also Jinga had him killed.[24] Whatever the truth – and legend credited Jinga with another murder at the same time, that of her nephew, with the additional titillating accusation that she subsequently ate his heart – it was certainly Jinga who benefited from these demises, since she now assumed power. Unlike Pocahontas, who remained 'the Lady Rebecca', the Angolan princess now re-nounced her convenient Christianity. Anna de Sousa was no more; Queen Jinga was born.

The next important stage in the story of this 'redoubtable Amazon', as C. R. Boxer has called her, was reached when the Portuguese declared war upon her.[25] They did so reluctantly. A tacit peaceful alliance in the business of producing and shipping slaves was infinitely more desirable. Queen Jinga however played by her own rules. In the end the Portuguese preferred to set up a puppet chief from another tribe on the Ndongo throne, and Jinga was driven out. The loyalty of her Mbandi people however remained steadfast: the puppet kings were scorned as the sons of slaves on the one hand, inadequate rainmakers on the other. And in 1630 Queen Jinga made an alliance with the neighbouring Kasanje kingdom, which had the effect of closing the vital slave routes to the Portuguese.

The Queen then led her people further east to the kingdom of Matamba, where she conquered the indigenous Jaga tribe, acquiring not only a useful base, but also the ferocious rituals associated with its members. The Jagas themselves have been described as indulging in cannibalism 'not merely as a ritual sacrifice, but as a matter of habit, convenience and conviction'. They also indulged in deliberate infanticide, in order to preserve the hardy nature of the tribe, turning for replenishments of their population to the children of their conquered enemies.[26]

Queen Jinga, following her take-over of the Jagas, indulged in the first practice, at least in public and at least for ritual effect. As it happens, we have an eyewitness account of the Queen as she appeared to the Dutch captain of her bodyguard, during her wars against the Portuguese in the late 1640s.[27] Captain Fuller, who was in command of sixty men put at the Queen's service for a period of years, referred to the deep importance attached to her by people: rumours of her death – the death of the Holy Figurehead – were always concealed from the Portuguese lest they take too much heart from them.

More crucially, he also witnessed Queen Jinga performing a ritual sacrifice. She wore, as she always did, 'man's apparel' for the occasion. She was also hung about with 'the skins of Beasts, before and behind', had a sword about her neck, an axe at her girdle and a bow and arrows in her hand. This awesome figure proceeded to leap 'according to the custom, now here, now there, as nimbly as the most active among her attendants' (Queen Jinga would by this date have been well over sixty). All the while she continued to strike the two iron bells which she used instead of drums. 'When she thinks she has made a show long enough, in a masculine manner . . . then she takes a broad feather and flicks it through the holes of her bored Nose, for a Sign of War.' This sinister gesture was the prelude to the first sacrifice: Queen Jinga selected the first victim, cut off his head and drank 'a great draught of his blood'.

As for male company, the Queen had evidently adopted that second practice of the Jagas: infanticide. According to Fuller, she kept fifty or sixty young men instead of husbands, who were in turn allowed as many wives as they pleased, 'with the proviso that if any became with child, they must kill the infant'. Jinga was also described as going further and clothing selected young men in women's clothes (shades of Radegunde, Spenser's Queen of the Amazons, with her 'unnatural order' of knights holding distaffs!). The clothing of her obedient favourites, in the pretence that they had become women, as she herself had been transformed by her 'man's apparel', enabled them to move freely among the other women of her household: 'and if they fail in their obligations, they seldom escape to tell further news'.

It is a vivid if intimidating picture. Yet as with the head-hunting of the Celts, and as with Boadicea's chilling sacrifices to Andraste, one must be wary of condemning the Jagas and Queen Jinga outside the standards of their own time and society; one should bear in mind also the slave trading which was the quite open practice of the alternative officially 'Christian' cultures of the Portuguese and Dutch.

In terms of the outside world at this date, Angola was indeed a mere pawn in the game played out between these two nations, each eager to supply much-needed slaves to the colonies of the New World. Its inhabitants were estimated as something lower than pawns: pieces without any significance so long as the supply was sufficient. About this time the captured Negroes destined for the slave ships and death, or a tormented exile of drudgery at best, were casually described by those responsible for their fate as 'brutes without intelligent understanding'.[28] That was not a description which anyone could or would have applied to Queen Jinga in the years of raiding against the Portuguese, aided by other tribes such as the Congolese and the Dembos, which followed.

Nor was she herself a pawn. Whatever the cruelties of her own practice, like Boadicea Jinga did at least stand for the independence of her race in the person of at least one individual (a female, as it happened). 'Every kind of display and power is necessary when dealing with this heathen', wrote Antonio de Oliveira Cadornego, about twenty years after Jinga's death;[29] but the reverse was of course also true for the Africans dealing with the European 'heathen'. In the late-twentieth-century meaning of the word, among so-called Mafia business organizations, Queen Jinga demanded and received 'respect'.

Captain Fuller's verdict on her, for all her 'Devilish Superstition and Idolatry', her ritual sacrifices and bizarre sexual habits, is fundamentally a respectful one. She was, he wrote, 'a cunning and prudent Virago, so much addicted to arms that she hardly uses other exercises; and withal so generously valiant that she never hurt a Portuguese after quarter given, and commanded all her slaves and soldiers alike'.[30] This is perceptibly the tone of the British Caratach praising his Roman enemy as a comrade-soldier in Fletcher's *Bonduca*; it is certainly not that of Caratach denouncing the Warrior Queen herself as a weak, boastful and shameless woman.

In the end the Queen was responsible, if indirectly, for the defeat of the Portuguese at the hands of the Dutch, by which Luanda fell to the latter in 1641. Her tactical withdrawal to the interior had obliged the Portuguese to penetrate too far from their own base in search of their slave-prey. Queen Jinga was now pleased to make allies of the Dutch. She set up camp on the

Dande river. From this vantage point she could both despatch caravans to the Dutch at Luanda – selling them her prisoners of war – and conduct a series of short campaigns on her own account, notably against the puppet monarch of Ndongo, Ngola Ari, and his Portuguese sponsors.

In 1643 Queen Jinga's forces routed the Portuguese outside Mbaka and there were further victories in 1647 and 1648. Unfortunately an intervening defeat inflicted by the Portuguese resulted in the capture of Jinga's sister Mukumbu (to them the Lady Barbara), a considerable blow to one who had none of Queen Elizabeth I's dislike of her own sex, but rather relied on the matriarchal family network. Jinga's other sister Kifunji (the Lady Grace), long a captive of the Portuguese, had justified the Queen's faith in this network by supplying her with intelligence: in October 1647, Kifunji was drowned by the Portuguese as they retreated, either out of fear of her efforts or in retaliation.

On 10 August 1648, in a reversal of the events which had led to the seizing of Luanda by the Dutch, the daring Brazilian land-owner Salvador de Sá recaptured the town for the Portuguese. This time it was the presence of two hundred Dutch soldiers at Jinga's side in her last victory of 1648 which had fatally weakened the garrison. With the return of Portuguese mastery to Luanda, Queen Jinga's finest hour was over. Yet even now, where the Kongo state made peace on humiliating terms, Jinga herself was able to retreat back to her Matamba heartlands. Here she was able to lie low for a few years; since the prime concern of the Portuguese remained their slave trade, and that depended on milking the interior, finally they had more to gain from negotiating with Jinga than battling against her. It was however the continued captivity of Mukumbu at the hands of the Portuguese which ultimately persuaded Jinga to agree to an official peace in October 1656.

One hundred and thirty slaves were formally exchanged for the person of 'the Lady Barbara', to be restored to her Mbundu *persona* for good. Other conditions imposed by the Portuguese were the establishment of 'trade fairs' along the borders of their

Portuguese territories, and the introduction of a Christian mission into Matamba. In return 'the ancient Virago' – now in her seventies – was to receive military help when she required it. Lastly, in a settlement which was certainly to the advantage of most of the parties concerned, the Jagas were to abandon their notoriously savage habits: there was to be no more infanticide, for example, and although the women of the tribe were still compelled to give birth outside the war-camp, at least they could now bring up their offspring.

This peace lasted until Queen Jinga's death in 1663. After her death her corpse, still richly arrayed in the royal robes encrusted with precious stones, still clutching a bow and arrow in its hand, as though to symbolize the majesty and ferocity which were Jinga's dominant qualities, was formally displayed to her subjects.[31] They viewed it with a mixture of apprehension, awe and sorrow. All three reactions can surely be justified.

Even in the short term, the effect of Queen Jinga's rule was beneficial to the prosperity of Matamba – compared for example to the puppet kingdom of Ndongo, whose fortunes went rapidly downhill and which was eliminated altogether as an independent entity in 1671.[32] Matamba benefited from the trade and the missions, and did not suffer direct European authority. In addition, there were the many long-term legacies of her career. The first of these was the undeniable 'respect' she had earned by her own capabilities. 'History furnishes very few instances of bravery, intelligence and perseverance equal to the famous Zhinga, the Negro queen of Angola': thus wrote Mrs Child in 1833, at the beginning of the American movement for the emancipation of slaves. Mrs Child, a liberal writer, issued *An Appeal in Favor of that Class of Americans called Africans*.[33] She was concerned in particular to refute one contemporary argument against such an emancipation, that the Negroes lacked the natural ability of the white race. Although Mrs Child granted that Queen Jinga had been a despot, and granted that she had committed murderous acts, she still cited the Queen's story as part of her impassioned plea, since her ability could hardly be doubted.

Then there is the 'pan-African' element to Jinga's rule, the fact that she did at certain points combine various tribes other than her own under her leadership (a leadership which in itself, being female, acts as an inspiration to a growing women's movement). Lastly, of course, and most importantly, in the People's Republic of Angola (established in 1975), there is the legacy of Jinga as the Warrior Queen who attempted gloriously but in vain to oust the Portuguese. Modern Angolan school textbooks naturally stress both of these aspects of Queen Jinga's heroic career.[*] 'She tried to unite the different peoples in the struggle against the foreign threat . . . After a few years of effort she succeeded in her aims, which were to unite the people of Ndongo, Matamba, Congo, Casnje, Dembos, Kissama and the Central Planalto. This was the greatest alliance ever formed to fight against the foreign colonialists.' Even if Queen Jinga was not successful then, her 'great dream did not disappear. Her idea of a union of the Angolan people in its struggle against colonialism is today realized.'

Some modern Angolan students of history are beginning to assess Queen Jinga's contribution more critically: such matters as her alliance with the Dutch, her co-operation at various stages with the Portuguese, her own involvement in the slave trade, even her own claim to the throne, are being subjected at least to scrutiny. On the other hand the best known of all the legends about the Queen explains the deathless quality of her popular image, and why it is not likely to be widely superseded.

There are many variants of this story, but they unite in taking place in the course of that visit by Queen Jinga to the Portuguese Governor Correira de Sousa in the early 1620s in which her public career was inaugurated. They also unite in having the Governor seated on his throne, while Jinga was required to remain standing; whereupon Jinga, in a gesture at once characteristically bold and characteristically imperious, ordered one of her

---

[*] These quotations (originally in Portuguese) are taken from a fourth-form history textbook in use in an elementary school in Luanda in 1987.

slaves to kneel on all fours to form a seat. After that she sat down. Did she refuse to take the slave away when she left the Governor's mansion, saying that she would not remove the Governor's furniture? Or did she refuse to remove the slave on the grounds that she never sat on the same chair twice? Was the slave actually a maidservant? In one version, she even went as far as to have the slave (or maidservant) executed on the same grounds: 'I have no further use for him [or her].'

The clear message of the story is the same in all its versions: even in her enforced national subjection, Queen Jinga's personal pride was equal, even superior, to that of the Portuguese Governor. And this pride proved to be prophetic:

> Rome for empire far renown'd
> Tramples on a thousand states
> Soon her pride shall kiss the ground, –
> Hark! the Gaul is at her gates.

Once again Cowper's lines for a British Boadicea are more appropriate to another Warrior Queen in another country than they were to Britain – and British women – in the age in which he wrote them.

CHAPTER FIFTEEN

Queen versus Monster

Let us fight the Monster, let us beat the Monster down

QUEEN LOUISE OF PRUSSIA on Napoleon

A woman with a pretty face, but little intelligence and
quite incapable of foreseeing the consequences of what
she does

NAPOLEON on Queen Louise of Prussia

Butterflies are not associated with battlefields (although they may actually be found there, fluttering incongruously amid the trampled corn and wildflowers of a long hot bloodstained summer's day). Napoleon Bonaparte thought that women did not belong there either: he had a profound dislike of anything approaching the Amazon in womankind, and theoretically even intriguing women met with his censure. As he assured his first wife Josephine, he liked women to be '*bonnes, douces et conciliantes*' and on another occasion '*bonnes, naïves et douces*'; adding, with more tact than accuracy, that that was because such good, sweet, naïve, soothing women resembled her.[1]

The object of Napoleon's disapproval was Queen Louise of Prussia. Ironically enough, she was by nature quite as gentle and submissive as the most exigent male could require, as well as being as lovely a princess as ever won the heart of a king. It was cruel destiny – a destiny incarnated by Napoleon himself – which transformed this harmless and iridescent creature into a Warrior Queen 'dressed as an Amazon' as Napoleon terms her in 1806, in the uniform of her regiment of dragoons: writing twenty incendiary letters every day, 'an Armida in her madness destroying her own palace with fire'. The reference was to Gluck's opera

Armide, popular with both French and Prussian audiences: it was in fact performed in Berlin for Louise's own wedding day. The eponymous heroine was a princess of Damascus at the time of the First Crusade, founded on Tasso's 'wily witch' in *Jerusalem Delivered* who, foiled by her lover, ended by calling on demons: 'destroy this palace!'[2]

Queen Louise's tragedy, in one sense, lay in the fact that she found herself matched against a man whom the Queen and her circle were inclined to sum up in one simple expression of horror as the 'Monster'. This was of course too simple a judgement: the real threat was not so much in Napoleon's perceived monstrosity of nature as in the brilliance of his military talent. Even one of Louise's staunchest confidantes ruefully admitted that war was Napoleon's trade: 'he understands it and we do not'.[3]

But there was another deeper layer to Louise's tragedy, which made of her a genuine martyr to her people's own zeal at the time, as well as a patriotic heroine and martyr to the generations which followed. If Napoleon was indeed a monster, then it was optimistic at best to match the frail Queen Louise against him. Why did the fact that she emerged crushed from the encounter, failing to save Prussia from his depredations, generate surprise as well as despair? This was a development which must always have been expected along the level of common sense. The answer lies in the false but exciting expectations sometimes aroused in the human breast by the sight of one type of Warrior Queen: 'sainted' and 'possessed of angelic goodness' – descriptions freely applied to Queen Louise – this Holy Figurehead of the Prussian armies must surely bless her people with victory over the forces of evil.

It is true that the Queen did have, apart from her beauty, the natural appeal of a female in distress, to which male soldiers traditionally reply by springing to arms. It is a point of view most famously expressed by Edmund Burke in his lament for another tragic queen, Marie Antoinette: 'I thought ten thousand swords must have leaped from their scabbards to avenge even a look that threatened her with insult'. In similar if less exotic terms Robert Wilson, a young British envoy at the Prussian court, wrote movingly of the spectacle of Louise's melancholy following the defeat at Jena in 1806: 'but soldiers must not reflect, and a beautiful woman in misfortune should animate to enterprise'. Besides, Louise's grief was a potent symbol of her nation's woe, for which reason 'a queen in distress is universally acknowledged to be a more tragical sight than the more disastrous and general calamities of the commonalty'.[4]

Despite this inspiration, Queen Louise's own powers as a Warrior Queen were, if challenged by the brutal reality of conflict and disaster, a mere illusion, vanishing into the mists of romance and chivalry from whence they came. Her story illustrates how the 'fancy dress' aspect of a Warrior Queen, so brilliantly developed by Elizabeth I at Tilbury to mask the possible weaknesses of her position as a female ruler in time of war, might come to be mistaken for the real thing: a passive queen allows herself to be used, ignorant of the true hollowness of her position because she has been trained by upbringing to female impotence, just as Boadicea, a doughty battling queen in literature at the end of the sixteenth century, becomes a modest and delicate princess two hundred years later, who conquers with a blush not a spear, rides in a litter not a chariot.

Under different circumstances – and with a different character involved – the 'distress' of a queen could indeed be used to good effect. Robert Wilson, suggesting that Louise's misfortunes should spur her supporters to military action on her behalf, recalled the example of Maria Theresa sixty years before: 'So thought and felt the nobles of Hungary, and Maria Theresa retrieved the fortunes of her house.' The reigns of two great empresses, Maria Theresa of Austria and Catherine the Great of Russia, spanned altogether over seventy years; 1740 to 1780 and 1762 to 1796 respectively. Gibbon was well able to write in his *Decline and Fall*, first printed in 1776, of those 'illustrious women' able to bear the weight of empire: 'nor is our own age destitute'.[5]

These great tracts of time were matched by the vast tracts of land over which each woman presided. At first sight, however, the resemblance between the two stops there; not only their characters but the circumstances which brought them to power were certainly very different. The Archduchess Maria Theresa was a young married woman of twenty-three when the death of her father the Emperor Charles VI brought the male Habsburg succession to an end; but by that treaty of 1713 known as the Pragmatic Sanction, the right of his eldest daughter to succeed had been theoretically accepted. Sophie-Auguste of Anhalt-Zerbst, born in 1729 and thus twelve years younger than Maria Theresa, was on the other hand an obscure German princess before her marriage to the Grand Duke Peter, heir to the Tsarina Elisabeth of Russia. By this union she was transformed first into the Grand Duchess Catherine, and then, following a dramatic coup in which her doltish husband was deposed, into the Tsarina Catherine II; she was by now in her early thirties, someone who could claim to have contributed strongly to her own surprising exaltation.

When time and various military endeavours had combined to establish Maria Theresa securely on her hereditary throne of Hungary, with her husband Francis of Lorraine beside her as the elected Holy Roman Emperor, she displayed in private a love of cosy royal family life with her apparent infinity of children. Personally chaste, she also showed an austerity, even Puritanism of temperament which recall the 'sainted' Isabella of Spain. The pleasures of Catherine II were, notoriously, rather different. This was Voltaire's 'Semiramis of the North', the Warrior Queen with a taste for magnificently strong guards officers as lovers, who in her day created a sensation for her debauchery: 'excesses which would dishonour any woman whatever her station in life' in the disapproving opinion of the British Ambassador to her court. She herself actually believed, engagingly enough, in frequent (and incidentally straightforward) sexual activity as a means to health; but she never denied that it was also enjoyable, and as such should be welcomed. 'Nothing in my opinion is more difficult to resist than what gives us pleasure', wrote Catherine. 'All arguments to the contrary are prudery.' It was a hedonistic point of view shared in no way by the pious and self-abnegatory Maria Theresa.[6]

Yet there *was* a further interesting resemblance between the two rulers despite their opposing personal morality. Both the Queen–Empress and the Tsarina encountered that familiar problem for a reigning female, the need to exert military leadership, or at least some kind of leadership in war (although the Russian Empire, unlike Austria, had known the rule of other women autocrats, including Catherine's own mother-in-law Elisabeth). In both cases, they made use of the skilful technique of Elizabeth I, putting on a show of glory, in which the appealing femininity was artfully contrasted with stern and indeed noble patriotic resolve. And neither of them, despite presiding over military victories, had that heroic love of war for its own sake which has marked so many male rulers: Louis XIV, who boasted in 1662 that glory was the principal aim of all his actions, recommended his great-grandson on his deathbed half a century later, 'Do not imitate my love of war.'[7]

The first challenge to Maria Theresa occurred when Frederick the Great of Prussia snatched her province of Silesia only seven weeks after her father's death. To Carlyle, this act of territorial rape, contrary to Frederick's promised word, was merely the Prussian King grabbing bravely at Opportunity as at a wild horse: 'rushing hitherward, swift, terrible, clothed with lightning like a courser of the gods; dare you catch *him* by the thunder-mane and fling yourself upon him . . .' Many may prefer the cooler estimate of Macaulay concerning the War of the Austrian Succession: 'The selfish rapacity of the King of Prussia gave the signal to his neighbours. The whole world sprang to arms . . .' (We might forgive Carlyle for his blithe cruelty towards one Warrior Queen, for the sake of that bright suggestion made to the young Miss Jane Welsh that Boadicea would be the ideal subject for her initial 'literary effort', with the comforting rider that 'she need not be "big" or "grim" unless you like' – except for the fact that bigness and grimness were the qualities that Carlyle evidently admired.)[8]

The young Maria Theresa was hailed as Queen of Hungary by her loyal subjects in that country, or rather by an oxymoron of a title – *domina et rex noster* (our mistress and our king), another variant of that familiar theme of gender transference. In her beleaguered state, the *domina–rex* was at least armed with one important weapon in the shape of an infant male heir; and she was quick to play upon the appealing possibilities of the image of the Warrior Queen as Young Mother. Sending a picture of herself and the child to General Khevenmüller in 1742 just after he had taken Munich on her behalf, Maria Theresa wrote this accompanying letter: 'Dear and faithful Khevenmüller – Here you behold a queen who knows what it is to be forsaken by the whole world. And here also is the heir to her throne. What do you think will become of this child?'[9] The next day the troops at Linz were shown both the picture and the letter, amid outbursts of wild enthusiasm.

At her coronation at Pressburg (Bratislava) in Hungary Maria Theresa mounted a huge black charger, and according to immemorial custom drew her sword to the four points of the compass, to signify her role as Hungary's protector. This was once again Elizabeth I at Tilbury, making the show stand for the substance, especially as Maria Theresa had to learn to ride astride specially for the event: furthermore, she had only just over a month in which to do so (following the invitation to Pressburg) and was in the process of recovering from the birth of her first son. Thereafter Maria Theresa continued to enjoy all the spectacles of military life such as reviews, parades and manoeuvres in which she could similarly display herself. She designed a uniform for herself and her ladies on these occasions which combined the practical chamois leather breeches and boots of the *rex* beneath, with the voluminous skirts of the *domina* above.

None of this amounted to a predilection for warmongering. The frequent battles she had to fight were more likely to be in defence of her own inheritance than in pursuit of others'. Indeed the Queen (in her own right) and Empress (by virtue of her husband's election) displayed on occasion a consciousness of the sheer immorality of national aggression which seems to have been rooted in her own personal piety. When the Polish Partition of 1772 was first suggested, Maria Theresa protested against the robbing of an innocent nation 'that it has hitherto been our boast to protect and support', adding 'The greatness and strength of a state will not be taken into consideration when we are called to render our final account.' Towards the end of her life the Empress protested vehemently against Austria's attempt to annex Bavaria: 'Let them call me a coward, a weakling, a dotard if they like [she was approaching sixty], nothing shall prevent me from extricating Europe from this perilous situation.' Afterwards she said: 'For me it is an inexpressible happiness to have prevented a great effusion of blood.'

More symbolic of her personal style than the image of the young Queen on the black charger at the beginning of the reign, is that presented by the statue erected in the nineteenth century opposite the Hofburg in Vienna. Here the Empress – 'the General and first Mother of the said Dominions', as she described herself – is seen presiding like an enormous benevolent muffin in her long dress and ceremonial robes (there is no glimpse of those practical chamois leather breeches and boots).[10] All about her, at the four corners of the statue, prance on horses, her male generals and ministers, both smaller and more active.

Unlike Maria Theresa, Catherine the Great did have, it is true, a penchant towards glory. When she told her adoring correspondent Voltaire in 1771 that 'the nation's glory is my own, that is my principle',[11] she summed up an intelligent philosophy which explained how she had come to rule the unwieldy Russias so successfully for the last nine years. This little German Princess had loved rough games as a child, hating to be fobbed off with dolls and cots instead of riding and shooting birds with the local children. As the unheeded bride of the Grand Duke Peter – their marriage was not consummated for nine years – she took her chief pleasure in riding, even in bed, by her own account, where she galloped away her frustration as 'a postilion on my pillow'.[12] When the Tsarina Elisabeth protested that riding like a man on a flat saddle led to sterility, the neglected wife replied pointedly that the more violent the exercise, the more she liked it. As Tsarina herself, Catherine put this caged energy to good use.

The coup against Catherine's husband, who had succeeded as the Tsar Peter III at the beginning of 1762, took place six months later. It was ten o'clock of the light northern night on 29 June, according to the Russian style of dating; there was thus scarcely any darkness to shroud the startling spectacle of the Grand Duchess Catherine, dressed in uniform, at the head of the rebel regiments whose members including prominently her current lover Grigory Orlov and his brother. When these rebels – disgusted by the Tsar's pro-German policies – had come for Catherine, she had borrowed the green and red uniform of a young officer, Captain Talietzin, in the Semeonovsky regiment, who was slight enough for his clothes to fit her. Her lady-in-waiting Princess Dashkova took the uniform of another young officer, Lieutenant Poushkin. According to the Princess's memoirs, it was she, Dashkova, who suggested that her mistress should now substitute the Order of St Andrew for that of St Catherine worn over her uniform: the order of St Andrew was theoretically worn only by the reigning sovereign, and the substitution was thus a dramatic gesture indicating the assumption of command.[13]

'For a man's work, you needed a man's outfit' was Catherine's official explanation for her masculine attire[14] (although since she had been accustomed to steal out of her palace in man's costume to meet her lover Stanislaus Poniatowski, it could clearly be used for a woman's work as well). The former tomboy easily mounted the mettlesome grey stallion brought for her use and mastered it. With her drawn sword and her long flowing hair beneath her black three-cornered hat lined with sable and decorated with oak leaves, the symbols of victory, Catherine now presented a very passable goddess of war at the head of her troops. The loyalty inspired by the sight was epitomized when a young NCO rushed forward to present her with a pennant for her naked sword. His name was Grigory Potemkin.

During her long reign, her triumphant progress towards

military victories galore – she listed seventy-eight of them – Catherine never failed to present herself wherever possible in the same heroic light. When the French diplomat the Comte de Ségur first saw her in 1785, he found her 'richly attired, her hand resting on a column'. Her majestic air, the pride in her expression and her 'slightly theatrical pose' so took him aback that he forgot his speech of welcome. So successful was this projection that the portrait painter Madame Vigée Le Brun, meeting her during a tour of Russia, was amazed to discover that the Tsarina was actually very short: 'I had fancied her prodigiously tall, as high as her grandeur'.[15]

Ségur described her in the course of that triumphal procession to Kiev of 1787 arranged by Potemkin, following the defeat of Turkey and Russia's annexation of the Crimea, which brought her both the fruitful steppes of the south and an invaluable access to the Black Sea. Stout and tiny in her military uniform, she was nevertheless 'a conquering empress', The descendants of the Tartars who had once swept across this territory (putting an end to the Georgian empire of Tamara) now prostrated themselves before 'a woman and a Christian'.[16] When a Georgian prince from Colchis brought presents to the foot of the Russian Tsarina Catherine's throne, it might be argued that the memory of Queen Tamara, in her sex if not her nationality, had been avenged.

Catherine, like Tamara six centuries before, understood how to make use of that deep mystical Slavic feeling towards the mother goddess, as well as the conquering goddess of war. To Orlov she was 'little mother' as well as 'most merciful sovereign lady'. To the later lover Potemkin she was 'Mother Tsarina Catherine . . . far more than a mother to me . . . my benefactress and my mother'. On the other hand, like Queen Elizabeth I, she did not consider that she belonged (unlike most mothers) to the 'weak, frivolous, whining species of women'; in this respect she was certainly the Warrior Queen as an honorary male. When Catherine founded an orphanage, for example, she ordered that the girls should learn to cook and make bread, following the much praised women of the Bible and those hard-working ones celebrated by Homer[17] (by which she definitely did not mean the Bible's sword-wielding Judith or Homer's flashing-eyed Athene, felling the war-god Ares with a stone).

At her accession, in fact, Catherine suffered from the same prudent dislike of war as Elizabeth I and for the same reason: the debts incurred by Russia during the Seven Years' War, which ended a year later in 1763. Even in 1770, after a successful campaign against the Turks, Catherine believed peace to be a fine thing, though she now admitted that war also had its 'fine moments'.[18]

Voltaire's correspondence with Catherine concerning the Turks was on a far more rambunctious level and there is a nice flavour of chivalry too: 'these barbarians deserve to be punished by a heroine for the lack of respect they have hitherto had for ladies', he wrote to the Tsarina in November 1768, a month after war had been declared by the Turks. 'Clearly, people who neglect all the fine arts and who lock up women, deserve to be exterminated.' A year later he was admonishing his 'Semiramis' and his 'Northern Star' in still more ardent terms: 'Come now, heir to the Caesars, head of the Holy Roman Empire, defender of the Latin Church, come now, this is your chance.' When there was news of a victory, he described himself as jumping out of bed in ecstasy: 'Your Imperial Majesty has brought me back to life by killing the Turks.' Voltaire's subsequent salute was a weird parody of the language of religion: for he began by crying 'Allah! Catherine!' and went on to sing 'Te Catharinam laudamus, te dominam confitemur'.[19]

Catherine herself had a more controlled appreciation of these tumultuous events. Did they serve the interest of Russian greatness (with which of course she identified herself)? That was her persistent concern. She had her own well-developed sense of Russian national pride – Russia, the country she had so successfully adopted. Not only did she display a taste for operas which celebrated Russian history, she also littered the imperial grounds at Tsarskoe Selo with monumental reminders of Russian military triumphs including obelisks and marble columns as well as war memorials. In 1771 she agreed with Voltaire that 'this army will win Russia a name for herself'. But when she declared that 'great events have never displeased me and great conquests have never tempted me', the second half of her statement was not quite as disingenuous as the list of her achievements and territorial acquisitions might indicate.[20]

Her own nominee on the throne of Poland and some of its territory annexed by Russia, further acquisitions on the Alaskan coast, to say nothing of the defeat of Turkey and Russia's surge into the Crimea, her revenues mightily increased: all this was brought about by only six years of war in her twenty-five-year reign. Nor, in all this, was Catherine a mere glittering figurehead of a Warrior Queen. Where military and naval matters were concerned, she played an active directing part. Attending twice-weekly meetings of the seven-man council which directed the war during the Crimean campaign, she herself was probably the originator of the daredevil plan whereby the Russian fleet in the Baltic sailed five thousand miles round the coasts of Western Europe to engage the Turks.

The results of this brilliantly executed expansionist policy for Russia were extraordinary: twenty million subjects owed Catherine loyalty at her coronation, compared to thirty-six million in 1795 shortly before her death. It was however expansion, not war itself with its manufactured heroics, which interested her, even if she could manufacture heroics herself with a will, where necessary. 'We need population not devastation': that was her philosophy. In short, as she herself declared, 'peace is necessary to this vast empire':[21] a perceptive comment on the vast Russian 'empire' at any stage of its history.

Where Warrior Queens are concerned, we return from the users – Maria Theresa and Catherine – to the used – Louise of Prussia. Although described by Napoleon as an 'Armida', there was by temperament nothing of Tasso's 'wily witch' and Gluck's destructive enchantress about Queen Louise of Prussia. 'Every day I realize that I am a weak woman,' she wrote during her early carefree years, 'and I am weak because I am kindhearted. I want everyone to be happy, and so I forgive, forget, and fail to scold when I should . . .'[22]

Like Catherine a minor German princess, Louise of Mecklenburg-Strelitz possessed, apart from this sweet feminine pliancy, the gift of beauty. On Louise's exquisite looks there is a remarkable agreement of testimony. In 1793, when she was seventeen, her ravishing appearance captured the heart of Frederick William, the shy young heir to the throne of Prussia: 'it is she, and if not she, no other creature in the world', he is reputed to have exclaimed at the mere sight of her (much as Isabella of Castile is supposed to have greeted Ferdinand). A decade later, seeing the Prussian Queen dressed as Statira, the Persian bride of Alexander the Great at a fête in Berlin, Madame de Staël was 'struck dumb by her beauty'. In 1801 Madame Vigée Le Brun, whose observant painter's eye was disappointed in the stature of Catherine the Great, alleged that her pen failed her in trying to describe Louise. The Queen happened to be in deep mourning on their first encounter, but her coronet of black jet served only to set off the dazzling whiteness of her complexion; as for the beauty of her 'heavenly' face Madame Vigée Le Brun compared it to that of a sixteen-year-old girl, with the perfect regularity and delicacy of the features, the grace of figure, neck and arms: 'all was enchanting beyond anything imaginable!'[23]

In life this perfect regularity of feature and the supple slender figure often led to Queen Louise being compared to a Greek statue. For once, the art by which later generations must judge confirms that does not disappoint: there is something neo-Hellenic about the many representations of her which have survived, enhanced naturally by the clinging Grecian style of contemporary fashion which suited her so well. We can accept with relief the verdict of the English diplomat Sir George Jackson that the Queen was 'really a beauty and would be thought so even if she did not sit upon a throne'. The chivalry she inspired is equally easy to understand: 'among the younger men especially', wrote Jackson, 'there prevails a feeling of chivalrous devotion towards her; and a sunny smile, or glance of her bright laughing eyes, is a mark of favour eagerly sought for'.[24]

At first it was all lightness at the Prussian court, Frederick William succeeding his father in 1797, four years after his marriage. Perhaps the Queen – who was after all young – danced a little too much (she danced at a court ball in 1803 within hours of giving birth) and she was also lightheartedly unpunctual. There are unpublished passages in the diary of Countess Sophie von Voss, Louise's battleaxe of a lady-in-waiting (already in her seventies, with a father who fought against Marlborough at Malplaquet) that criticize the Queen's frivolity and even her petulance in these early years; but Countess Voss's final verdict was to be very different: 'all the loveliest virtues of woman and the most pleasing to God'.[25]

On the other hand Louise's surely admirable attempts at enlarging her perfunctory education with a study of German literature, to which more intellectual ladies-in-waiting introduced her, were greeted with boorish mockery by Frederick William. He described one of these intellectuals, Caroline von Berg, as 'vain, trivial . . . and forever gushing poetry'. Nor was the reputation of Goethe sacred to the Prussian King. 'Wha's 'is name, t'great man from Weimar?' Frederick William would enquire, aping the local dialect. Another of these ladies, Marie von Kleist, aunt by marriage to the poet and playwright Heinrich von Kleist, persuaded the Queen to patronize her nephew; he received an honorarium under oath of secrecy.[26] Schiller became a special favourite: the Queen wanted him as Poet Laureate. She also read Shakespeare in translation.

The Queen's tentative efforts at intellectual independence had however little in common with that kind of Amazonian behaviour described with all the richness of sexual violence in Kleist's *Penthesilea*: 'A nation has arisen, a nation of women, Bound to no overlord . . .'[27] Louise's submissiveness, her wifely wish to please, was most notably demonstrated by the continuous procession of children that she bore. Ten years after her marriage she had already borne seven; two of the children had died and there were also various miscarriages. Louise gave birth to a total of nine children in fourteen years, the last of them less than a year before her death.

When Madame Vigée Le Brun met the Queen in 1801, she could not make an appointment before noon because, as Louise explained, 'the King reviews the troops at ten every morning and likes me to attend'. The only blight on this picture of domestic and marital bliss appeared to be the plain looks of Louise's numerous children. 'They are not pretty,' murmured the Queen sadly. 'Their faces have a great deal of character', was the painter's tactful comment. Privately, she thought the youthful princes and princesses of Prussia downright ugly.[28]

But for Prussia and its king – if not yet its queen – already problems existed along more serious lines than those of a military review or a homely royal family. The rise of Napoleonic France had placed Prussia in a quandary: neutrality? And if not neutrality, alliance with which of the various great powers involved? It was a profound Prussian conviction of the time that its army, built up by Frederick William's great-uncle Frederick the Great, remained the finest in Europe. Time would test the validity of that belief. In the meantime Frederick William's indecisive nature led him to see his fine army as a bastion of Prussia's neutrality rather than as anything more aggressive.

The King's personal quandary however – neutrality versus alliance – remained. And it was this quandary, finally, which brought Louise to play the role of Warrior Queen. In 1803 the French forces occupied Hanover, a state which on the one hand Prussia was pledged to protect as a neutral zone, and on the other coveted for itself. Prussia was offered Hanover in return for a treaty with France. Frederick William hesitated unhappily. Napoleon made good use of his dilemma of conscience. The French judicial murder of the young Bourbon Prince the Duc d'Enghien on 21 March 1804 for alleged conspiracy horrified all royal Europe: but Louise was persuaded not to wear mourning for the Duc by the new Prussian Foreign Minister, the veteran statesman Carl-August von Hardenberg, who hoped to secure Hanover peaceably.

Louise's martial instincts were still nascent. Placatory gifts of dresses from the newly created Empress Josephine (Napoleon assumed the title of Emperor on 18 May) were accepted: pale grey satin magnificently embroidered with steel, and white satin embroidered with gold thread, further adorned with Alençon lace and Brussels point. The Queen's attempts at influencing the King towards war were dated nearly a year later by Sir George Jackson to February 1805. It was not until September of the same year that she was generally reputed to head the 'war party'.[29]

What brought about the transformation? Napoleon himself angrily and publicly ascribed the change to another charismatic man: the Tsar Alexander I. There had been that magic summer at the Baltic coastal resort of Memel in 1802, the year following the accession of the young Tsar. The grandson of Catherine the Great, Alexander was an intensely attractive figure: even the crabby Countess Voss found him at this stage 'irresistible', with his handsome appearance and striking fair colouring (he was of course genetically far more German than Slav, his mother like his grandmother having been born a German princess).[30] Memel, symbolically enough, was not only on the Baltic, but also on the borders of Prussia and Russia: here the two courts mingled and the two youthful royal families – already interrelated – relaxed together.

Louise flowered. 'She was today more beautiful than ever', wrote Countess Voss of one particular June evening. There was dancing every night, and presents for Louise from the Tsar including earrings of her favourite pearls (even Countess Voss got a pearl necklace). No wonder the Countess wrote that she was 'quite grieved that these pleasant days should come to an end'.[31] But further delightful co-celebrations were planned by Alexander, such as a pageant based on the happy days at Memel for Louise's birthday the following March; Louise's current baby would be named Alexandrina with the Tsar as her godfather.

For all Napoleon's subsequent excoriations in which he vowed that the Prussian Queen had been 'so good, so gentle' until the Tsar's baleful influence made her desert 'the serious occupation of her dressing-table' for politics,³² the story of an actual affair between Alexander and Louise was certainly a calumny. That primitive desire to find a Warrior Queen either preternaturally lustful or preternaturally chaste (Louise came in for both charges) may have played its part. The truth of Louise's feelings for Alexander was probably subtler. What a contrast the romantic young Tsar – born in 1777, he was a year younger than Louise – presented to the vacillating and uncultured Frederick William! For Louise, well knowing her duty both as a wife and a queen, her unacknowledged sentimental devotion to the Tsar could be safely expressed in a public admiration for his policies and a trust in his political objectives. 'I believe in you as I believe in God', she wrote to Alexander at one point:³³ this idolatry was not the outburst of a voluptuous and satisfied woman.

The late summer of 1805 brought persistent murmurs of war in the Prussian capital of Berlin. How could Prussia stand aloof while the French devoured half Europe? Frederick William reflected gloomily concerning his impossible position on 12 September: 'Many a king has fallen because he loved war too well, but I may fall because I am in love with peace.'³⁴ There was no doubt that the general Prussian mood veered towards war. Napoleon's enemy the Tsar was cheered wildly at the opera in Berlin (the performance incidentally was of *Armide*). And when a secret pact was finally concluded between Russia and Prussia, agreeing to send an ultimatum to Napoleon, Louise's influence over Frederick William was generally believed by those in the know to have brought it about. The treaty was signed on 3 November 1805. That night the three friends – Alexander, Louise and Frederick William – went secretly together to visit the tomb of Frederick the Great at the Tsar's request (a popular contemporary print would depict them standing reverently beside the historic sepulchre). The episode represented the romantic culmination of Louise's hopes that war would not only stop the unstoppable Napoleon, but bring honour to the Prussian King at last, by uniting him with the brave and honourable Tsar of Russia.

At the beginning of the next month it was Louise's turn to be cheered wildly as she stood on the palace balcony to watch the Prussian troops leaving Berlin, the banners dipping as they passed. Her popularity with the army at this point knew no bounds. Here was their beloved patroness, she who had in peacetime attended those morning parades, danced at their balls, befriended young officers in trouble; now she was to be not only their queen but their goddess of victory. Moreover Louise herself had always reciprocated these feelings. When the Tsar praised her good relationships with the military, the Queen replied that 'such a respected estate, whose vocation brought such toil and changes of fortune could not be admired enough'.[35]

Unknown to the Queen on her balcony, one of those swift changes of fortune which would affect the destiny of the bonny Prussian soldiers beneath her had already taken place. In late October Napoleon had secured the capitulation of the Austrians at Ulm; on 13 November he entered Vienna; on 2 December, in a brilliant striking manoeuvre, he had utterly crushed the Austrian and Russian forces at Austerlitz. When the news reached the Queen in Berlin, she exclaimed that 'no one who is a German can hear of this and not be moved'. She was right to see the chilling significance of the defeat. Prussia for her part was simply told she must accept the territorial changes imposed: Hanover for example could be retained, but Ausbach ('the cradle of the Hohenzollern race' as Louise tearfully told Frederick William), Neuchâtel and Cleves with its fortress of Wesel must be given up. In June 1806 the Holy Roman Empire would be brutally ended, the Confederation of the Rhine put in its place.

The Queen, passionately opposed to the ratification of this Treaty, wrote: 'There is only one thing to be done, let us fight the Monster, let us beat the Monster down, and then we can talk of worries!'[36] Her words became a patriotic slogan for the party still resolutely opposed to dealing with Napoleon, just as the Queen herself was increasingly credited with all the qualities of inspiration the King so signally lacked. Prince Louis Ferdinand, Frederick William's clever raffish cousin, remarked that if the people knew how much Louise had done, they would raise altars to her everywhere. Even without the benefit of altars, popular admiration expressed itself in a thousand ways. One unit demanded that its name be changed to the Queen's Cuirassiers! Let Louise lead them!

With a weak king and a valiant queen, there was the inevitable emergence of the Better-Man Syndrome. After this period of debate and anxiety was over, Hardenberg would quote the famous words of Catherine de Foix to her husband Jean d'Albret: 'If we had been born, you Catherine and I Don Jean, we would not have lost our kingdom.' Queen Louise, he said, had an equal right to address her husband thus.[37]

It was not until the autumn of 1806 that the Prussian King's hopes of treating with France were formally abandoned; he agreed at last to combine with the allies including Russia, Austria and England, to try to beat the 'Monster'. By this time Queen Louise's personal fixation against Napoleon as the source of all their woes had begun to be matched by the anger of the Emperor at what the Prussians considered her patriotic fervour but he deemed her womanly interference in dragging Prussia away from France. The Bulletin of the Army, an official propaganda publication, printed a conversation Napoleon was said to have had with Marshal Berthier: 'a beautiful queen wants to see a battle, so let us be gallant. Let us march off at once to Saxony.' It went on to report Napoleon's outburst quoted earlier concerning the Queen with her army 'dressed as an Amazon'. On another occasion: 'So – Mademoiselle de Mecklenburg [an allusion to Louise's birth outside Prussia] wants to make war on me, does she? Let her come! I am not afraid of women.'[38]

This elevation of Queen Louise to something more than a pretty woman attired from time to time in a becoming adaptation of military uniform suited both sides, in fact. But the Queen's true intentions were probably better interpreted by Thomas Hardy later in his poetic drama *The Dynasts*, than by Napoleon. Here Hardy has the loyal Berliners protest against Napoleon's insulting epithet of Amazon: 'Her whose each act Shows but a mettled modest woman's zeal . . . To fend off ill from home!'[39] Alas, the mettled but modest Louise, like Armida, but for very different reasons, would all too soon find that very home laid low.

The French victory over Prussia at the double battle Jena–Auerstädt on 14 October 1806 virtually obliterated the Prussian army, that force which had, under Frederick the Great – dead only twenty years before – terrorized Europe. In the wake of the general destruction, the Queen found herself enquiring wildly for her husband: 'Where is the King?' 'I don't know, Your Majesty.' 'But, my God, isn't the King with the army?' 'The army? It no longer exists.'[40] The Prussian army, Prussia itself and for that matter Queen Louise were none of them ever to be quite the same after this ghastly day of national humiliation. (The French Marshal Davout would be made Duc d'Auerstädt for defeating an army twice his own strength.) A week before the battle, Frederick von Gentz, the philosopher–politician, had an interview with the Queen at the Prussian war camp in which she expressed herself 'with a precision, a firmness and energy, and at the same time with a restraint and wisdom, that would have enchanted me in a man'.[41] Afterwards, the Queen was transformed into both a fugitive and an invalid.

Her flight from the French was real enough. Napoleon had hoped that the Queen who had defied him would be captured. Although he was cross that she had escaped, he was at least able to exult in the Bulletin of the Army: 'She has been driven headlong from danger to danger . . . she wanted to see blood, and the most precious blood in the kingdom has been shed.' As for Louise's health, that finally collapsed as she made her painful way via Berlin and Königsberg to Memel, safe on the borders of Russia but already wrapped in the Baltic winter. Snow was falling in heavy flakes as her husband's cousin Princess Anton Radziwill watched Louise depart from Königsberg, lying down in her coach, barely able to wave a hand in farewell.[42]

What was the Queen doing at the war camp in the first place? The Duke of Brunswick, the Commander-in-Chief of the army, was appalled to find her there, on the scene of battle, in her little carriage. 'What are you doing here, Madame? For God's sake, what are you doing here?' he exclaimed. Then he pointed at the fortress occupied by the French: 'Tomorrow we will have a bloody decisive day.' The Queen departed very early the next morning with the noise of the cannonades in her ears: already the French could distinctly perceive her amid the Prussian lines, and in the event missed capturing her by a mere hour. (Later the Queen would remark wryly that the Duke of Brunswick's order to retreat was the first time she ever heard him express himself either positively or energetically.)[43]

Queen Louise's official explanation for her presence was the King's need of her support; Gentz at least accepted this, as did General Kalkreuth. She propped up the King's waning confidence, he believed, and besides her presence had its usual encouraging effect on the soldiers. Kalkreuth's reasoning was undoubtedly correct. Yet the grim truth was that on a battlefield, for the Prussians, King and soldiers alike, the encouragement of their goddess could avail little against the superior French. And a fancy-dress Warrior Queen, however patriotic, had little place there, when she might have been captured and given cause for still further exultation on the part of her enemies.

Queen Louise's tribulations were not at an end with her flight to Memel. How freezing, how forlorn and how horribly crowded with refugees was beloved Memel now, compared to that sweet summer place where she had danced with the Tsar four years earlier! The Queen herself was ill most of the time. She was still recovering from typhus, while that combination of a weak heart and congestion of the lungs which would finally kill her was beginning to take its toll. Diplomatic negotiations to save something for Prussia from the wreck of its defeat caused her further anguish, as the Prussian King and his advisers struggled to conciliate France while not antagonizing Russia. Perhaps the Queen derived some ironic amusement from her riposte to the hated French Marshal Bertrand who asked her to use her influence to bring about a proper peace between France and Prussia. 'Women have no voice in the making of war and peace', replied the Queen, with dignity. When Frederick William sent her a soldier's pigtail, to indicate that the sacred but old-fashioned costume of the Prussian army was at last being modernized, Louise both laughed and wept. But by June tears were constantly dripping down the Queen's cheeks, 'despite her brave little games' as the British envoy, Lord Granville Leveson-Gower, noted.[44]

Meanwhile the 'Monster', in the Queen's own room at Weimar, gloated over the notes and reports which he found in her drawers, mixed with the other more delicate objects of her toilette, still perfumed by the musk which was used to scent them. 'It seems as if what they say of her is true', he noted. 'She was here to fan the flames of war.' Then he dismissed Louise as 'a woman with a pretty face, but little intelligence and quite incapable of foreseeing the consequences of what she does'. He even managed a kind of compassion: 'Now she is to be pitied rather than blamed, for she must be suffering agonies of remorse for all the evil she has done to her country and to her husband, who, everyone agrees, is an honourable man, wanting only the peace and welfare of his subjects.'[45]

But at the City Hall in Berlin, Napoleon ranted on concerning the excellent example of the Turks who kept women out of politics (shades of Voltaire's salute to that 'woman and a Christian', Catherine the Great!) and would not listen to two elderly ecclesiastics who praised their queen's kindness and goodness. When the wife of Prince Hatzfeld pleaded on her knees for her husband's life, on the other hand, Napoleon was pleased to grant the request and issued a picture commemorating the incident; that presumably was the proper position for a woman. Queen Louise was already suffering furious humiliation at Napoleon's insinuations concerning her relationship with the Tsar. She burst out in a letter otherwise written in French: *Und man lebt und kann die Schmach nicht rächen*' (And one lives and cannot take revenge for the humiliation).[46] She was now further punished by the issue of a very different picture. At the tomb of Frederick the Great, in a caricature of that secret night visit and its vows depicted in the popular print, Louise was shown in the guise of Lady Hamilton to the Tsar's Nelson. Since Lady Hamilton was then notorious in Europe as the late Nelson's mistress, the implication was clear.

It was at this time that Queen Louise was traditionally supposed to have transcribed this harpist's song (set by Schubert) from Goethe's *Wilhelm Meister*, with its mournful quatrain:

> Who never ate his bread in sorrow
> Who never spent the darksome hours
> Weeping and watching for the morrow
> He knows ye not, ye heavenly powers![47]

But the greatest humiliation lay ahead. Its prelude was another crushing defeat: that of the Russian army under General Bennigsen at Friedland, twenty-seven miles south of Königsberg, on 15 June 1807. A week later it was the Tsar Alexander's turn to negotiate a truce. This was the prayer of Louise to Alexander before the battle: 'You are our only hope: do not abandon us, not for my sake, but for my husband's sake, for the sake of my children, their future and their destiny.' Her prayer would go for nothing compared to the crudeness of *Realpolitik*. Louise's 'only hope' was indeed about to abandon them, as she would shortly discover.

At Tilsit, while the Emperor Napoleon of France and the Tsar Alexander of Russia met on an island in the middle of the river, King Frederick William of Prussia was condemned to await their summons standing in the pouring rain, on the shore. His unhappy stance perfectly illustrated the comment of the Austrian Prince Metternich: at Tilsit Prussia descended from the first rank 'to be ranged among powers of the Third Order'.[48] What was Prussia's fate likely to be – what territorial sacrifices, what financial reparations would be demanded at a treaty negotiated under such unpromising circumstances?

It was at this point that someone at the Prussian court, convinced that the Queen's 'fascinating affability' would win over 'this Monster vomited from hell' (the King's phrase on this occasion), had the idea of sending for Louise. One German biographer suggests that it was Hardenberg and General Kalkreuth who decided to use the Queen. Another name proposed is that of Murat, working on Frederick William. But on the French side Talleyrand was certainly very much against it and, accepting Louise's putative powers as an enchantress, enquired of Napoleon angrily: 'Sire, will you jeopardize your greatest conquest for a pair of beautiful eyes?'[49]

We know from the testimony of those young British diplomats stationed at Memel – all of them half in love with the Queen – how reluctant she was to go. Her health alone might have precluded such an ordeal. To the King, however, Louise wrote that her arrival would be a proof of her love for him: for as she confided to her diary, 'this burden is demanded', whatever it might cost her to be pleasant and courteous towards Napoleon.[50] Louise was condemned to the 'burden' by the romantic Prussian belief, which she herself obviously shared, that she could succeed where male diplomacy failed. Furthermore, hopeful signs elicited, as it seemed, from the 'Monster' only underlined the general atmosphere of expectation: he drank the Queen's health and asked with some tenderness after her family's welfare.

Perhaps it was as well that the Prussian courtiers could not read Napoleon's reassuring letter to Josephine on the subject of the Prussian Queen's 'coquetting': 'I am like cere-cloth, along which everything of this sort slides without penetrating. It would cost me too dear to play the gallant on this subject.' The Queen herself might have been more affronted by the merry gossip of the time in London where bets were being taken on whether she would get Napoleon to fall in love with her. The playwright Sheridan took, on the other hand, the cynical line that Louise would fall in love with Napoleon: from an empress to a housemaid, 'all women are dazzled by glory, and sure to be in love with a Man whom they begin by hating and who has treated them ill . . .'[51]

In the event what happened satisfied neither the optimists, the romantics nor the cynics. The Queen arrived in Tilsit on 6 July.[52] Napoleon behaved extremely courteously all along, ending dinner especially early out of regard for her delicate health. When the Queen gently taxed him, 'Sire, I know you accuse me of meddling in politics', Napoleon responded gallantly, 'Ah, Madame, you must not believe that I listen only to malicious gossip' (thus splendidly ignoring the subject of his own Bulletins of the Army). Nor did Louise herself find the 'Monster' as odious as she had expected (although she certainly did not fall in love with him).

But while Louise saw it as her role to plead with him, as the traditional Queen-in-distress – 'I am a wife and mother and it is by these titles that I appeal for your mercy on behalf of Prussia' – Napoleon responded blandly with compliments on her white embroidered crêpe de Chine dress made in Breslau, and the superb collar she wore of her favourite pearls. After Louise's death, Countess Voss would comment sadly on the Queen's love of pearls, with their connotation of tears, as opposed to diamonds, which stood for prosperity; certainly there were tears enough to be shed on this occasion. Again and again the Queen tried to steer the conversation away from clothes back to the fate of Prussia itself. Privately, Napoleon rather admired her for her polite tenacity, how she always got back to her subject: 'perhaps even too much so, and yet with perfect propriety and in a manner that aroused no antagonism'. He even went as far to admit that 'In truth, the matter was an important one to her . . .' Publicly, he would have none of it.

There is a celebrated story concerning the occasion following the dinner when Napoleon went to call on Louise in her Tilsit lodgings; like many celebrated stories which sum up the popular image of a particular character (or characters) – the story of Queen Jinga and her royal 'chair' is another noted example – it has several variants. It seems that the Queen pleaded with Napoleon to exclude certain Prussian possessions from the confiscation which was planned as part of the peace treaty. Those to be reallocated included all the Prussian territories west of the Elbe, not omitting Magdeburg itself, on the river, most of Prussian Poland (to be reconstituted as the Napoleonic Duchy of Warsaw) and the Silesian fortresses. It is not known for certain exactly which provinces the Queen named to Napoleon, but attention has generally focused on Magdeburg.

The most colourful version of the story has Napoleon asking for a single rose from the Queen's arrangement of flowers. In reply, the Queen asked for an exchange: 'A rose for Magdeburg, Sire.' Some biographers have found this behaviour on the part of the Queen to be uncharacteristically arch. In another version (which accords better with Napoleon's own description of Louise as relentless – but dignified – in pursuit of her aims) the Queen struck a tragic note more or less on Napoleon's arrival: 'Sire, Justice! Justice! Magdeburg! Magdeburg!' There is no dispute however about the Queen's lack of success in securing from Napoleon even the slightest diminution of the harsh terms imposed upon Prussia, including an enormous bill of financial reparation. (Ironically enough, her reproaches to the Tsar for abandoning them did move him guiltily to plead for an alleviation of the Prussian punishment;[3] Louise, however, had been brought to Tilsit to woo Napoleon, not to reproach the Tsar.)

Everyone had been wrong: Frederick William, Hardenberg, General Kalkreuth, all those who had pinned their hopes on the 'fascinating affability' of their Queen. Three years before, seeing Louise dressed as Statira, wife of Alexander the Great (on that same occasion when she had struck Madame de Staël dumb with her beauty), Sir George Jackson had reflected that 'our queen of beauty' too would have conquered Alexander, 'had the hero the happiness of seeing her'. But the Queen of beauty had not conquered the Alexander of the hour: Napoleon. Much later, on St Helena, Napoleon referred to her 'winning ways' as well as her attempts to win him over. The Queen on the other hand wept bitterly and continuously afterwards, according to Countess Voss, referring over and over again to her 'deception' and reading her favourite Schiller (*The Thirty Years' War*) for comfort. 'In that house', she told one of the young Englishmen at Memel, referring to Tilsit, 'I was cruelly deceived.'[54] Napoleon had become once more the 'Monster', 'this inhuman being' who must be beaten down for the sake of the future of Prussia, of her husband and of her children.

Queen Louise did not survive to see the 'Monster' beaten down, although Frederick William did. She died of a pulmonary embolism in July 1810, having given birth to two more children, on 1 February 1808 – she must have been once again in the early stages of pregnancy at Tilsit – and 4 October 1809. But it was widely thought that she had died of a broken heart, to which her humiliation at Tilsit, symbolizing the humiliation of Prussia, had contributed. Her last years were marked by the inevitable sorrow of Prussia's grievous political situation, as well as by her persistent attempts to bolster up Frederick William. Heinrich von Kleist gives a moving picture of her at this time: 'She has developed a truly royal character . . . She, who a short time ago had nothing better to do than amuse herself with dancing or riding horseback, has gathered about her all our great men whom the King neglects and who alone can bring us salvation. Yes, it is she who sustains what has not collapsed.'[55]

The Queen also made earnest attempts to study history – Hume, Robertson and Gibbon – as though to try to make sense of the great if tragic events she had lived through. As with the whole of Louise's brief life – she was thirty-four when she died – there is a touching quality about the enterprise. 'I am so stupid and I hate the stupidity,' she exclaimed. 'What was the Punic War? Was it against Carthage? Who were the Gracchi and what were their troubles? What does hierarchy mean?' Even here, patriotism was never forgotten: Louise admired Theodoric for instance as 'a genuine *German*', with his love of justice, his upright character and his magnanimity.[56]

Like Queen Jinga of Angola, however – albeit a very different kind of Warrior Queen – Queen Louise of Prussia was to have another whole life as a national heroine, far more enduring than her actual life on earth. To the grieving King, she quickly became his 'sainted Louise', while he was always firm against charges of political interference: she had 'never quitted her own sphere of feminine usefulness'. Her popularity with the army was deliberately invoked when he instituted the order of the Iron Cross for military valour on the anniversary of her birth in 1813. (The *Luisenorde* for ladies, on the other hand, instituted on his own birthday – 'we are determined to do honour to the female sex' – concentrated on women who relieved suffering, not warriors; and the medal showed the late Queen in silver on a pale blue background, with a crown of stars – not in military uniform). When the 'Monster' was despatched to Elba, a hymn was composed in the Queen's honour beginning: 'Oh Saint in bliss . . . Thy tears are dried at last' and ending with the refrain:

> Louise, the protectress of our right,
> Louise, still the watchword of our fight.[57]

Classically, the ordinary soldiers in the Prussian army refused to believe in their beloved Queen's death for years afterwards; as for the rest of the nation, Princess Anton Radziwill wrote that twenty-five years later 'still the same regrets are given to the memory of that angel of goodness!' And an English author, Mrs Charles Richardson, who toured Prussia in the 1840s, subsequently dedicating her biography of Louise to Queen Victoria as another one distinguished 'for pre-eminence in female excellence', found many local traditions of the Queen as a guardian angel in time of war, 'a lovely vision' who appeared and then disappeared back to heaven.[58]

Nor did the cult of the holy and patriotic Warrior Queen stop there. Queen Louise may claim to have possessed a genuine sense of Prussia's importance as part of the German whole: she was not after all born a Prussian, and throughout Prussia's troubles retained a conviction that its triumph or defeat should be seen as affecting Germany itself (her remark concerning Theodoric was not uncharacteristic). It was therefore not inappropriate that in the late nineteenth century, continuing into the twentieth, she should come to be regarded as the Holy (departed) Figurehead of the resurgent and mighty Prussian-led Germany. On the sixtieth anniversary of her death, 19 July 1870, her son, then still King William of Prussia, went to pray at her grave; this was the day on which war was declared against France, that war from which he would return as German Emperor. Louise's son was convinced that he had thus fulfilled her dearest dreams and hopes, she who could be viewed 'as a martyr to her love for the Fatherland'.[59]

The Queen's verdict on herself was both more modest and more poignant.[60] 'If posterity will not place my name amongst those of celebrated women [she might have instanced Maria Theresa or Catherine the Great] yet those who were acquainted with the troubles of these times, will know what I have gone through and will say "She suffered much and endured with patience".'

CHAPTER SIXTEEN

The Valiant Rani

~

On every parapet a gun she set
Raining fire of hell,
How well like a man fought the Rani of Jhansi
How valiantly and well!

Indian folk song of 1857

The story of the Rani of Jhansi, which ended with her death leading her men in the course of the Indian Rebellion, or 'Mutiny', began like that of Boadicea, with an injustice. In this case, however, the injustice was British, not Roman.

In Britain itself – two or three months away even by steamer – preparations were already under way for that huge ceremonial sculpture commemorating Boadicea and her daughters which stands today on the Embankment of the Thames. The sculptor Thomas Thornycroft and his wife – also a sculptress – were favourites of the British royal family. She had immortalized the young Princess Alice as 'Spring' and the Prince of Wales as 'Winter'; he had produced public pieces such as 'Alfred the Great encouraged to the pursuit of learning by his mother' and an equestrian statue of the Queen. In 1856, under the patronage of Albert, the Prince Consort, who lent horses from his own stable as models and often visited the sculptor's studio to measure progress, Thornycroft embarked on the Boadicean group.[1]

Although, as we shall see, it was to be half a century before Boadicea, her daughters and her chariot achieved their present resting place (the Prince Consort had envisaged the central arch of the entrance to Hyde Park) the accession of another queen regnant in the shape of Victoria had had its predictable effect in drawing attention to Boadicea's fortunes. In the winter of 1859 the Poet Laureate Lord Tennyson read aloud to his wife what he described as 'a fiercely brilliant poem', constructed in an unusual and extremely difficult metre adapted from the Latin of Catullus.[2] That poem was *Boädicea*:

> So the Queen Boädicéa, standing loftily charioted,
> Brandishing in her hand a dart and rolling glances lioness-like,
> Yell'd and shriek'd between her daughters in her fierce volubility
> Till her people all around the royal chariot agitated . . .

The poem ended with a sombre picture of the Roman colony awaiting the British holocaust and reflecting in silence on their misdeeds which had brought it about:

> Out of evil evil flourishes, out of tyranny tyranny buds.
> Ran the land with Roman slaughter, multitudinous agonies.
> Perish'd many a maid and matron, many a valorous legionary,
> Fell the colony, city, and citadel, London, Verulam, Cámuldodúne.

In truth, there was little real parallel to be drawn between Tennyson's 'loftily charioted', yelling and shrieking Boadicea, and Victoria, whose own conception of being a Warrior Queen was more that of Maria Theresa. On the one hand Queen Victoria displayed throughout her long reign a real affection for her ordinary soldiers and devotion to what she perceived as their interests; on the other hand, despite bursts of emotion – 'Oh, if the Queen were a man!' – she was in no sense a warmonger. When she urged on Mr Gladstone in 1871 over the Franco–Prussian war 'the necessity for great prudence and for not departing from our neutral position',[3] above all not to take action alone, one can sense the cautious shade of Queen Elizabeth I at her shoulder.

Yet ironically enough, within Queen Victoria's increasingly vast dominions – that 'empire . . . on us bestow'd' celebrated by Cowper – a situation had arisen which did parallel, almost exactly, that of Boadicea and the Romans. At the time the Rani of Jhansi was compared, not to Boadicea, but to another very different warrior-woman, Joan of Arc. Sir Hugh Rose, the British commander who finally defeated her at Gwalior, himself used the phrase 'a sort of Indian Joan of Arc' to the Commander-in-Chief of the army, the Duke of Cambridge.[4] Since Boadicea had now become a patriotic symbol of British rule on the one hand and an established queen regnant on the other, it was perhaps scarcely surprising that British contemporaries of the Rani did not note the similarities of their two stories.

The parallels however were and remain remarkable. The injustice with which the story of the Rani of Jhansi began was not only dealt out to her by a dominant 'occupying' power of another race, but was also dealt out to her as a young or youngish widow. (As with Boadicea, the Rani's exact date of birth is unknown.) This was not a case of physical brutality – scourging or rape; but there was a clear element of violation, according to Hindu law, in the way the Rani's claims to rule Jhansi in the name of her late husband's adopted son were ignored.

'I have always considered Jhansi among the native states of the Bundelkhand as a kind of oasis in the desert': this was the verdict (in his memoirs) of Sir William Sleeman, long stationed at the court of the Rani's husband, Gangadhar Rao.[5] It is important to realize that the small Mahratta principality of Jhansi, in the Bundelkhand hill country of northern India, had a history of friendship towards the British interest, just as the Iceni's resentment at their treatment was fuelled by memories of their voluntary submission to Caesar. Jhansi had been raised by the British to princely status by that treaty of 1817 which brought the Mahratta Confederacy to an end although its dynasty had in fact been sovereign for nearly a hundred years. Thereafter the Rajah of Jhansi considered himself to be its independent and hereditary ruler; but he also inherited a tradition of benevolence towards and dependence upon the British government. In 1825 Gangadhar Rao's grandfather, Ramachandra Rao, was granted the title of maharajah and 'devoted servant of the glorious King of England' (George IV) for aiding the British against some rebels.

When Gangadhar Rao's own succession in 1838 was disputed within the family, the British backed his claim.[6]

Prosperity and peace followed for Jhansi, in both cases assured by the efficient supervision of British officials. Gangadhar Rao himself liked to spend his time in the theatre, both directing and acting: he played female parts and was reputed to wear female dress offstage as well. Not necessarily for these reasons alone, Gangadhar Rao was believed to be homosexual. Be that as it might, it was more to the point that he did not manage to produce an heir: his first wife died childless. In 1842 Gangadhar Rao married again. His bride was she who would be known to history as Lakshmi Bai, the Rani of Jhansi.

Lakshmi Bai was probably born in about 1830: estimates vary between 1827 and 1835, with the British authorities tending to go for the earlier and the Indians for the later figure.[7] Her original name was Manukarnika – one of the many names of the holy river Ganges – and she was brought up in the wing of a palace in Benares on the south bank of the great river itself. This was because her father, Moropant Tambe, a brahmin official, acted as chief political adviser to the brother of the last Peshwa of Bithur, whose court had come to rest in Benares after his deposition.

A web of legends surrounds the childhood of little 'Manu'. Her horoscope is said to have indicated an important marriage. It is also scarcely surprising to find that many of these legends feature her one way or another as a tomboy. Here once again are the familiar stories of the future Warrior Queen wrestling with boys and disdaining the company of girls (except to insist on always playing the role of leader among them). A favourite if probably apocryphal tale has 'Manu' demanding a seat on the howdah of an elephant when playing with the adopted son of the Peshwa, Dhondu Pant, later known as Nana Sahib (he was surely too old to have acted as her playmate in childhood, despite the dramatic destiny which would one day link their names). The little girl was rebuked for her presumption: 'You were not born to ride on an elephant.' At which the future Rani shouted at the future Nana

Sahib: 'I'll show you! For your one elephant, I will have ten. Remember my words.'

On a more elevated level, Lakshmi Bai's convenient birth in the very 'lap of Mother Ganges' meant that her birth could later be imbued with a religious significance: here was the pure incarnation of the sacred river, come to save India by destroying the heathen British. On this level, she was said to have been an assiduous attender at the Temple of Vishweshwar with her parents. Future places of pilgrimage were being provided, her pride in the Hindu religion underlined. A typical story, told of the Rani at the height of her triumph, had her encountering a brahmin by a well and, in spite of her thirst, refusing to let him pull up the clay pot for her: 'You are a learned brahmin and it does not befit you to do this. I will do it myself.' Concerning the Hindu religion, she informed the brahmin: 'for this I have sacrificed all attachment for wealth, life, everything'.[8]

For all the curtailed freedoms – both sexual and social – of the female in the Hindu religion, as laid down by its brahmin lawgivers, little 'Manu', she who had boldly demanded a seat upon the elephant, came from a culture where powerful intelligent women were not unknown.[9] Some of these belonged to history: there were folk memories of well-educated Hindu princesses and intrepid women at the Indian courts in the past who had ridden armed with the men. After her death, the Rani would indeed be described to Queen Victoria by Lady Canning, her former lady-in-waiting, now wife of the Governor-General of India, as having kept up the tradition of the Mahratta women for being both 'brave and clever' (although this particular Mahratta woman had been 'wicked' as well).[10]

Even within the confines of the Hindu religion itself, there were sundry menacing goddesses, whose mythical behaviour hinted at a very different female nature from that of the gentle and unselfish Sita. This was the heroine of the Ramayana epic who, having been abducted forcibly, was repudiated by her husband, only to prove her continuing love for him (and her virtue) by immolating herself in fire.[11] The goddess Durga, for example, wife of Siva, although seen as basically benevolent and maternal and endowed with a serenely beautiful face, also displayed a remarkable capacity for aggression, with the help of her ten arms, each bearing a different weapon, and her eight accompanying demonesses. (It was to Durga, riding on her tiger, that Mrs Gandhi in her turn would sometimes be picturesquely compared.) As for another version of Siva's wife, the much-venerated goddess Kali, the black one: here was the force of destruction represented in its most terrifying form: four arms ending in bloodstained hands, fang-like teeth and protruding blood-dripping tongue.

Where the powers of women were concerned, the unconscious influence of Hindu mythology was underlined by public Indian example. Moreover, roughly contemporary with the Rani herself were two remarkable Indian Muslim female rulers. One of these, the Begum of Bhopal, was described to Queen Victoria by Lady Canning in 1861 as 'A really clever upright character': she looked after the affairs of her country herself and ruled it admirably. 'No one disputes her power or her justice.' When the Order of the Star of India was founded, the Begum of Bhopal was one of the twenty-five 'Knights' appointed to it.

Hazrat Mahal, the Begum of Oudh, on the other hand, was also formidably clever – but not morally upright. John Low of the East India Company called her 'one of those tigress women, more virile than their husbands, who when finding themselves in a position to gratify their lust for power, have played a considerable part in oriental history'. Yet the courageous part played by the Begum as Queen Regent, in the defence of Lucknow against British attack, could not be denied. The *Times* correspondent, W. H. Russell, referred to her as 'Penthesilea', an Amazonion image confirmed by the female sepoys who guarded the entrance to the Begum's harem, wearing military jackets and white duck trousers, with muskets and bayonets, cross-belts and cartridge boxes. Russell reflected: 'it appears from the energetic characters of these Ranees and Begums that they acquire in their zenanas and harems a considerable amount of actual mental power . . .'[12]

After her enthronement, the Begum of Oudh was received by Queen Victoria in England. It was a development greeted with angry cynicism by Ernest Jones, the Chartist poet and leader (whose father, in contrast or perhaps in explanation, had been a royal equerry). Despite the Begum's notorious 'peccadilloes', once she had been dethroned, he exclaimed, moral scruples had been thrown out of the window in face of her rank: 'and the dusky royalty hobnobs with the pallid'.[13] One might look at it from another angle and see in Queen Victoria's persistent welcome to various Indian royalties her attractive lack of racism, in the sense that so many British people of the time practised it.

There is yet another possible angle. The career of Hazrat Mahal, long-reigning Queen Cartimandua to the Rani's more dramatic Boadicea, reminds one how differently matters might have gone for Lakshmi Bai . . . Given her energy, courage and determination, given that female rule was not of its nature inimical at this point to the British, how might she not have fared under another set of stars – another horoscope? As it was, Manukarnika, who took on her marriage the name of Lakshmi, the lovely goddess of fortune and prosperity, would one day be transformed further into powerful Durga riding upon her tiger – and even, maybe, bloodstained Kali herself.

One legend concerns Lakshmi Bai's actual wedding day. When the priest – according to tradition – tied the ends of her various gowns together, the bride shocked those present with her boldness. 'Make the knot very firm,' she said. But whatever the state of the knot, the new Rani did not succeed in presenting Gangadhar Rao with an heir, although a baby boy was said to have died at the age of three months. Then in 1853 Gangadhar Rao fell seriously ill. In the absence of an existing heir, one was adopted. Damodar Rao, as he became known, was five years old: a descendant of Gangadhar's grandfather and thus a member of the royal family.

The ruler now proceeded to dictate his will and have it read aloud to Major Ellis, the British Political Agent in Jhansi: 'Should

I not survive, I trust that in consideration of the fidelity I have evinced towards the British government, favour may be shown to this child and that my widow during her lifetime may be considered the Regent of the State (*Malika*) and mother of this child, and that she may not be molested in any way.' Major Ellis replied that he would do everything possible to bring this about. The substance of this will was then repeated in a letter to Major Malcolm, the Political Agent for Gwalior and the Bundelkhand, in which Gangadhar Rao referred once more to that treaty which had guaranteed the throne of Jhansi to Ramachandra Rao 'and his heirs and successors'.[14]

Gangadhar Rao died on 21 November 1853. Not long afterwards the Governor-General of India, the Marquess of Dalhousie, announced that under the policy of 'lapse', Jhansi was to be annexed by the British government. That is, since Gangadhar Rao had left no heir or successor – adoption did not count – the state of Jhansi reverted by treaty to the East India Company (no longer an independent corporation but largely under governmental control).

The only possible defence of Dalhousie's 'policy of lapse', in this instance, is that of expediency, if defence it be. Certainly expediency had long been the watchword of the East India Company when the possibility of annexation arose; to that extent it could be argued that Dalhousie was only implementing a policy which others had conceived.[15] But if Dalhousie's policy had its roots in the past, it was also to cast its black shadow upon the future.

Dalhousie had already annexed Satara in 1848, the year of his arrival in India, on the same grounds of 'lapse' (once again there was the question of an adopted heir). This move too had aroused deep resentment – and also bewilderment. The resentment was due to the unfair prohibition of a practice – adoption – allowed by Hindu law. The bewilderment sprang from the known religious significance of adoption in the Hindu religion. The sacrifices of a son were an essential duty, if the father was not to be condemned to punishment – the hell called Put – after death.

But an adopted son could perform these vital sacrifices equally with a natural one.

Colonel, later Major-General Sir John Low, who had been Political Agent at Gwalior and Lucknow, reported in his memoirs this general anguish which followed the annexation of Satara. 'What crime did the late Rajah commit that his country should be seized by the Company?' was the one question which every Indian put to him.[16] Similarly in Jhansi in 1853 little Damodar Rao was unarguably the late ruler's 'son' in Hindu law; as such he was surely his 'successor' under the terms of the earlier treaty. To regard him otherwise was 'so ungenerous, and being so ungenerous, so unwise'. These were the terms which would be used by the distinguished British military historian Sir John Kaye (who worked for the East India Company and later the India Office) in his *History of the Sepoy War in India 1857–1858*, published in 1880.[17] Significantly, Dalhousie's wiser successor Lord Canning – derisively nicknamed 'Clemency' at the time, a name he has since borne with honour in the roll of history – explicitly stressed the Indian rulers' right of adoption at his healing durbar of 1859.[18]

Meanwhile in 1856, the year of his own departure from India, Dalhousie would go further and annex the much larger state of Oudh: as early as 1848 he had described it as being 'on the highroad to be taken under our management'. On this occasion, the pretext was not the lack of heirs to the Nawab – there was an heir – but the Nawab's numerous transgressions against his subjects. It was a rather more sympathetic excuse. Nevertheless an Indian ruler had once again been removed. A leading Indian historian of the events of 1857 has judged Dalhousie's policy of annexation as one of the main contributory facts to the rebellion and 'perhaps the decisive one'.[19]

We return to Lakshmi Bai, she who had expected to rule Jhansi during the boyhood of Damodar Rao and was now consigned to the unenviable fate of a childless Hindu widow. Was she perhaps inadequate to the task of the regency, at least in the view of the British? But only a week after Gangadhar Rao's death, the Political Agent Major Malcolm wrote that his widow, 'in whose hands he has expressed a wish that the government should be placed during her lifetime, is a woman highly respected and esteemed, and I believe fully capable of doing justice to such a charge'. Other witnesses confirm that the Rani comported herself as 'a brave-minded woman had to do in her position', being in herself 'quite capable of discussing her affairs with a Committee or a government'.[20]

Moreover her behaviour was perfectly discreet: she kept purdah where the British were concerned, although not at home (later she would indeed encourage women to take part in the defence of Jhansi). Her life was disciplined in the extreme: she would rise at 3 a.m., supervise work in the political and military offices, and then at her court listen to religious readings. One is reminded indeed of the application and austerity of another female ruler called from a secluded life to greatness: Isabella of Spain.

All this time, the Rani was hoping – even perhaps expecting – that the terms of Gangadhar Rao's will would be allowed to prevail. Two petitions appealing against Dalhousie's decision were sent, in late 1853 and early 1854, the Rani herself being credited with composing them.[21] Attention was drawn to the position of the adopted son in the Hindu religion, his ability to make sacrifices on behalf of his late father, equal to that of a natural son. In the second petition, the difference between 'heirs' and 'successors' in the original treaty was argued; for if Damodar Rao was not one, he was certainly the other. It was significant of the justice of the Rani's case that Major Ellis, the Political Agent at Jhansi, himself endorsed her petition. Unfortunately – or possibly due to malevolence – this vital letter was not forwarded to Dalhousie. For Major Malcolm, who did not choose to forward it, now believed the petition should be refused. Dalhousie's decision was dated 27 February 1854. Adoption, he considered, was valid only in the case of sovereign princes, and he held firmly to Jhansi's dependent status (an argument which has since been convincingly demolished by Indian writers).

When the document was read to the Rani on 15 March 1854,

she cried out loudly: '*Mera Jhansi Nahin Denge.*' (I will not give up my Jhansi.) Then she shut herself away, refusing food or water. But if the Rani despaired, it was only a temporary state. With remarkable pertinacity, she continued to argue her cause, employing a British counsel, John Lang, who advised her to appeal to London. It was not until 1854 that the appeal too was turned down. At Malcolm's suggestion, the Rani was granted a pension of five thousand rupees monthly from the Treasury at Jhansi; the palace and the state jewels and funds which her husband had willed to her were also to be handed over. Even at this point, the British administration managed to arouse further resentment: with what Sir John Kaye described as 'extraordinary meanness', it was now laid down that the Rani should pay her husband's debts before receiving her emoluments.[22]

So the Rani, with no other choice before her, fell back for the next three years into private life. Dalhousie left India. He once told a correspondent in England – whom he termed his 'safety valve' – of his feelings about the great subcontinent he ruled: 'I don't deny that I detest the country and many of the people in it. I don't proclaim it; but I don't doubt that my face does not conceal it from those I have to do with.' It was not likely that such a man – one who would come out of his dying coma in order to learn the score in the Eton and Harrow cricket match – would spare much thought for the feelings or resolves of an obscure Hindu widow.[23]

Jhansi itself, like its Rani, was judged unimportant for the future. Its prosperity inevitably declined with the disappearance of the princely court. Another brisk British judgement from the centre was the discontinuance of the state revenues paid to the Temple of Lakshmi, just outside the city; although once again Major Ellis, the man on the spot, had suggested that the practice should be maintained. As to the garrison of such an important place, a few hundred soldiers were surely all that were necessary nowadays. A safe farewell could be bidden to the thousands of troops who had once added to the lustre of Jhansi's princely ruler – could it not?

*

In 1855, the year before Lord Canning arrived in India to replace Dalhousie, he gave a speech in London to the Court of Directors of the East India Company. It contained this remarkably prophetic passage: 'We must not forget that in the sky of India, serene as it is, a cloud may arise, at first no bigger than a man's hand, but which growing bigger and bigger, may at last threaten to overwhelm us with ruin.'[24] By the summer of 1857, that cloud had indeed arisen.

The causes of the Indian Rebellion – or Mutiny – are not the subject of the present work; suffice it to say that on the Indian side, the case of the Rani of Jhansi, the mixture of injustice, insensitivity and indifference displayed by the British administration towards entrenched Indian customs and interests, might perhaps stand as a microcosm of the whole. On the British side, the case of Jhansi itself, the unexpected uprising of supposedly loyal troops, coupled with the treacherous slaughter of British women and children (as well as soldiers and officials) might equally stand for what was most dreadful in India wherever the Mutiny occurred.

Canning's words were prophetic. They had not however prepared him for the event itself. In April 1857 Lady Canning was happily telling Queen Victoria of the 'ridiculous stories' being circulated that the Governor-General had signed a bond saying that he would make all the Indians into Christians within three years. She added that there was 'an odd mysterious thing going on, still unexplained', by which she referred to the circulation of some native chupatties or biscuits from district to district (a strange episode whose precise relevance to the events of 1857 – were the chupatties coded signals? – has never been totally explained). Only five months later Queen Victoria would write in her turn to the King of the Belgians, 'we are in sad anxiety about India, which engrosses all our attention'; although even now, characteristically, she spared a thought for the feelings of her protégé, the dispossessed Indian Prince Duleep Singh, who had been virtually raised with her own sons: 'What can it be for him to hear his fellow countrymen called *fiends* and *monsters*?'[25]

In keeping with its reputation for pro-British tranquillity, Jhansi was not in the forefront of the rebellion. As late as 18 May, following the first weeks of disruption elsewhere, Captain Skene, the Political and Administrative Officer of Jhansi, was able to write, 'I do not think there is any cause for alarm about this neighbourhood.'[26] It was not until 4 June that some of the garrison at Jhansi (drawn from the Twelfth Bengal Native Infantry and the Fourteenth Irregular Cavalry and commanded by a Captain Gordon) actually mutinied. Under a rebel sergeant, Gurbash Singh, they invaded the Star Fort; in the battle to seize it, they killed all the British officers they found there except a Lieutenant Taylor, who, despite being badly wounded, managed to escape to the City Fort. This was the place appointed by Captain Skene for some British and Eurasians in Jhansi – some sixty people all told, over half of them women and children – to take refuge.

With the mutineers seemingly impregnable in the vastly superior Star Fort (which contained Jhansi's magazine as well as its treasure chest), who would now come to the aid of this vulnerable fragment of humanity? Ironically enough, the only possible bastion for the Europeans at this point against the rage of the sepoys was none other than the deposed Rani herself. She had earlier been allowed a few troops of her own as security against the disturbances which were sweeping across India. Now Captain Gordon appealed to her in the following terms. Given the extreme danger to the European and Eurasian community, who might all be killed by the mutineers the next day, 'we suggest', he wrote, 'that you take your kingdom [*sic* – shades of Lord Dalhousie] and hold it, along with the adjoining territory, until the British authority is established'. He added, 'We shall be eternally grateful if you will also protect our lives.'[27]

It cannot be known for certain what if anything the Rani replied to this appeal. The most plausible version, given her circumstances, has her answering, 'What can I do? . . . If you wish to save yourself, abandon the fort, no one will injure you.' The most damning version has the Rani promising a safe conduct which she had no intention of carrying out.[28] Whatever the Rani's reactions – for there are numerous contradictory versions, mainly based on hearsay – the tragedy which followed is not in dispute.

On 7 July the City Fort was duly besieged by the mutineers, and Captain Gordon, the commander of the garrison, killed in the assault. Captain Skene, the Political Agent, then gave the signal of surrender. A safe retreat from the fort itself was now promised to the remaining Europeans inside if they would lay down their arms. This they agreed to do. So the British, defenceless but hopeful, filed out of the City Fort. A little column was just outside the walls of Jhansi itself, when the rebel leader, Risaldar Kala Khan, ordered them all to be killed. One of the Europeans still surviving in Jhansi (who had not gone to the fort) was a Mrs Mutlow, who by her own account was concealed by her Indian ayah in the native quarter, and by another account was able to adopt Indian dress successfully since she was herself a Eurasian, although her husband and brother went to the fort and were killed. (We shall return to the testimony of Mrs Mutlow.) For the moment it is enough to say that a frightful massacre had just been carried out by the rebel sepoys: their victims were mainly civilians, and the majority of them of course women or children.

It is inconceivable that the Rani encouraged this piece of wanton mayhem. Leaving aside her actions at a later stage, the Rani in these first days of mutiny at Jhansi rightly considered the sepoys to be a frightening force outside her own control, and indeed outside anyone else's. It may well be that she did give the rebels money – 35,000 rupees – as well as two elephants and five horses. She probably had little choice. According to one report, the rebels threatened to execute her if she did not comply. The charge of aiding the sepoys in this manner was made against the Rani by Mr Thornton, the Deputy-Collector of Jhansi, on 18 August, and it does have a ring of truth; but in the wake of the bloodbath Thornton went further and added the *post hoc propter hoc* remark that the slaughter had taken place 'wholly at the instigation' of the Rani of Jhansi. It was this statement, incorporated in the official British report on 20 November 1858, which was to prove damaging to the Rani's reputation in the estimates of British historians (some of whom further embellished Thornton's statement to make the Rani responsible for the *original* mutiny of 5/6 June – which Thornton had not even suggested).[29]

An important part of this myth of the Rani's responsibility for the Jhansi massacre was the treachery she was said to have displayed in that false promise of a safe conduct. But the existence of this safe conduct rests either on hearsay or on the testimony of Mrs Mutlow; as has been pointed out by Dr Surendra Nath Sen, who sifted through the mass of evidence in the National Archives of India for his authoritative centenary study *1857*, the document which Mrs Mutlow is supposed to have seen, written in the first person and signed by the Rani personally, is quite implausible.[30]

Although Mrs Mutlow would not have known this, the Rani, as an Indian ruler, would never write in the first person and in any case invariably signed her official documents with a seal. Another colourful piece of the myth had the Rani exclaiming that she would have nothing to do with those 'swine' the British, when Captain Skene implored her protection. But as the (nameless) clerk who provided the evidence obviously did not know, the Rani's language was Maratti, not English, and in Maratti the word 'swine' was not one of abuse. Thirty years after these blood-stained happenings, one T. A. Martin, a resident of Jhansi who escaped the siege, wrote a letter to the Rani's adopted son Damodar Rao in the Rani's defence: 'Your poor mother was very unjustly and cruelly dealt with – and no one knows her true case as I do.'[31] Unfortunately – by a further piece of irony in a career already marked by such – it was the Rani's alleged implication in the massacre, her guilt in the eyes of the British authorities, which finally persuaded her many months later that she had nothing to lose by siding against the British.

For the moment however the Rani in Jhansi was seen – including by the British – as bringing order into a disorderly situation. She formed a government which included her own father. She also wrote an account of the whole ghastly business of the massacre to Major Erskine, the Commander at Sagar, in two letters of 12 and 14 June. The Rani roundly condemned the 'faithlessness, cruelty and violence' which the troops had displayed towards the Europeans and regretted that she had not had sufficient soldiers and guns of her own to help them (thanks, of course, to the withdrawal of the previous strong garrison). The Rani explained that the sepoys had threatened to blow up her own palace and for this, to save her 'life and honour', she had given them sums of money to depart. Since then, in the absence of any British officer (they had all been killed, although some civilians survived by one means and another in the town) she had taken over the government.[32]

There is no reason to doubt the truth of this account nor did Erskine himself do so. He forwarded the letters to the central government with the covering note that their content 'agrees with what I have heard from other sources'. On 2 July he asked the Rani to continue to manage the district including collecting revenues and recruiting police, until a new supervisor should arrive.[33] For a few halcyon months, interrupted only by certain successful military campaigns against the neighbouring states (in which all parties claimed to be supporting the British in paying off old scores), the Rani was able at last to enjoy what she had so long desired, the rulership of 'my Jhansi'.

Her court was conducted with traditional splendour and dignity. The Rani herself would be seated behind a curtain on a raised seat. Previously she had worn a plain white muslin dress drawn about her tightly to reveal her figure: 'and a remarkably fine figure she had', commented her lawyer John Lang. Now, somewhat stouter – 'but not too stout' – she adopted a costume which symbolically combined the elements of a warrior with those of a queen: jodhpurs, a silk blouse with a low-cut bodice, a red silk cap with a loose turban (or puggree) round it. She wore diamond bangles and large diamond rings on her small hands: but a short bejewelled sword and two silver pistols were stuck into her cummerbund.[34]

'A woman of about middle size', the Rani must have been quite beautiful when she was younger, thought Lang: she was at this point around thirty. Even now her 'particularly fine' expressive eyes and a nose 'very delicately shaped' gave her countenance many charms. Lang added: what spoiled her was her voice. This was later described as 'somewhere between a whine and a croak' – but then, as has been noted, Warrior Queens have always had trouble with their voices, either from their enemies or from those of another race (to her fellow Indians, the Rani's voice was on the contrary 'melodious'). Other estimates described the Rani without qualification as 'a very handsome woman', although her complexion ('not very fair but far from black', according to Lang) had been marred by smallpox. Her grace in particular impressed the British.[35]

For the moment the Rani – with her diamonds but also her pistols – was free to enact Lakshmi, rather than Durga or Kali. A library was formed, plays once more encouraged. But either from natural inclination since her tomboy childhood or from pre-science, she also studied the martial arts. Her daily round included shooting at a target with a rifle and a pistol, and of course riding. Lady Canning heard later that her riding was 'wonderful'. In an interesting link with history, one Turab Ali, who was taken in Jhansi and who died in 1943 aged 113, survived long enough to tell tales of his youth when he had watched the Rani practising the art of managing her horse with the reins in her teeth and two swords in her hands.[36]

There was however a cloud on the Rani's horizon, as there had once been on the horizon of the British in India. As the latter gradually pressed back the rebels into submission, recapturing Delhi and Oudh, still no official proclamation had come to Jhansi confirming that the Rani had been put in charge of the district in July. The arrival of Sir Robert Hamilton from England, to resume his work as Political Agent for Central India, prompted the Rani to write to him on 1 January 1858, giving once again her side of the story. This was a nervous communication; the Rani was well aware that the recapture of Delhi and Oudh meant that Jhansi would not be tolerated much longer as a kind of unofficial rebel state – or was it? She was anxious to make it clear that it was not. On the other hand she was equally anxious to maintain her own position of power.

In any case it was too late; perhaps it had always been too late. Despite Erskine's judgement, despite the Rani's own pleas, despite Sir Robert Hamilton's confidence in the veracity of one of the rebels under sentence of death – 'she was obliged to yield' – the Rani was already believed to be guilty of complicity in the massacre. Her official guilt was even now in the process of being established. (One of the pieces of damning evidence cited to Erskine, who was 'forgiven' for originally crediting the Rani's story, was a telegraphic message from Major Ellis, dated 26 June; but he actually referred to the mutineers as 'having at last forced the Ranee to assist them with Guns and Elephants' – evidence surely of duress rather than complicity.)[37]

There is cause to believe that the Rani's reputation also suffered from guilt by association. Later, as we shall see, she would join forces with 'that fiend' Nana Sahib, he who was held responsible for another frightful massacre, that of Cawnpore, which took place on 27 June.[38] Nana Sahib was another with a grievance against the British: as the adopted son of the last Peshwa of Bithur, he was allowed to be styled maharajah as a courtesy, but not to enjoy the Peshwa's pension.

It is not clear exactly at what point the Nana joined forces with the rebels within Cawnpore, a wealthy city lying about 260 miles east of Delhi, guarding the road to Lucknow; subsequently many of the British would believe that the Nana had been 'at the races and sipping coffee etc. with our officers and all the time planning the mutiny'. That may not be quite how it happened. Possibly a character of mysterious origins who went under the pseudonym Tatya Tope was actually the 'master butcher', as one later British investigation suggested, the Nana being offered an even starker choice than was the Rani by the sepoys: a kingdom if he joined them, death if he didn't.[39] But if that was the case, Nana Sahib certainly did not hesitate. The massacre of Europeans and Eurasians at Cawnpore took place in roughly similarly circumstances to that of Jhansi, with all the indications of treachery, captives going trusting and all unknowing to their deaths.

It is impossible to exaggerate the feelings of horror aroused by this grisly episode in the hearts and minds of the British community not only then but long afterwards; quite regardless of the fact, as Indian historians have pointed out, that in the meantime they themselves had performed acts of equal savagery in retaliation. For the Indian men, women and children who died subsequently in Cawnpore, ten times the number of the slaughtered Europeans, are hardly registered in the British consciousness.[40] A parallel may once again be drawn between the Britons' rampant slaughter of the Romans at Colchester – vividly reported by the Roman Tacitus – and his bald account of the extinction of the Britons, including their womenfolk, at the final battle.

Many years later the British Field-Marshal, Lord Roberts, described his feelings as a young soldier on returning to Cawnpore in the autumn of 1857. As ever, the small things were the most poignant: 'tresses of hair, pieces of ladies' dresses, books crumpled and torn, bits of work and scraps of music, just as they had been left that fatal morning . . .' It is easy to believe Roberts's verdict: 'the sights which met our eyes, and the reflections they gave rise to, were quite maddening'. In vain Queen Victoria spoke out against 'any retribution' which 'I should deeply deprecate': officers and men, by abandoning the prospect, should show 'the difference between Christians and Hindoos or Musselmen'. G. O. Trevelyan, in a study, *Cawnpore*, published in 1865, compared the British soldiers' behaviour to that of Telemachus slaughtering his mother's maids and he added the comment that it was 'curious' that his 'Pagan' act should be revived by 'a Christian warrior' (Brigadier-General Neill) after twenty-five centuries.[41]

The recapture of Jhansi lay ahead; but it was not to be expected that the British behaviour there would be marked by any 'maudlin clemency'. These were the words with which Dr Thomas Lowe, who was present as the Medical Officer to the Corps of Sappers and Miners, would choose to dismiss the quality of mercy, *pace* his sovereign, in an account of it all published in 1860. As for the Rani herself, once officially implicated in the Jhansi massacre, her likely fate, were she to be captured, was death (her father, who was captured, was hanged). To Lowe, as to many others not imbued with the spirit of Queen Victoria, the Rani had become 'the Jezebel of India . . . the young, energetic, proud, unbending, uncompromising Ranee, and upon her head rested the blood of the slain, and a punishment as awful awaited her'.[42]

Perhaps Tennyson's sad verdict in *Boädicea* is the fairest on the state of India during the frenzied months of the Rebellion, when the land certainly ran with slaughter – Indian as well as British – and 'many a maid and matron' of both races did suffer 'multitudinous agonies' before perishing: 'Out of evil evil flourishes, out of tyranny tyranny buds.'

In the new year, Sir Hugh Rose, in the process of mopping up the remaining rebel encampments, set off for Jhansi. It was time for the Rani to put aside the peaceful mien of Lakshmi and mount the tiger of Durga. To this end she began to recruit a large army of her own, securing fourteen thousand volunteers from a population of some two hundred and twenty thousand, as well as fifteen hundred sepoys. She also strengthened the defences of the city itself. The siege of Jhansi began on 20 March 1858. One eyewitness, an Indian, told of the fierce British fire, including 'red-hot balls' which thundered over the city walls 'like the rains in autumn'. [43]

An attempt by Tatya Tope to relieve Jhansi from Kalpi, ended in a disastrous defeat at the Betwa river, with many Indian casualties, or as Thomas Lowe put it: 'a bloody day for not a man of the enemy asked for quarter or received it'.[44] Jhansi, it seemed, stood alone, with Rose determined not to allow the rebels to escape (as had happened at certain other fortresses *en route*) and the Rani, supported by the inhabitants, determined not to surrender.

On the British side, the energetic quality of the defence, Indian soldiers scurrying about with more vigour than they had ever been seen to display under British orders, was especially noted. 'They worked like bees,' wrote Lowe, apparently surprised. The women of Jhansi, organized by the Rani, joined in; they were seen by the British working the batteries, carrying ammunition and otherwise bringing food and water to the soldiers.[45]

As for the Rani herself, whose standard flew proudly from one white turret, she was constantly visible both to her own followers and to the enemy. To the one she was a source of encouragement, to the other not entirely a source of abhorrence for all the mutterings of 'Jezebel': for already the strange double standard which could sometimes protect a Warrior Queen, where it would not protect her male counterpart, was in operation. There was wonderment and even admiration there too.

It is said that one of the bombardiers told Rose that 'he had covered the Queen and her ladies with his gun'; he asked permission to fire. To this Rose chivalrously replied that he did not approve of that kind of warfare.[46] Yet this was a woman who, it is suggested, would have been executed if she had been captured. There is certainly, from this point on, a dichotomy between the reactions of the soldiers who fought against her – who, in sum, admired her for her pluck, 'a perfect Amazon in bravery . . . just the sort of daredevil woman soldiers admire', as the historical records of the 14th Light Dragoons described her[47] – and those who preferred to write about her in the vivid terms of the Voracity Syndrome, recalling those charges of sexual licence which Semiramis, Cleopatra and other Warrior Queens in the past had incurred. Both these types of judgement were of course directly inspired by her sex, and for better or for worse would not have been applied to a man.

Afterwards Sir John Kaye summarily dismissed the tradition of the Rani's 'intemperance', as he phrased it, as 'a myth' based on contemporary prejudice. It is true that tales of the hot-blooded Indian, avid to lay his fingers upon Anglo-Saxon womanhood, widely embellished the true horrors of the Mutiny with further not-quite-unspeakable (and untrue) details. For the coming of the white womenfolk to British India had brought to an end those jolly eighteenth-century days when a young Englishman would happily set his heart on 'A lass and a lakh a day' – to adapt the conventional lament – a lakh being 100,000 rupees and the lass being Indian. As the races drew apart, the customs of child marriage and polygamy seemed to give credence to the notion of Indian lustfulness.[48] Once again the Rani, for all the discretion of her personal behaviour, suffered by association.

A typical comment was that of Ellen C. Clayton (author of *Celebrated Women, Notable Women*, etc.) in her omnibus study *Female Warriors* published in 1879, the year before Sir John's own more judicious work: 'All agreed as to the extreme licentiousness and immorality of her [the Rani's] habits; and the rooms in her palace are said to have been hung with pictures "such as pleased Tiberius at Capri"' – the delicate Victorian allusion is to pornographic art, although the Rani's keen detractor Lowe, who actually saw her apartments, mentioned no such titillatory detail in his own full description. One of the most damning – but equally quite unsupported – judgements was that of George W. Forrest in *A History of the Indian Mutiny*, published between 1904 and 1912, since his former position as the Director of Records for the government of India naturally carried weight. Picking eagerly on the phrase 'the Jezebel of India', he wrote that 'to speak of her [the Rani], as some have done, as "The Indian Joan of Arc" is indeed a libel on the fair name of the Maid of Orleans'. (Given Forrest's nationality, a somewhat self-righteous comment in any case.)[49]

He who had so described her – Sir Hugh Rose in two letters back to his royal Commander-in-Chief, the Duke of Cambridge – and had just spared her life, was granted no similar mercy by the lady in question. He watched the Rani first firing in his direction and then peering through a telescope to see what harm she had done. 'Like the 3rd Europeans and the 86th she requires a good deal of drilling,' commented Rose sardonically, 'nobody having been able to discover where the Ranee's shot went.'[50] But these days of mutual observation and raining fire could not last for ever. The British assault upon Jhansi, which was to be both fierce and final, took place on 3 April. It may have been prompted by knowledge of a weakness in the defence supplied from inside: all accounts agree that the Rani herself was in the thick of the fighting.

At some point that night, however, the Rani escaped with about four followers, including her father. It is sometimes supposed that Rose laid a trap for her by allowing her to escape: but if there was a trap, she certainly eluded that too.[51] Riding hard, outdistancing her pursuers, in particular one Lieutenant Bowker, she succeeded by stages in reaching the fortress of Kalpi. She had travelled over one hundred miles in twenty-four hours. Here were congregated, among Indian rulers who had joined the rebels, not only Nana Sahib but the Nana's nephew, Pandurang Rao, known as Rao Sahib, as well as Tatya Tope.

Lieutenant Bowker's own story has him perceiving the Rani aloft on her celebrated grey (or white) horse and pursuing her with Rose's permission. A shot – possibly but not certainly fired by the Rani herself – disabled him, and so 'the lady escaped for the time being'. Indian sources have the Rani wounding the Lieutenant in a sword fight at Bhander, a small village where she stopped for food; some of these accounts take on the already heady quality of incantation, as in this one written by a barrister and published in Calcutta in 1930: 'But Lakshmi, put your horse now into a gallop. For Lieutenant Bowker is galloping behind, followed by select horsemen, in order to capture you. And you, O Horse, fortunate on account of the sacred treasure you carry, gallop on! . . . The dawn has now broken. So, heroic goddess, flying all night on the wings of the wind, test thee!'[52]

There can be no question that Lakshmi Bai was right to escape both from her own point of view and that of her cause. The vengeance taken in Jhansi was frightful by any standards; some

British historians have suggested that while four to five thousand died in battle, the civilians were spared. But Vishnu Godse, a priest from Bombay who was present, recalled four days of fire, pillage, murder and looting without distinction; it was difficult to breathe, he wrote, for the stink of burning flesh. Lowe's words, that the enemy were slain in their 'puffed up thousands . . . such was the retribution meted out to this Jezebel Ranee and her people . . .' do not suggest there was much of a distinction between soldiers and civilians.[53]

In his description of the vanished Rani's personal apartments, however, Lowe dipped his pen into the ink of Sir Walter Scott, as he described the palace doors inlaid with plate-glass, mirrors, chandeliers, velvet and satin beds, bedsteads with silver feet, velvet-cushioned chairs, brazen throne, gold- and silver-handled tulwars, spears, silver bird cages, ivory footstools, dozens of shawls, silver candlesticks 'and a thousand other things such as a luxurious woman would have' (although there is no mention of pictures 'such as pleased Tiberius'). All these accoutrements, as well as the works of Horace, Longfellow and Browning said to have belonged to the dead officers, 'lay here and there in chaotic confusion in every part of the building'. 'The soldiery went to and fro tramping over and through these things and kicking them about as they would any heap of rubbish', wrote Lowe, 'until order was somewhat restored.' Meanwhile the rebels fought like tigers 'so the bayonetting went on till after sunset'. The fate of the Rani might not have been so summary as that of her luxurious belongings but it is difficult to believe she would in the end have fared much better.[54]

While the Union Jack flew once more over Jhansi, in Kalpi, in contrast, the Rani was given an honoured reception by Rao Sahib, with a special parade of his soldiers. The next engagement which followed was that of Kalpi itself, to which Sir Hugh Rose and his army patiently slogged their way in heat so great that big tears trickled down the cheeks of the patient elephants and the very camels groaned. It is sometimes suggested that if Rao Sahib had given the command to the Rani, not to Tatya Tope, the result of the battle – another total defeat for the Indians – might have been different.[55] Another expression of the general admiration for the Rani is the widespread belief that she was responsible, as 'their most determined, spirited and influential head', for the Indians' next plan, one of extreme daring, to seize the fortress of Gwalior (although Tatya Tope, with contacts inside Gwalior, is perhaps a more likely author).[56] As a manoeuvre it was certainly remarkably successful, at a time when the rebel fortunes were badly in need of some coup to rally them. Gwalior was seized, and there the coronation of Rao Sahib took place. From the great regalia of Scindia, which resided in the Treasury at Gwalior, the Rani was granted by Rao Sahib a fabulous pearl necklace. Like the torc of Boadicea, it was to prove an ornament of ritual significance.

For all the daring which had attended its seizure. Gwalior could not expect to remain long immune from reprisal. When that attack came, the Rani was said to have been put in charge of the eastern side of the defence. She wore her armour, her sword with its jewelled scabbard – and her wonderful new acquisition, the pearl necklace. According to tradition, she took as her motto on this occasion the celebrated verse: 'If killed in battle we enter the heaven and if victorious, we rule the earth.'

Of the two alternatives, it seemed that the Rani of Jhansi was not destined to rule the earth. She was killed at some point in the fierce but ultimately unsuccessful battle to defend Gwalior: the most likely date being 17 June – the second day of the fighting. As Boadicea's daughters traditionally died with their mother, two of the Rani's 'maids of honour' – in the British phrase – were said to have died with her: Indian sources give their names as Mandar and Kashi. One was described as 'most beautiful' and in her last agony stripped off her clothes.[57]

The exact manner of the Rani's death is not known for certain, nor who actually killed her. The British clearly took some trouble afterwards to find out. Three independent accounts written within a week of her death agree that she was mortally wounded as a result of a blow received during hand-to-hand fighting.[58] As J. Henry Sylvester, who was present, wrote: 'the gallant Queen of

Jhansi fell from a carbine wound, and was carried to the rear, where she expired, and was burnt according to the custom of the Hindoos'. This is probably the truth although some local Indian ballads and songs have the Rani carried by faithful servants to the nearby monastery of Baba Gangadas and whispering to the Baba as he put the Ganges water in her mouth: 'I leave my [son] Damodar in your charge.'

A small locked notebook was found among Lord Canning's papers after his death (in 1862: like Lord Dalhousie, who died in 1860, he did not long survive his Indian experience). Canning had jotted down the following observations:[59] '*Ranee of Jhansi.* Killed by a trooper of 8th Hussars, who was never discovered. Shot in the back, her horse baulked. She then fired at the man and he passed his sword through her . . . She used to wear gold anklets, and Sindia's pearl necklace, plundered from Gwalior. (Sindia says its value is untold.) These when dying she distributed among the soldiery, when taken to die under the mango clump.' (Sir Hugh Rose told the Duke of Cambridge, apropos 'these ornaments', that Tatya Tope had 'intercepted' the necklace.)[60]

Lord Canning went on: 'The army mourned her for two days.' But even in this terse report he paid tribute by implication to the Rani's gallantry – and to her continued femininity: 'The Infantry attacked the Cavalry for allowing her to be killed. The Cavalry said she would ride too far in front.' He added: 'Her tent was very coquettish.'

At the time, Sir Hugh Rose's report back to the Duke of Cambridge in England confirmed the story of the Rani's speedy immolation. After burning, she was buried 'with great ceremony, under a tamarind tree under the Rock of Gwalior, where I saw her bones and ashes'. His own epitaph contained the generous tribute of one soldier to another: 'The Ranee was remarkable for her bravery, cleverness and perseverance; her generosity to her Subordinates was unbounded. These qualities, combined with her rank, rendered her the most dangerous of all the rebel leaders.' In its regimental history, the 8th Hussars, at whose hands the Rani probably died (the squadron commander was granted a VC for his conduct in the course of that charge), reiterated Sir Hugh Rose's praise: 'in her death the rebels lost their bravest and best military leader'.[61]

The Rani's epitaph at the hands of her own people was to be nobler yet. The verdict of Colonel Malleson, who continued the work of Sir John Kaye in his own history of the mutiny published in 1896, proved correct: 'Whatever her [the Rani's] faults in British eyes may have been, her countrymen will ever remember that she was driven by ill-treatment into rebellion and that she lived and died for her country.'[62]

Nana Sahib, that master of 'ferocity and slaughter', escaped to Nepal where his legendary adventures as a wandering fakir inspired Jules Verne. Since his exact date of death was unknown, false Nanas were to reappear throughout the nineteenth century.[63] The Rani's adopted son Damodar Rao had a more prosaic but happier fate: he surrendered to the British in March 1860 and was subsequently granted a pension.[*] But the Rani's reputation passed into the airy world of ballad and song. There are statues of the Rani – at Gwalior as well as Jhansi – and nowadays innumerable highly coloured pictorial representations of the celebrated Warrior Queen. Nevertheless, it is by the ballads that the Rani of Jhansi is preserved in the Indian folk memory. A study by P. C. Joshi – *Folk Songs of '1857'* – published as part of a symposium in 1957 to mark the centenary,[65] explains why: 'The Rani's noble example and supreme sacrifice have blazed the path for countless sons and daughters of India to join the freedom struggle. She is one of the immortals of our national movement and such songs have kept her alive in our memory.'

> The song of joy, the song of freedom rises
> In every corner of the land this song is heard
> Here fought Lakshmi Bai and Peshwa Nana . . .[66]

---

[*] In 1957, to mark the centenary, his descendant was also given a symbolic monetary reward by the Indian state.[64]

Some of these songs have a fairy-tale quality: the Rani moulds her army from clay and stones, she makes swords from mere wood. Others dwell on the loyalty of her followers: the chief gunner guarding the main gates of Jhansi who tells his companion that 'we have to die one day, brother' and 'I shall choose today, For our Queen I shall lay down my life'. The old names ride again, but in a different guise. Here is 'Proud Hugh Rose' begging for 'one pot of water' to quench his thirst. The heroism of the Rani is however a constant element:

Old India was filled again with the bloom of youth . . .

wrote Subhadra Kumari Chauhan,

> The old sword flashed once more in fifty-seven
> This is the story we have heard
> From the Bundelas who worship Shiva
> The Rani of Jhansi fought valorously and well.

One popular ballad in particular calls attention to the salient characteristic of a heroine who, like Boadicea, will never be forgotten by her own people: that, for all the apparent weakness of her sex, she was in fact in courage the equivalent of any hero:

> How valiantly like a man fought she,
>   The Rani of Jhansi
> On every parapet a gun she set
>   Raining fire of hell,
> How well like a man fought the Rani of Jhansi
>   How valiantly and well!

CHAPTER SEVENTEEN

Iron Ladies

The Iron Lady of the Western World! Me? A Cold
Warrior? Well, yes – if that is how *they* wish to interpret
my defence of values and freedoms fundamental to our
way of life.

MARGARET THATCHER (1976)

When Queen Boadicea, courtesy of the sculptor Thornycroft, did finally take up her position upon the Thames Embankment in 1902, it was as an embodiment of the age of empire. Lest the message be missed, Cowper's proud lines of prophecy were inscribed upon the plinth:[*]

Regions Caesar never knew
Thy Posterity shall sway.

Queen Victoria had died early in the previous year, at the ripe age of eighty-one. The role of the female ruler, provided it did not involve the actual battlefield, appeared to be conducive to longevity. In 1900 a very different kind of Warrior Queen, Tz'u-Hsi, the so-called Dragon Empress of China, had the impudence to solicit support from Queen Victoria during the Boxer Rebellion which she herself had done much to foment on this very basis: 'two old women', so ran her telegram, should understand each other's difficulties.[2] (Born in 1835, an approximate

---

[*] It was not missed. As late as the Second World War, Prime Minister Churchill's Private Secretary, John Colville, strolling through London in the Blitz to inspect landmarks he might not see again, described Boadicea's statue as 'a monument to successful imperialism'.[1]

contemporary of the Rani of Jhansi, the Dragon Empress was sixteen years younger than Victoria.) Nevertheless even in 1902 the erection of the Boadicean monument should still be seen as celebrating the kind of maternal imperialism – indistinguishable to its practitioners from patriotism – personified by Victoria herself.

Curiously enough, the Embankment site was a second, or if one remembers Prince Albert's original suggestion of the Hyde Park Arch nearly a half century before, a third choice.[3] Thornycroft's project had passed through various vicissitudes following the Prince's premature death in 1861. To be sure, there was a melancholy bonus in a series of equestrian portraits of his former patron; but Thornycroft had toiled on the Boadicean group for fifteen years before a favourable review of it in *The Times* in 1871 suggested the possibility of a government commission. The sculptor resumed work in 1883, but died two years later, at which point his family offered the group to the public, together with a contribution to the heavy cost of casting.

It was a spurt of interest in the supposed burial place of Boadicea near the end of the century which was responsible for the final step. The London County Council proposed to erect the statue at the top of Parliament Fields, on the grounds that a tumulus there was the traditional site; a subscription of £2,800 was raised to have Thornycroft's statue cast in bronze, with a further £1,500 for a pedestal by J. G. Jackson. Intervention from the Society of Antiquaries, who rejected the Parliament Fields tradition, left the Boadicean group once more siteless, until 1902 when it reached its present resting place, near Westminster Bridge, and within sight of the Houses of Parliament.

Beyond Cowper's significant lines, the inscription beneath the statue kept various other options open. The subject of the monument was described as 'Boadicea (Boudicca) Queen of the Iceni Who died AD 61 after leading her people against the Roman invader'. Boadicea's daughters, however, although shown as part of the group – two strapping females, bare-breasted as Amazons for the fight – suffered from their usual official disregard and were not named or even mentioned. As for the Iceni Queen herself (her hair in a neat pageboy style rather than flowing), 'One really must admire her sang-froid', wrote Lord Edward Gleichen in 1928 in a study of London's open-air statuary. For the horses, modelled – not too closely one hopes – on those of Prince Albert's stables, are galloping wildly, but Boadicea has no reins with which to control them, as she stands coolly aloft with her spear.[4]

This belief in the nobility of empire, attached to the idealized character of a patriotic woman, was to be one important element in the survival of the Boadicean legend.[5] The year 1900 for example saw the publication of *Britain's Greatness Foretold*, the story of Boadicea by Marie Trevelyan, which traced the foundations of 'our present freedom' back to those ancient struggles against the Romans.[6] (The South African War against the Boers had begun while Marie Trevelyan was in the process of writing.) The book is redolent with direct comparisons between Boadicea and Queen Victoria: also characteristic of the time is the general emphasis placed upon the inspiring femininity of both queens.

British colonization, Marie Trevelyan pointed out, was the task of families, not soldiers, 'just as it was the woman Boadicea who rallied all the tribes of Britain round her in her day'. Led by Queen Victoria, it was the women of Great Britain who had materially helped to spread and maintain the British Empire. As for Marie Trevelyan's Boadicea, even in war she never surrendered her natural tenderness: at the last battle indeed the 'majestic queen' was described as being 'lost in the weeping woman'. On the other hand, when Boadicea's men responded loudly to her speech with the rallying cry 'For Britain, Boadicea and freedom', they were of course intent on making aggressive war rather than domestic peace.

So Boadicea, aided both by late Victorian perceptions concerning women and empire, and by the image of Queen Victoria herself, passed into the pantheon of idealized patriotic women. It is a place she has not lost in the century since the erection of her statue and is not likely to lose, so long as national crises arise, demanding reference to comforting historic symbols of courage and endurance.

Patriotic fervour helped to make up one part of the modern Boadicean plinth. At the same time, as women stirred in their struggle for general recognition as a sex (rather than as privileged individuals) Boadicea's protean legend began to be employed in quite a different connection. Pageants had become increasingly popular in late Victorian and Edwardian times; in this manner the British aristocracy was able to show off both its adequate historical knowledge and its more than adequate historical fancy dress, in a pleasurable real-life example of zeugma. But *The Pageant of Great Women*, first performed on 10 November 1909 at the Scala Theatre, London, was a pageant with a difference, since it was performed in the suffragette cause.[7] This was two months after the Prime Minister, Asquith, had instructed the prison doctors to feed suffragette hunger-strikers forcibly. Originally produced by the play department of the Actresses' Franchise League, written by Cicely Hamilton, designed and directed by Edith Craig, the pageant subsequently toured the country.

Boadicea, 'a Briton in arms', was one of the most prominent characters. When she appeared, spectators were adjured to 'look on her who stood . . . and spat defiance at the hosts of Rome!' A photograph of the event in the *Daily Mirror* shows what they saw: a stalwart Boadicea, towering over her companions and got up more or less according to Dio Cassius' instructions, with flowing tresses over a barbaric robe, a torc and other jewels, and an enormous spear in her hand (another possible comparison, to Ellen Terry's famous portrait as Lady Macbeth, reminds one that Edith Craig was Ellen Terry's daughter).

The character of Prejudice was played by a man. Otherwise the familiar stage army – in this case literally so – of great women was paraded in categories which included 'Learned Women', 'Artists' and 'Saintly Women' as well as 'Rulers' and 'Warriors'. Here Queen Zenobia 'of the hero's heart' was placed among the Rulers; but the Rani of Jhansi – 'though but a child in years' – found her place among the Warriors together with Boadicea, Joan of Arc and the fourteenth-century Scot Agnes Dunbar. It was intended by this appeal to the rich past to draw public attention to the 'physical, intellectual, creative and ethical' strengths of women, in contrast to Prejudice's contemptuous declaration that Woman's innate stupidity made her incapable of thought. Fifty-two actresses took part.

In order to facilitate touring, it was Edith Craig's plan that such a pageant should contain only three speaking parts, all allegorical; these were performed by professionals. Otherwise members of suffragette societies on the spot would supply the colourful heroines, Edith Craig arriving to dress them. This ingenious arrangement was not without its little local difficulties: the extreme popularity of the role of Joan of Arc constituted one of them. Another of a rather different nature was encountered when the members of a suffrage society in a university town thought they knew enough for no one to be anxious to play Catherine the Great: who, 'whatever may have been her merits as a ruler, was renowned for the scandals of her private life'. Finally a girl was found who presumably shared Edith Craig's view that a good part was a good part for all that.

The pageant ended with Prejudice taking his stand on force as 'the last and ultimate judge', and claiming that force for man alone 'who takes the sword – The sword that must decide!' Woman on the other hand, declared Prejudice, 'Fears the white glint of it and cowers away'. It was at this point that the Warriors, led by Boadicea, were paraded in rebuttal. The stage directions read: 'Then Prejudice slinks away.'

But Prejudice, if he left the stage of the Scala Theatre, did not slink far, let alone slink away altogether, even with the winning of the vote for women at various dates in various countries across the world. Seventy years after the *Pageant of Great Women* an extraordinary exhibition was shown in San Francisco for the first time before embarking upon a worldwide tour to packed attendance.*

The Dinner Party was conceived by the American artist and craftswoman Judy Chicago and executed by her over five years with 'a working community of women and men'.[8] The exhibition consisted of thirty-nine 'place settings' upon a large open triangular banqueting table, which in turn rested upon a porcelain 'Heritage Floor', bearing the names of 999 women, grouped into categories. Its aim – an avowedly feminist one – was not only to 'symbolize the long history of female achievement' but also to remind its audience that 'the history of Western civilization, as we have understood it, has failed to represent the experience of half the human race'.

The Dinner Party's categories include 'Primordial Goddess' and 'Fertile Goddess' but also 'Kali', a category described as a 'traditionally positive view of female power misrepresented as a destructive force' (such as Celtic Britain's Rhiannon). 'Boadicea d. 62 AD' (*sic*) is, like 'Kali', the name which heads a category standing for 'the tradition of warrior queens extending back to legendary times'. Other Boadiceas include Cartimandua, Artemisia, Cleopatra, defined as a 'Ruler–Deity', Medb of Connacht, Tomyris and Zenobia, given the full panoply of description as 'Queen, warrior, military strategist and scholar'.

Give or take changes in the language of female protest between 1909 and 1979, there is an obvious and significant similarity between the suffragette pageant and the feminist exhibition in method of execution. It is not just that certain devaluations of the nature of women – her innate stupidity and cowardice for example as denounced by the pageant's male figure of Prejudice – are clearly still perceived to need rebuttal in the late twentieth century, as they have been rebutted by bold spirits throughout history. Further than that, the appeal in both cases to

---

* There were, for example, long queues in London when it was shown at a converted warehouse in White Lion Street, Islington, in the spring of 1986.

'Triumphant Women' of the past bears witness once again to the enduring importance of heroines such as Boadicea, mythical or actual, to women combating their own inferior status; and this despite the passionate desire of many women to help forward *all* their sex, not merely the potential leaders.

With the coming of the Women's Movement, such heroines naturally take on new guises. In *The Dinner Party*, for example, 'Elizabeth R', like 'Boadicea d. 62 AD', constitutes a category: the first Elizabeth is described as 'One of the greatest female rulers who ever lived, distinguished stateswoman and scholar.' While not dissenting from the verdict, one cannot help wondering what Elizabetha Triumphans herself would have made of the all-female company, she who was accustomed to pikes being couched and ensigns lowered in devotion as she passed, 'to she alone and none but only she'; to say nothing of her calculated boast of having the heart and stomach of a *man*. Boadicea, on the other hand, has come to symbolize a kind of female freedom and even sexual liberation.

The discovery by the feminist poet Judy Grahn – to her own satisfaction – that the name Boadicea (in its original Boudica form) was the origin of the word 'bulldike', may stand as an extreme example of this.[9] Grahn, in an article of 1980 entitled 'The Queens of Bulldikery', described how in years past the mystery of the word 'bulldike' had 'burbled and thickened' in her mind; deciding that it stemmed from Old English, she therefore searched for a historical people who once worshipped and valued bulls. From here to Boadicea ('Bo' means 'cow' in Irish while English friends assured her that 'bull' was pronounced 'Boa') and thence happily to Boudica, was a short leap of Grahn's creative imagination.

'Boudica was a barbarian and a Celt,' wrote Grahn, 'and her pudenda would have been active, unashamed, and radiating with female power all her life . . . Considering Celtic customs it would have been unnatural of Queen Boudica *not* to be a lesbian. She was, after all, a queen and a military leader of her people.' With an even greater leap of the imagination, Grahn also drew attention to the large number of puns surrounding Boadicea's name, such as the soldiers' *dikes* which they made in AD 61, and her statue called 'Boadicea on the Embankment', embankment being a synonym for dike.

Grahn however derided Dio Cassius' description of the atrocities committed under Boadicea's command – the laceration of the women's breasts in particular – as being 'too much like the typical patriarchal response to women warriors in general to be believed'. (This point of view, incidentally, provides Grahn with an ally in the shape of Milton, however unlikely the combination; he too dismissed such invented details by which historians hoped to 'embellish' their work.)[10] The next leap is to transfer the word 'bulldike' to the United States: Grahn's explanation lies in the slang of Newgate Prison, from which many indentured criminals proceeded westwards, a high percentage of them, according to Grahn, Celts, who remembered their ancestors as homosexual 'as a matter of course'.

It is too easy to dismiss all this as ludicrously unhistorical (which of course it is). For one might observe with truth that Grahn's imaginative reconstruction is really no more ludicrous than some of the other theories which have been proposed about Boadicea in the past, including, famously, her 'rich burial' at Stonehenge, actually erected nearly two millennia before, but believed as an article of faith in the early seventeenth century. Nor is Grahn's bold lesbian Celt, 'radiating with female power all her life', necessarily further away from the original than Purcell's meekly apologetic late-seventeenth-century princess ('My Fortune wound my Female Soul too high And lifted me above myself').[11]

Be that as it may, Grahn's alluring but fantastical theory has its own importance: for it draws attention to the Warrior Queen, here epitomized by Boadicea, as a symbol of sexual freedom as well as female independence. At the same time, such an image looks back to the remote past. Grahn's poem, written in 1972, 'She Who', acts as the epigraph of her article:

I am the wall at the lip of the water
I am the rock that refused to be battered
I am the dyke in the matter, the other . . .
and I have been many a wicked grandmother
and I shall be many a wicked daughter . . .

This is once again the language, proud, mystical and ferocious, of the Ptolemaic creed of Isis, invoked to adorn the image of Cleopatra: 'I am she that rises in the Dog star, she who is called Goddess by women . . . I am the queen of war, I am the queen of the thunderbolt . . .'[12]

Liberated sexuality in general – not merely homosexuality – contributes to the modern image of the Warrior Queen. *Boadicea: A Tragedy of War* by Robert Reynolds, issued by the Poets Press in New York in 1941, has a heroine who is seldom mentioned without a reference to her heavy breasts 'like pillows . . .' and her frank sexual desires characteristic of Celtic women: 'Yet she attracted the younger tribesmen. She was the eternal, fecund woman of their songs and stories, and their myths.' Henry Treece's heroine, in an English novel of 1958, *Red Queen, White Queen*, has not only Boadicea but her daughters (Gwynedd and Siara), all three of them plump and buxom and blonde, sleeping with whoever pleases them 'in the old fashion'. In 1986 a British television programme on 'Imaginary Women' conducted by Marina Warner, showed Toyah Wilcox, twenty-five-year-old rock singer turned actress and film star, driving a chariot; her hair – an appropriate modern version of Dio's 'tawny' – was a violent punk red.[13] Toyah Wilcox, who had accepted the role of Boadicea – 'a character I greatly admire' – in a film the year before, now described her heroine as a 'free liberated sexual woman'.

Such a picture of a free-wheeling female rebel against patriarchal attitudes may seem in quaint contrast to the statuesque image inherited from late Victorian times, gravely maternal, deeply imperialist. Yet once again, as in the case of Grahn, the idea of the rebel, give or take her sexuality (the true nature of

Boadicea's sexuality is one of the many things about her which are likely to remain forever obscure), is, of the two, the more in keeping with the few known facts of Boadicea's career.

There is still a further element in the mythology of Boadicea which has ensured the survival of interest in her image into modern times. That is the emergence of the political female leader. At first sight an elected woman Prime Minister may seem to have little in common with a Warrior Queen of ancient or even more recent times. Yet there is still an equivocal relationship perceived to exist between women and force which can rise to a head whenever a woman is voted into power, or even (significantly in modern democracies) *might* be voted into power. This equivocal relationship brings the notion of Boadicea, or some other legendary Warrior Queen, into play once more.

In the suffragette pageant of 1909, Prejudice had claimed force for Man alone, on the grounds that Woman traditionally cowered away from 'the white glint' of the sword; he also claimed force as 'the last and ultimate judge', effectively debarring timorous Woman from the exercise of power. Or in General de Gaulle's nobler version of the same sentiment, quoted in Chapter One, force was described as watching over civilization and ruling empires, 'the fighting spirit' being an integral part of man's inheritance. On the stage in 1909 Prejudice had been easily roused by the appearance of the defiant Boadicea, epitomizing Woman's ability to handle any martial matter. But the reality was very different and remains so. The question of what Kleist in *Penthesilea* called 'Fate's iron tongue, the sword' will not go away.[14]

Can women, if voted into power, handle the great issues of war (and death) and peace? Are they not too tender, if not actually too timid? Female leaders of the second half of the twentieth century have conspicuously found themselves having to prove their credentials in this respect by one means or another, not only after election but during the process leading up to it. Geraldine Ferraro was the Democratic Vice-Presidential candidate in the United States presidential election of 1984: the first woman to

figure in such an outstanding position (and at the time of writing
– 1988 – the year of the next round of presidential elections, the
only one). Her account of her experiences campaigning, as related
in *My Story*, published in 1986, makes illuminating reading. For it
shows clearly that deep, primitive fears of women's potential
timidity or weakness lurked in certain quarters of her country.
Nothing in the political development of women elsewhere or
even in America's own vigorous Women's Movement had
affected this.[15]

Such fears were not exactly nursed in secret. In her confrontation on nationwide television with her opposite number, the
sitting Republican Vice-President George Bush, on 11 October
1984, Geraldine Ferraro described herself facing 'the final and
inevitable question'. Thus Vice-President Bush: 'Congresswoman
Ferraro, you have had little or no experience in military matters
and yet you might some day find yourself Commander-in-Chief
of the armed forces. How can you convince the American people
and the potential enemy that you would know what to do to
protect this nation's security, and do you think in any way that the
Soviets might be tempted to try to take advantage of you simply
because you are a woman?' (This question was posed incidentally
five years after Mrs Thatcher had become Prime Minister of
Great Britain, hardly a good example of a woman of whom the
Soviets had successfully taken advantage!)

'I didn't hesitate,' wrote Geraldine Ferraro. ' "Are you saying
that I would have to have fought in a war in order to love peace?"
I shot back . . .' And she did of course assure the questioner of
her confidence in her own ability to handle such a situation. But
she admitted that it was a terribly important question 'and I had
thought a great deal about how to answer it'. George Bush for his
part emphasized his own combat experience in the Second World
War – for which Geraldine Ferraro, born in 1934, would of
course have been too young, quite apart from her gender: 'Yes, I
did serve in combat, I was shot down when I was a young kid,
scared to death. And all that . . . heightened my convictions
about peace.'

Marvin Kalb on *Meet the Press* put the question to Geraldine Ferraro in an even simpler form: 'Are you strong enough to push the button?' (Another legitimate question – to candidates of both sexes – might be: Are you strong enough *not* to push the button? But this was not posed.) Although Ferraro gave the obvious reply that she could do whatever was necessary for the protection of her country, privately she found it endlessly annoying to be presumed weak and indecisive just because she was a woman. There was a bigger underlying issue: if her candidacy was really being judged on the same level as a man's, she would hardly be asked to answer questions like that. Nor indeed was this question asked of any other candidates, other than members of Congress who were religious ministers.

But of course Geraldine Ferraro's candidacy – in the event unsuccessful since the election was won by the Republicans in a landslide – was not being judged on the same level as a man's. And those elected female leaders who have emerged triumphant have needed to pull the mantle of the Warrior Queen about them, where appropriate, and use it to lend further mythic authority to the role of mere Prime Minister: sex has had to be made a subtle advantage, instead of a crude disadvantage.

Indira Gandhi became Prime Minister of India on 24 January 1966 at the age of forty-eight. She was not in fact the first woman in the world to occupy the position: that honour had already gone to Mrs Gandhi's contemporary, Sirimavo Bandaraneike of Sri Lanka, who was elected in July 1960. Interestingly enough, at their inception, the careers of both Mrs Gandhi and Mrs Bandaraneike indicate that the Appendage Syndrome common to so many Warrior Queens continued to operate under elective conditions as it had done under the hereditary system in the past. That is to say, although the London *Evening News* wrote concerning Mrs Bandaraneike of the need for a new word – 'Presumably we shall have to call her a Stateswoman' – the comment of the *News Chronicle* was considerably more apt: 'Gentle widow heads for job as premier'.[16]

For Mrs Bandaraneike, Rani-like, was the widow of the veteran

Sri Lankan statesman Solomon W. R. D. Bandaraneike, eighteen
years her senior, who had acted as premier for three and a half
years before he was assassinated in 1959 by a Buddhist monk. An
inconclusive political election the following March was followed
by an invitation to Mrs Bandaraneike to head the government:
'she was the symbol, the figurehead that was necessary; the spark
to ignite the flame', in the words of her biographer.[17] (There is an
obvious modern comparison to be made with Mrs Corazon
Aquino, grieving widow of an assassinated opposition Filipino
leader, whose symbolic presence heading a political party, at a
time when her remarkable personal qualities were largely unknown, provided the spark to sweep away President Marcos in
1986.)

As for Indira Gandhi, coming from a Kashmiri brahmin
family, the only child of Pandit Nehru, she could in a sense be
said to have been born to rule: a princess who inherited from her
parent, as Matilda of Tuscany inherited from her father Boniface
II, or Tamara of Georgia from Giorgi III. Prior to her election,
Indira Gandhi, the shy child of a brilliant father, absent much of
her childhood in prison, and of an uneducated mother of lower
social standing, had indeed held only one political position: she
had been President of the Congress Party in 1959, but resigned
after less than a year in favour of her maternal duties. Indira
Gandhi actually became Prime Minister when Lal Bahadour
Shastri died suddenly in office of a heart attack. In this uneasy
situation, it was a symbol of that same continuity which Queen
Elizabeth I constantly sought to establish with references to her
sire 'Great Harry', that the crowds in 1966 shouted not only
'Indira ki jai!' (Long live Indira!) but also *'Jawa-harlal ki jai!'* (Long
live Nehru!).[18]

Mrs Gandhi, the beneficiary of the Appendage Syndrome,
quickly became part of another familiar syndrome – that of the
Better-Man: in her first year of office, for example, she was
described as 'the only man in the cabinet of old women'. She also
received much of the same 'heroic' treatment concerning her
youth from her admiring biographers, as well as herself stressing

such early heroic self-identifications in what was surely a calculated manner. An early girlhood identification with Joan of Arc for example is frequently mentioned even by her family, and confirmed by Mrs Gandhi herself in a letter to her lifelong friend Dorothy Norman: she was 'a great heroine of mine . . . one of the first people I read about with enthusiasm'.[19]

In other interviews, as with the celebrated Italian journalist Oriana Fallaci, Mrs Gandhi underlined a tomboy past: she revealed that her very doll play had been militarily oriented: 'I had many dolls. And I played with them, not necessarily seeing them as babies to feed. In fact I used them as men and women to perform insurrections, battles and so on.' She told a would-be biographer that sometimes her dolls were arranged to perform a struggle between the Satyagrahis and the police, with the bride-groom doll playing the Satyagrahi leader, while the little Indira shouted slogans such as '*Mahatma Gandhi ki jai!*' Mrs Gandhi's 'male' aggressive role was by her own account encouraged by her mother, who had resented the constrictions on her own life, as well as by her father: 'I was brought up as a boy when I was small. I climbed trees, I ran and I never had any feeling of inferiority or weakness.'[20]

It was politically adroit of Mrs Gandhi, faced with the problem of being a woman premier in a country which was 83 per cent Hindu, to hint at the honorary male in such statements about herself. Officially however she took a slightly different stance: 'As Prime Minister, I am not a woman. I am a human being.' (Although her confidence to Dorothy Norman – 'I am in no sense a feminist but I believe in women being able to do everything' – may have come nearer to representing her real feelings on this complicated subject.) Again she stated: 'I do not regard myself as a woman but as a person with a job to do.' Golda Meir's version of this, incidentally, when asked how it felt to be a female Foreign Minister, was to crack back, 'I don't know, I've never been a male Foreign Minister.' A short biography of Mrs Gandhi 'for young boys and girls' by R. Sundara Raju, published in New Delhi in 1980, begins with the prophecy of a dying old man, Sarojini Naidu, at her birth that she would be the 'Nightingale (the new soul) of India'. Later Indira Gandhi declared that 'Being a woman has neither helped nor hindered me. During the struggle for independence, nobody was concerned about being beaten up or shot at or anything. Nobody said: "This is a woman and we won't shoot." It would be unfair if, later on, this question were to crop up.'[21]

Yet since inevitably it did crop up and would always do so, Mrs Gandhi also employed that other expedient of the Warrior Queen by which she made a virtue of necessity with wonderful dexterity. That is to say, she assumed the role, even the title, of 'The Mother', so deeply embedded in the Hindu consciousness, with the aura of those goddesses bright and dark, Durga and Kali, rulers of fertility and destruction, hovering about her. History, or folk memories of history as described in Chapter Sixteen with regard to the Rani of Jhansi, could be said to be on her side, to make of her in the minds of the less educated the last in a long line of queens and empresses, rather than the first woman Prime Minister. Moreover in 1966 Mrs Gandhi possessed to the simple mind the hopeful imperial quality of being the mother of sons – Rajiv Gandhi, later Prime Minister of India in his turn after his mother's assassination in 1986, was twenty-two at the time. One remembers Isabella of Spain, bolstered up in authority by the birth of an heir during the civil war.

It was however war – the successful Indian war against Pakistan of 1971 – which gave Mrs Gandhi her ultimate prestige and also her ultimate kind of deification, as Durga on the one hand, an imposing leader of her country on the other. Afterwards, as Dom Moraes wrote, 'She had achieved the status of a myth. She was Joan [of Arc] without the inconvenience of prison, fire and cross.'[22] It was not a war of Mrs Gandhi's seeking (in fact it can be argued that the female premiers of the twentieth century, like the eighteenth- and nineteenth-century queens regnant, have not been of their nature belligerent – merely determined to do their belligerent best in war when it comes – that is to say, to be as good as men if not better). Yet following the first Pakistani air raids against India in December 1971, no one could ever again ask, in India at least: how will this woman react in a crisis? Will she be too timid, or if not too timid, too tender?

Golda Meir, born in 1898, and thus nearly twenty years older than Indira Gandhi, became Prime Minister of Israel in 1969, having served as Minister for Foreign Affairs from 1956 to 1965. She had previously been the first Israeli Ambassador to the Soviet Union and Minister of Labour and would also serve as Secretary-General of the Labour Party. Early in her career Golda Meir had also shown herself capable of oratory on the (imagined) Boadicean scale. On 21 January 1948 she spoke eloquently to the Council of Jewish Federations in Chicago, appealing for funds without which the future state could not survive. It was a speech subsequently praised by the first premier of Israel, David Ben-Gurion: 'Some day when history will be written, it will be said that there was a Jewish woman who got the money which made the state possible.'[23] To British ears, at least, it has a Churchillian ring: 'I am not exaggerating when I say that the Yishiv in Palestine will fight in the Negev and will fight in Galilee and will fight on the outskirts of Jerusalem till the very end. You cannot decide whether we should fight or not. We will . . . You can only decide one thing: whether we shall be victorious in this fight or whether the Mufti will be victorious. That decision American Jews can make. It has to be made quickly within hours, within days . . .' Golda Meir returned to Palestine with promises of fifty million dollars.

As with Mrs Bandaraneike, the choice of Mrs Meir was intended to be a healing one, in view of the rival claims of Moshe Dayan and Yigel Allon; and once again Mrs Meir's elevation followed an unexpected death, that of the premier Levi Eshkol. Otherwise, there was one very important difference: here at last was a female leader who owed nothing to the Appendage Syndrome, one who was neither the daughter or widow of a famous man, nor the regent-mother for some form of infant princeling. To secure her place without the benefit of any specific male connection was in itself a remarkable achievement on the part of Golda Meir; and one far rarer in the history of women than is generally supposed. One can appreciate the judgement of Mrs Meir's political adviser Simcha Dinitz, later Director-General of the Prime Minister's Office (and Ambassador to Washington 1973 to 1978), that she had 'the best qualities of a woman – intuition, insight, sensitivity, compassion – plus the best qualities of a man – strength, determination, practicality, purposefulness'.[24]

Nevertheless for all the self-made quality of her position, the kind of questions – sometimes innocent, sometimes not – which Mrs Meir faced concerning the implications of her reaching high office have as ever a familiar ring. In *My Life*, published in 1975, Golda Meir described a visit to the National Press Club in Washington when she was Foreign Minister: 'there were only two queries that were at all new'. The first concerned Israel's intention – or otherwise – to employ nuclear weapons if its survival was in jeopardy. The second went as follows: 'Mrs Meir, your grandson Gideon says you make the best *gefilte* fish in the world. Would you reveal your recipe to us?' This was naïve behaviour at worst, and it made Mrs Meir laugh at the time. On the other hand the Jordanian newspaper which mocked Mrs Meir in 1969 for asking for negotiations before war, as 'a grandmother, telling bedtime stories to her grandchildren' (she was indeed a grandmother at this point, not surprisingly for a woman in her early seventies), was not naïve but calculating.[25] Once again, it is impossible to envisage a male leader being subject to this particular diatribe.

And yet the ambiguity at the centre of the whole subject of the Warrior Queen remains. Mrs Meir also derived strength, surely, from her 'grandmotherly' image, not least among her own strongly matriarchal people. It was after all perfectly possible that the president of the Washington Press Club genuinely wanted that recipe, and admired Mrs Meir for her alleged skill: months later in Los Angeles, when she answered a question on television about her chicken soup, 40,000 people wrote in for the recipe! That juxtaposition of Israel's survival with a recipe could have been evinced only by the sight of a woman minister. And there was indeed something matriarchal – grandmotherly even – about the way she ran her government. To quote Chaim Herzog (later President of Israel), another who knew her well and worked under her, Golda Meir had a particular style of government in which her personality was the deciding factor: and that personality was very much that of 'the overbearing mother who ruled the roost with her iron hand'.[26]

This was not always, in his opinion, to the benefit of her government. With little idea of orderly administration, she preferred to work closely with cronies in an *ad hoc* framework that soon came to be known as her 'kitchen' – so named for good reason, since Golda Meir was wont to make coffee and tea there for her associates throughout the long night hours (as well as making coffee at 4 a.m. for her guards). At the same time one might most easily rebut the Jordanian sneer by observing that in the Arab–Israeli War of 1973 – the War of Atonement – the 'grandmother' acquitted herself both gallantly and expertly. To quote Chaim Herzog again on her conduct during the war: 'on many occasions she [Golda Meir], a woman who had reached seventy-five, found herself thrust into a position where she had to decide between differing military options proposed by professionals. She decided, and invariably decided well, drawing on a large measure of common sense which had stood her in good stead.'[27] Her stubborn decisiveness proved a national asset during the war, even if her doctrinaire approach to problems and to the operation of government contributed to the failings of that government before it.

And then there was that special rapport which Golda Meir had with the ordinary soldiers of Israel, something bringing her close to Isabella of Spain or Tamara of Georgia. When Golda Meir wept at the Wailing Wall on the fifth day of the Six Day War for the sacrifices of Israel's youth, the soldiers watched her and wept too.[28] There is however one twentieth-century female political leader who has had to be extremely cautious at any overt suggestion of queenship – warrior or otherwise. That is not to say that the subject in all its emotive strength does not arise.

Margaret Thatcher, then aged fifty-three, became Prime Minister of Great Britain in May 1979, the first woman to occupy the position, as five years earlier she had been the first woman to lead any British political party. By this date, Queen Elizabeth II, a mere six months younger than the new Prime Minister, had already been on the throne for over twenty-seven years.

'This nation loves a monarch', a committee of the House of Commons had advised Lord Protector Oliver Cromwell in 1657, suggesting that he should regularize his position by accepting a crown himself. In the words of Secretary Thurloe advocating the same course: 'it's the office which is known to the laws and this people. They know their duty to a King and his to them.'[29] Certainly the British love their monarchy, and certainly they love their present monarch, Queen Elizabeth II, who regularly tops polls as the most admired British woman. They also know their duty to her: just as she knows hers to them, the Queen's conspicuous sense of duty being among the qualities which have endeared her to her subjects in the course of a reign whose span, at the celebration of her golden jubilee in 2002, surpassed by several years that of her illustrious predecessor, the first Elizabeth. It is Queen Elizabeth II who enacts the role of the Holy (Armed) Figurehead to her people in her frequent ceremonial appearances at military parades, naval reviews and so forth; of which her presence for many years in uniform and on horseback at the Trooping of the Colour is probably the best-known.

Under the circumstances one can understand the alarm, both public and private, which Mrs Thatcher displayed at any suggestion of encroachment on the royal role on her own part. She was obviously well aware of the resentment she might have unleashed.[30] 'You don't do that to me, my dear, I'm only in politics', she observed hastily to an unwary Spanish tourist who curtseyed to her, when the Prime Minister was glimpsed on a shopping tour in 1987.[31]

But, once again, the issue is not so simple. The existence of queens regnant in British history, and the tradition of national prosperity under two of them, the long-reigning Elizabeth I and Victoria, means that every British schoolchild – the one who knows about the knives on the wheels of Boadicea's chariot – also knows that it is not out of the question for a woman to rule Britain, much as Mrs Gandhi benefited from Hindu traditions of powerful women in religion, literature and history, despite the theoretically inferior position of women in Hindu society.

In January 1988, when Mrs Thatcher became the longest-serving Prime Minister in twentieth-century Britain, there was a plethora of commentaries and comparisons: but after lip-service had been paid to Prime Minister Asquith – whose record she had just beaten – the main comparisons were made unashamedly to British reigning queens. As Robert Harris wrote rather despairingly in the *Observer*: 'It is not sexist to use a regal analogy to describe her impact on the country. It is not particularly facetious. It is simply the nearest thing we have to an historical parallel.' Lord Hailsham, Lord Chancellor in Mrs Thatcher's government for eight years, openly described his premier as being in the same category as Mary Tudor, Elizabeth I, Queen Anne and Queen Victoria, favouring Elizabeth I especially 'in her handling of men'.[32]

So Mrs Thatcher, without visibly seeking it – rather to the contrary – did benefit from that tradition expressed long ago by Tacitus concerning the Britons and Boadicea: 'they did not discriminate against women in matters of command'. There is a kind of justice in this. For Mrs Thatcher also had to contend with many of those problems special to the Warrior Queen – or Queen Regnant – which have been mentioned throughout this book.

The female voice of command, which grates on the male ear for reasons which are as much psychological as physiological, is one of these problems, from Boadicea's allegedly 'harsh' voice onwards. The disadvantage to Mrs Thatcher of her female lightly timbred voice in a massively male-dominated House of Commons – which means of course deep-male-voice-dominated – is not one to be dismissed lightly, since it entailed exactly that kind of screeching in making herself heard most disliked by men (and many women).

Mrs Thatcher acknowledged this herself: 'Yes, I do have to shout to make myself heard,' she admitted in an interview in 1986, 'and sometimes I say, "I am not going to shout any more like I did last time, I will just stand there until they are quiet".' In the same year the Labour Shadow Minister Gerald Kaufman drew attention to what he called Mrs Thatcher's 'fishwife' act in the House of Commons: 'screaming away in a shrill, strident voice, with her face absolutely contorted'. The Liberal leader David Steel made the same point – and independently used the same epithet: 'I don't personally like her House of Commons style. I don't think that the "fishwife" approach . . . is at all effective or impressive.' It was however in vain that Kaufman hoped his own comment was made 'in an unsexist way': for the point is indeed a sexist one, whether intended as such or not, in that no man could possibly be subject to the same criticism. (One cannot help recalling Leonardi Bruno's quattrocento advice to Battista Malatesta about a woman who 'increases the volume of her speech with greater forcefulness': she will appear 'threateningly insane and requiring restraint'.)[33] A man bellowing to make himself heard in the House of Commons, as many men do, does not sound either to his own side or to his opponents like a 'fishwife' – that traditional English misogynist term of abuse going back to the fourteenth century – let alone as though requiring restraint.

There is no obvious solution to this particular problem of a female leader's voice except of course more women members of Parliament – after the 1987 general election, there were forty-one women to six hundred and nine men. But another lingering problem, the problem which will not go away (to judge from Geraldine Ferraro's experience) – how resolute can a female leader be expected to show herself against a nation's enemies? – was solved for Mrs Thatcher from an unexpected quarter: the Soviet Union, ironically enough the most likely candidate at the time for the title of Britain's enemy.

In January 1976, just under a year after she had been elected leader of the Conservative Party, Mrs Thatcher made a major speech in London which described the Soviet Union as a serious threat, both military and political, to which threat it was vital that the West should respond with strength and confidence. It was the Soviet Union's response, attacking her as the 'Iron Lady' in *Red Star*, the official journal of the Red Army, which presented Mrs Thatcher with what rapidly became, for good tactical reasons, her favourite sobriquet. It was immediately given wide prominence, not only in the Western Press, but by the victorious victim herself. 'I have the reputation of being the Iron Lady,' she would say on US television at the time of the Falklands War. 'I have great resolve.' (A cartoon in the *Daily Express* of her visit to the United States on this occasion showed Mrs Thatcher as Boadicea, long sword raised, iron breastplates prominent, with President Reagan at her chariot wheels in a cowboy hat.)[34]

Even if Mrs Thatcher had been variously dubbed 'Iron Maiden' and 'Iron Lady' by Majorie Proops in the London *Daily Mirror* as early as 1973, it was the Soviet Union's adoption (or spontaneous invention) of the phrase which gave it exactly the endorsement which Mrs Thatcher needed to emerge as a Warrior Queen, at any rate in the estimation of Britain's 'enemies'. As Bruce Arnold wrote in a hostile work, *Margaret Thatcher: A Study in Power*, published in 1984 (that memorable line 'the female of the species is more deadly than the male' acts as the epigraph), Mrs Thatcher's baptism as the Iron Lady 'effectively created the political reputation on international affairs which, by their dismissal, her Labour opponents had denied her, up to that point'.[35] 'The Iron Lady of the Western World! Me? A Cold Warrior?' she was able to riposte publicly. 'Well, yes – if that is how *they* [the Russians] wish to interpret my defence of values and freedoms fundamental to our way of life.'[36]

What propaganda had so felicitously – from Mrs Thatcher's point of view – begun, war itself was to confirm. Certainly the fact that the Falklands campaign would be the crucible of Mrs

Thatcher's reputation as a leader was appreciated in advance. In the House of Commons in the opening debate following the Argentinian invasion, on 3 April 1982, Enoch Powell (no longer a member of the Conservative Party) actually referred to the phrase 'Iron Lady' in order to add: 'In the next week or two this House, the nation and the Right Honourable Lady herself will learn of what metal she is made.' It is said that Mrs Thatcher nodded her head in agreement.[37]

Another observer of the political spectrum hostile to Mrs Thatcher, Anthony Barnett, author of *Iron Britannia: Why Parliament Waged its Falklands War* (the epigraph this time was merely the biblical name JUDITH in heavy black type), wrote cogently that Mrs Thatcher remained 'a misfit' until the 3 April debate 'elevated her into the war-leader of a bipartisan consensus'. An important inside testimony, on the other hand, is that of Patrick Cosgrave, the author of three successive biographical studies of Mrs Thatcher, since he worked for her as her Special Adviser for four years. In 1985 Cosgrave wrote that not only did the period between 2 April and 14 June 1982 show the Prime Minister at her most typically daring and resolute, but 'the war in the South Atlantic will undoubtedly be seen in the future, as it was at the time, as bearing witness to Margaret Thatcher as most truly herself'.[38]

As a result of the British campaign in the South Atlantic to recover the Falkland Islands from the Argentine invader saw Mrs Thatcher's personal popularity as a leader jump from 36 per cent approval in March 1982 to 59 per cent after the war – a staggering leap. There can be no starker illustration of the continuing potency of the image of the Warrior Queen in a nation's consciousness. As for the armed forces themselves, and the men who lead them, they have been described as responding to her as a war-leader 'in a way that hasn't been known since the time of Elizabeth 1, with a passion and loyalty that few male generals have ever inspired or commanded'. For the army at least Mrs Thatcher began to have her own *mana* as a goddess: an apparition transcending that of the Armed Figurehead, for example, holy or otherwise, because of its sheer personal strength. It was suggested (by Selina Hastings in the *Sunday Telegraph*) that in view of 'the aphrodisiac pull of power itself . . . for the armed forces she is far and away the favourite object of sexual fantasy'.[39]

Equally, for those for whom power is not necessarily thrilling (Mrs Thatcher at the time being the most powerful woman in the world), she sometimes seemed like Kali, 'the grim Indian goddess of destruction', as she ruthlessly demolished 'old ideas, policies and personalities', while at the same time exercised her other talents as 'the great creative stateswoman, the Blessed Margaret'. This remarkable double-headed comparison to the goddess-destroyer on the one hand and the sainted female was that of the historian and political journalist Paul Johnson on the eve of the Conservative Party Conference in 1987. He warned discontented Tories: 'Don't get caught under the wheels of the juggernaut. Blessed Margaret the creative-radical is driving it, but Kali-Thatcher the Destroyer is at hand – if required.'[40]

Opinions vary about what use Mrs Thatcher actually made of her own unavoidable femininity, consciously or unconsciously, and what difference the whole intricate topic made to her premiership. Commentators of both sexes and all shades of political opinion have gazed at her with fascinated awe: some seeing in Mrs Thatcher that Medusa on the 'snaky-headed Gorgon shield' wielded by 'wise Minerva', which froze her foes to stone; others viewing her with more admiration as wise Minerva herself, whose own 'rigid looks of chaste austerity and noble grace', as Milton pointed out in *Comus*, were enough to dash 'brute violence' without need of any Gorgon shield. But there has been remarkable unanimity among commentators and biographers that it did make *some* difference. Hugo Young and Anne Sloman, for example, in *The Thatcher Phenomenon* of 1986, agreed that her style of leadership turned heavily on her being a woman – without being sure how.[41]

While the independent-minded Conservative MP Julian

Critchley described her as deploying her feminine qualities 'like artillery pieces', one biographer summed it up more ambivalently thus: 'she has played the matter of being a woman, and that of woman's place in modern society, in a variety of not always very clear-cut ways'.[42] The explanation for this lack of clear-cutness lies surely in Mrs Thatcher's own intuition concerning her situation. As the brilliantly instinctive politician she undoubtedly is, Mrs Thatcher realized either consciously, or unconsciously (the effect is the same) that if the issue were to be clear-cut, it would rob her of a great deal of support on the one hand, a good deal of manoeuvrability on the other.

On the one hand she played the role of the 'honorary male' with all the aplomb of Queen Elizabeth 1, as when in 1979 on a visit to Northern Ireland following the murder of Lord Mountbatten and a number of British soldiers, Mrs Thatcher adopted the red beret and flak jacket of the Parachute Regiment (thus pleasing the regiment itself but not the Northern Ireland Office). This can be directly compared to Queen Elizabeth 1's choice of a silver cuirass and plumed helmet for her appearance at Tilbury, since neither lady actually intended to take to the battlefield. There were to be numerous other carefully organized sightings of Mrs Thatcher in military situations, particularly in the early days of her premiership, where her symbolic presence as a Warrior Queen was hard to miss.

Like Queen Elizabeth again, Mrs Thatcher displayed another interesting characteristic of the honorary male; she had no visible preference for the advancement of her own sex. After nine years of Mrs Thatcher's premiership, only one other woman was to be appointed to the Cabinet, and she incidentally a member of the non-competitive House of Lords, not Commons: Baroness (Janet) Young's two-year stint, in her capacity as Leader of the House of Lords, included the period of the Falklands War, a fact which Mrs Thatcher either had temporarily forgotten, or chose grandly to ignore, when she told her Cabinet on 2 April 1982: 'Gentlemen, we shall have to fight.' It ended when Baroness Young was demoted to a minor role in the Government outside the Cabinet. It was percipiently observed that the presence of *another* woman in the Cabinet photograph spoiled the radiance which the leader alone possessed in photographic terms, making her so clearly unmistakable in her visible female dress.[43] At some very primitive level, did Mrs Thatcher resent Baroness Young's presence?

For there is the element of chivalry which the woman in a man's world traditionally evokes (an honorary male perhaps, but not sacrificing any of the prerequisites allowed by society to the female). At Mrs Thatcher's first Party Conference as Conservative leader, in October 1975, Barbara Castle, a prominent Labour politician in the Wilson government who had yet to see her own party elect a female leader, confided to her diary, possibly not without a small jealous pang, that Mrs Thatcher now displayed a special bloom, produced by 'the vitamin of power'. In March she had written, 'Margaret's election has stirred up her own side wonderfully: all her backbenchers perform like knights jousting a tourney for a lady's favours, showing off their paces by making an unholy row at every opportunity over everything that the [Labour] Government does.' Thirteen years later, the official photograph to commemorate Mrs Thatcher's long-serving record certainly did give her a remarkable air of a Tudor sovereign, in her long gold brocade dress, surrounded by males including Cabinet ministers, top civil servants and her own husband: twenty-six black-and-white (dinner-jacketed) knights.[44]

Then there is Mrs Thatcher's celebrated reaction to a question concerning Women's Liberation, at her first Press conference as Conservative leader: 'What's it ever done for me?' Queen Victoria, among past female rulers, might have approved of this disdain, with her well-known antipathy to Women's Rights in principle and professional women in practice. But in her own time such contempt earned Mrs Thatcher the justified dislike and disapproval of the Women's Movement. An editorial of August 1982 in *Spare Rib*, a leading feminist magazine, criticized the way 'masculinity' had been propagated throughout the whole

Falklands crisis, military and sexual powers mixed up together as glorious, most notably by the (female) Prime Minister: 'We are not saying women should avoid positions of power, but that unless we direct our efforts to the good of all women . . . we are likely to promote rather than challenge the current notions of masculinity.' In short, there is the 'very real danger of leading to more Margaret Thatchers'.[45]

On the other hand, with Mrs Thatcher's denial of any specifically female qualities went an ability to capitalize on them where necessary – once again, probably successful just because it was instinctive. (One has to admit that even her reaction to Women's Liberation may, fortunately or unfortunately depending upon one's view of the subject, have gained her far more support than she lost in Britain in 1975.) Nor can Mrs Thatcher fairly be blamed for capitalizing on her sex, since she has had to suffer a good many slings and arrows on the subject, from the first moment when Labour supporters shouted 'Ditch the bitch!' until honourably restrained by women members of the Labour movement.

During the Falklands campaign, insults in the Argentine Press varied from 'chicken brain' (because she was a woman) to 'go back to knitting' and 'stay in the kitchen'. Although such outbursts were smoothly dismissed by President Galtieri of Argentina in an interview, once more with Oriana Fallaci, on the grounds that 'humour and caricature belong to the Latin temperament', the area of attack chosen was surely significant.[*][47] Under the circumstances, Mrs Thatcher was well entitled to use that metaphorical knitting needle, to which she was told to return, as an offensive weapon.

As early as 1979, on the eve of her first general election as Conservative leader, Mrs Thatcher emphasized the practical value

---

[*] Nor was the 'kitchen' reference confined to the Latin temperament. The puppet Iron Lady, as depicted by Luck and Flaw, the British cartoonists, on television in November 1976, had her breastplate and armour created out of colanders and other pieces of kitchen equipment.[46]

of her female domesticity: 'I know what it is to run a home and a job . . .' and quoted the recent example of Golda Meir for authority, that characteristic technique of the female leader through history, back to Zenobia stressing her descent from Cleopatra. In an important and prominent interview with George Gale in the *Daily Express*, shortly after the Falklands War was over, Mrs Thatcher directly compared the running of the campaign to household management – something on which she, as a woman, could be presumed to be an expert, or at least by implication more expert than the men surrounding her.[48] This was in answer to the question: 'Did being a woman make any difference?' 'It may just be that many, many women make naturally good managers and organizers. You might not think of it that way, George,' she went on sweetly, 'but each woman who runs a house is a manager and an organizer. We thought forward each day, and we did it in a routine way and we were on the job twenty-four hours a day.'

Mrs Thatcher's reaction to George Gale's next topic is however a perfect illustration of the kind of manoeuvrability she allowed herself. 'Was it difficult for a woman to issue orders involving blood being shed?' he asked. 'We were thinking in terms of saving lives,' she answered (without directly replying to the question), 'but bearing in mind that our people had been invaded by a pretty awful dictatorship. One lived with the agony of the troops who were going down on the supply line on ships. One lived with the agony of the soldiers. But we didn't look only at the agony: we also looked at the professionalism, the loyalty and the devotion of our troops.' In a trice, the cosy super-feminine housekeeper has become the dedicated Warrior Queen, the 'singular exception' in Gibbon's phrase, the woman ruling proudly in the man's world.

So Boadicea marched on in her third modern personification, not the abstract patriotic symbol of empire, not the independent woman, free of shackles which may be political or sexual, but the elected female Prime Minister and occasional war-leader, whose existence continues to enrage, fascinate and inspire, in equal quantities, beyond any capacity of her male contemporaries to do these same three things. The innumerable allusions and comparisons to Boadicea during Mrs Thatcher's premiership, far from being monolithically favourable in intention (or unfavourable), in fact illustrate just this many-sided aspect of her own image, as well as that of Boadicea herself.

At the time of the Falklands campaign, the left-wing *New Statesman* in a critical editorial called Mrs Thatcher 'this Boadicea' who would have to come back into 'the real world' when the war was over. Adam Raphael in the *Observer* also called her Boadicea at roughly the same date (late May): 'every time she opens her mouth she castrates one of her ministers'. When the action was over, however, she would need 'to pipe down'. In 1985 however *Woman's Own* magazine interviewed a lady who had just been voted 'the most feminine woman of the year' for believing that a woman's place is not in the office but to stay at home having babies. The happy winner also professed herself a great admirer of Mrs Thatcher. When it was pointed out that this was a contradiction in view of Mrs Thatcher's manifest career as Prime Minister, 'the most feminine woman' was at first nonplussed; then she took refuge in a safe historical comparison: 'Well, ideally she shouldn't be there [in office], but she is an extremely exceptional woman and the exceptions will always find their way to the top. Look at Boadicea . . .'[49]

The most potent image is a visual one, that of the cartoonist Gale in the *Daily Telegraph* (the foremost newspaper of Conservative sympathies) on polling day, 11 June 1987. Mrs Thatcher is seen dressed as Boadicea, late-twentieth-century version, in a Celtic robe but with pearl necklace and stud earrings (as Thomas Heywood's seventeenth-century heroine wore the lambent pearls of her own day). As the leader urges forward her chariot towards the third-term Conservative victory – which would in fact resoundingly be hers by the next day – the huge knives set in its wheels dominate the foreground of the picture. Meanwhile sundry small male figures in chains from other political parties drag behind; even Mrs Thatcher's own recognizable jubilant supporters are tiny in stature compared to the dominant figure of the Warrior Queen.

CHAPTER EIGHTEEN

Unbecoming in a Woman?

~

Fell, from those funeral flames
A golden mist; which token is, from high gods
Of their unending glory to endure.

CHARLES DOUGHTY on the funeral pyre of Boadicea and her
daughters, *The Dawn in Britain*, 1906

'Tis no less unbecoming [in] a Woman . . . to conduct
an Army, to give a Signal to the Battle, than it is for a
Man to tease Wool, to handle the Distaff . . .

GEORGE BUCHANAN, *History of Scotland*, 1571

Boudica of the Iceni was not a savage and she was a patriotic leader; that is to answer two of the questions originally posed about her in Chapter One. A courageous widow, she led her oppressed people in an uprising against a foreign occupation, having herself – and her daughters – been foully treated at the hands of the conqueror. The details of the uprising were not pretty, as such things seldom are. At the end of it, following a last battle, Boudica met her death, most probably at her own hand and again most probably carrying her daughters with her. She is buried in an unknown grave. All this – the known or supposed facts about Boudica – took place around AD 60.

Queen Boadicea on the other hand has had a far longer and more varied history. If not all female things to all men, she has certainly been a good many of them, and recently she has also represented a good many different things to many very different women. To the sixth-century monk Gildas, for example, Boadicea, far from being a patriot, was a 'deceitful lioness' for daring to oppose her morally superior Roman rulers.[1] Falling soon after that into a long sleep of obscurity, due to the vanishing of the Classical records, Boadicea awakened to the kiss of humanist scholarship in the sixteenth century to find herself a patriot once more, and on a far grander scale than that of a mere tribal queen.

For now she was the heroic leader of the *Britons* in their resolve to recover 'their old liberty', in Camden's phrase. Most importantly, Boadicea as a woman valorous had become a prefiguration of the patriot currently on the English throne, Elizabetha Triumphans: one of those rare women lifted, according to Spenser, to 'lawful sovereignty', as opposed to all the rest of her sex, whose destiny from birth to death was 'base humility'.[2] The long fruitful inter-relationship with Boadicea with the queens regnant (or female leaders) of this country had begun.

Alas for the all-British heroine! It was not only as Camden's high-minded patriot that Boadicea would survive. The seventeenth-century Queen, in accordance with the general estimate of women at that time, veered from Fletcher's boastful venal creature at the beginning (described by her ally Caratach as 'beastly' and by the Romans as 'unnatural') to a fragile blossom, whose very voice was too soft 'to accent the rough Laws of War'.[3]

At least these very differing Warrior Queens had some kind of human character, however inappropriate to the truth. The idealized Boadiceas of eighteenth-century poetry stood for a special kind of national pride, rather than anything more personal. In the case of James Thomson, whose 'Liberty' was written around 1730, his was nostalgia for 'a stubborn isle, disputed hard and never quite subdued' by the Romans. Thomson was one of the several men of letters patronized by the 'Patriot King' movement centred round Frederick Prince of Wales. When he went on to praise Boadicea for her 'Sparkling ardent flame' of rebellion, and ended with a vision of the Goddess of Liberty, he wished to show how ill all this accorded with the times in which he lived. Cowper, half a century later, looked to the past in order to issue a hymn to the British

Empire.[4] But in both cases the woman herself had departed for that allegorical sphere where her feminine gender made her suitable for such an inspiring role, not unsuitable, as it would otherwise have done in real life.

Nor did the nineteenth-century growth of empire – and imperial values – rescue Boadicea from such an idealization, although the increase in historical novel-writing in the reign of Victoria did bring an inevitable crop of 'womanly' Boadiceas, a tribute to the sovereign if not the art. These were in keeping with that belief in the sweetness of feminine influence enunciated by Mrs Matthew Hall in her preface to *The Queens Before the Conquest* of 1854: 'Woman has thrown a bright light over the dark history of the first eleven centuries of our annals.'[5] (Although according to Victorian rules for women's conduct neither Boadicea nor Cartimandua really cast much bright light on Britain's dark first-century history.)

It was the suffragette movement first, and the Women's Movement generally, which created a demand for a new kind of heroine, an independent woman operating successfully in what was generally held to be a man's sphere. Queen Boadicea, still trailing her clouds of patriotic endeavour, fitted neatly into such a mould, just as her imagined Celtic free living made her for others an exciting figure with which to combat the perpetual encroachments of patriarchy.

Such a brief summary of the fortunes of the legendary Boadicea does not however of itself explain the persistence of the legend. For on one level these fortunes have merely echoed intriguingly the fortunes of 'women's worth', in Anne Bradstreet's eloquent phrase. The endurance of the story is another matter.

> High ride the flames, now giddy bowering wave;
> Which licks, with golden throat, the Summer woods,
> Surging to heaven; wherein ascend their spirits,
> Like unto like: whence now, immortal pure,
> They look from stars.

This is the 'timeless death' of Boadicea and her daughters, described by Charles Doughty in *The Dawn in Britain*. He recounts her story at length under the name of Boudicca – 'commonly but *mendosè* written Boadicea' – in an epic poem, full of strange imagery. It was written between 1866 and 1875, but first published in 1906. It was also reissued in 1943 when a British wartime generation read again of 'a furious scour of [British] women warriors' defying Rome: at a time when women were an integral and essential part in the defence of the nation, or in the words of a spirited 'woman warrior' of that period, 'it had to be done and women were as good at it as men'.[6]

Having taken poison, Doughty's three royal women fall upon a huge funeral pyre as the menacing Romans under Suetonius approach; soon their dead bodies are seen by the mourning Britons to 'wreathe' like holly in a herdsman's fire. The scene of the immolation is one to which Wagner might have done justice in music and setting; certainly Doughty, far more than Tennyson, whose own *Boädicea* was written roughly a decade earlier, captures that magical and mythical quality of the legend. He concludes:

> Fell, from those funeral flames
> A golden mist; which token is, from high gods
> Of their unending glory to endure.

For it is finally to her presence in the great pantheon of Valkyries, rather than to her actual historic significance (about which so little is known for certain), that the British Brünnhilde owes her own 'unending glory' or at least her enduring reputation. In order to comprehend her survival further it is time to try to catch hold of this shimmering phenomenon of the Warrior Queen.

At the heart of the matter lies the feeling, almost if not entirely universal in history, that war itself is 'conduct unbecoming' in a woman. When George Buchanan attacked female government, especially in time of war, in the late sixteenth century, he explicitly contrasted the established roles of the two sexes. ' 'Tis no less unbecoming [in] a Woman', he wrote, 'to levy Forces, to conduct an Army, to give a Signal to the Battle, than it is for a Man to tease Wool, to handle the Distaff, to Spin or Card, and to perform the other Services of the Weaker Sex.' When a woman did take part in such unnatural (to her sex) procedures, the effects were dire: for that which was reckoned 'Fortitude and Severity' in a man, was liable to turn to 'Madness and Cruelty' in a woman.[7]

It is not difficult to see why this philosophy should be widely held. 'The act of giving birth itself' has been considered throughout history to be 'profoundly incompatible with the act of dealing death'; thus wrote Nancy Huston in a 1986 symposium of 'contemporary perspectives' entitled *The Female Body in Western Culture*.[8] Biology alone – or by extension let us call it chivalry – provides an obvious explanation: if women, as the mothers of the race, need physical protection which they in turn extend to their young, then surely it is unreasonable, even unkind, to expect them to take part in war as well. From women's weaker physical strength, a more or less universal estimate, springs the concept of their tenderness, again an almost if not entirely universally held opinion; an extension of this is their timidity. (Why not be timid if physically so much weaker than a potential aggressor? It is a reasonable reaction.) And from their tenderness in one sense is derived another sense of their tenderness: woman the nurse, the nurturer, the succourer . . .

The epitaph to Pocahontas in St George's churchyard, Gravesend, on the outskirts of London, where she lies buried, is a perfect case in point: 'Gentle and humane, she was the friend of the earliest struggling English colonists whom she boldly rescued, protected and helped.' It was an early American feminist writer, Margaret Fuller, who commented on the universal appeal of the American Indian Princess: 'All men love Pocahontas for the angelic impulse of tenderness and pity that impelled her to the rescue of Smith', she wrote in *The Great Lawsuit: Man v. Woman*, first published in *The Dial*, Boston, in 1843; while women pity her for 'being thus made a main agent in the destruction of her own people'.[9] Compared to Boadicea, with those threatening knives on the wheels of her chariot, Pocahontas is a heroine who fulfils the highest expectations concerning her sex in general.

The problems of 'masculinity' in a woman – inevitable in some sense in a woman who leads in war – were argued by Helene Deutsch, one of the first four women to be analysed by Freud. *The Psychology of Women* was a comprehensive study of the female lifecycle and emotional life, which extended and modified Freud's own postulates. In it, Helene Deutsch devoted considerable discussion to what she called 'The "Active" Woman' and her 'Masculinity Complex' which 'originates in a surplus of aggressive forces that were not subjected to inhibition and that lack the possibility of an outlet such as is open to man. For this reason the masculine woman is also the aggressive woman.' This view stretches back at least as far as the wild, untamed and basically anarchic conception of the female in Athenian drama, at a time when woman's physical nature was itself thought to be unstable (based on the demands of her reproductive system).[10]

Although *The Psychology of Women* was published in 1944 (in the United States whither Helene Deutsch had fled in 1933), time and political events have not diminished the strong perceived connection between 'masculinity' – activity – in a woman and an 'aggression' felt by many to be unsuitable in one of her sex.

It is the leading role upon the stage which is felt to be unnatural in a woman, as opposed to any role. Many men all through history have after all been content to accept and even approve the ambitions of Fulvia, wife to Antony, as described by Plutarch: 'her desire was to govern those who governed or to command a commander-in-chief'. Cleopatra the dominatrix (and the seducer) is another matter. Boadicea herself may have acted the Fulvia before the death of her husband Prasutagus: we cannot know, *pace* Judy Grahn's freewheeling lesbian Celt. When women have been compelled by circumstances to take a dominating role, they are expected to surrender it gracefully afterwards; the 'natural' behaviour is that of Spenser's Britomart, the chaste warrior-maid who finally dropped her shield when her purpose was fulfilled and became 'a gentle courteous Dame'. As for the unnatural Amazons whom Britomart subdued, 'that liberty' being removed from them, which they as women had wrongfully usurped, they were returned to 'men's subjection'.[11]

The strong contention of many theorists of the Women's Movement that war itself is the product of aggressive *masculine* values, and might even be eliminated if 'the whole wide world' were under 'a woman's hand' (one of the Sibylline prophecies linked to Cleopatra), meshes of course with these more primitive feelings.[12] *Spare Rib*'s denunciation of Mrs Thatcher following the Falklands War for promoting such values will be recalled, but the point is inclined to emerge whenever women, outraged by the depredations of war, manage to find a voice.

Militarism versus Feminism was written in 1915, the anguished product of feminist pacifism in response to the first terrible months of carnage in the First World War.[13] It was in effect a plea for internationalism – the Hague Women's Peace Conference of that year – in the cause of peace. The three authors, Mary Sargent Florence, Catherine E. Marshall and C. K. Ogden, argued not only that war was man's creation (as opposed to woman's) but also that man used war as a weapon in order to keep the other sex in perpetual subjection, since in time of war he was the manifest ruler. Catherine Marshall in particular, a prime mover behind the setting up of the conference, referred to the 'deep horror of war' which had entered into the soul of the organized women's movement, adding her belief that 'women's experience as mothers and heads of households' had given them 'just the outlook on human affairs' which was needed in such a process of international and creative reconstruction. (This is the argument which Mrs Thatcher, following the Falklands War, stood on its head by announcing that it was just her practical feminine abilities as a homemaker which had enabled her to keep going in the direction of military affairs.)

'But if woman climbed up to the clearer air above the battlefield', wrote Catherine Marshall in 1915, 'and cried aloud in her anguish to her sisters afar off: "These things must not be, they shall never be again!", would man indeed say, "Down with her!" Would he not allow her prerogative? Would he not even wish to climb up, too?' Once again, the experience of women sixty or seventy years later protesting at Greenham Common against nuclear weapons in the cause of peace does not suggest that man necessarily allows woman her prerogative in this respect. Nor does it propose that all men (any more than all women) wish to climb up to the clearer air above the battlefield.

Nevertheless the sheer appalling magnitude of the disaster to humankind inherent in any actual use of nuclear weapons suggests an interesting possibility. John Keegan, at the end of *The Mask of Command* (1987), a study in heroic leadership, calls for a new 'Post-heroic leadership'; he points out that the old inspiring 'heroic' leader, at the forefront of the battle itself, has been rendered obsolete and even dangerous by the advent of nuclear weapons. 'Today the best must find convictions to play the hero no more'; leaders should now be chosen for 'intellectuality' and the capacity for making decisions.[14] Women might now make more suitable political leaders than men (being strong enough *not* to press the button), provided of course that the conventional view of woman the peacemaker is accepted.

Certainly for many feminists the connection between women and peace remains 'some sort of "given"' – the phrase is that of the more sceptical Lynne Segal. As Petra Kelly for example wrote in 1984 in *Fighting for Hope*: 'Woman must lead the efforts in education for peace awareness, because only she can . . . go back to her womb, her roots, her natural rhythms, her inner search for harmony and peace . . .' Woman's pacific nature can however only be taken as some sort of given so long as any outstanding woman who does not seem to suffer from conspicuously peaceful inclinations is treated as an honorary male. According to this argument, which has a circular quality, Tomyris, issuing her plea to Cyrus of Persia, 'Rule your own people, and try to bear the sight of me ruling mine', is acting in accordance with her true feminist nature, whereas the same Queen Tomyris who had Cyrus put bloodily to death was acting as a man.[15] In the absence of an all-female-ruled state (with all-female-ruled neighbours) the thesis must remain unproved. But the importance of the argument from the point of view of a study of Warrior Queens is that it represents the meeting point of visionary feminism and its direct opposite: war is an unnatural occupation for a woman.

We return to the question of motherhood, at the source of this unease. The idea of female dominion, that authority posed in childhood from which happy infants must one day escape for the sake of their own maturity, is surely also at the source of the implicit threat posed by the notion of the Warrior Queen. Many percipient women writers and activists have drawn attention to this phenomenon, from Margaret Fuller in 1843 who wrote, 'Man is of Woman born and her face bends over him in infancy with an expression he can never quite forget', to Gloria Steinem in 1987 who suggested that part of the antagonism towards Mrs Thatcher 'may be because, in a deep sense, we fear women having power in the world because we associate that with childhood'.[16]

Dorothy Dinnerstein, in a classic of feminist psychological analysis first published in the United States in 1976, drew attention to woman's primary role in infant care as being responsible for early memories of her domination. For while woman continues to be the parent who is the 'first [remembered] boss' in most societies in the world, her relationship to other adults will be unfavourably affected by these memories. 'The right to be straightforwardly bossy – the right to exercise will head-on . . . – cannot reside as comfortably in a woman as a man', wrote Dorothy Dinnerstein.[17]

That this is true at least in some measure is indicated most recently by the innumerable references to Mrs Thatcher as 'Nanny', one famed for her 'bossiness'. (The equivalent words used for a male prime minister might be 'autocrat' and 'authoritativeness'.) It is therefore fascinating to observe the ways in which the Warrior Queens in history have felt their way to a solution to the problem. At the same time, these solutions, universally adopted, also do suggest that there was (and is) such a universal problem.

Adopting the role of an honorary male has been only one among the expedients employed by the Warrior Queens with instinctive or calculated cunning, a quality which they have certainly needed in order to survive in what has always been realistically a man's world. It has however been one of the most successful – to act the King of Kartli as Tamara did, the Catholic King of Spain like Isabella, a mighty prince like Elizabeth I, *rex noster* of Hungary like Maria Theresa. The frequency with which the Tomboy Syndrome is found in accounts of the childhood of a given Warrior Queen testifies to the same deliberate process. The type of Camilla of the Volsci ('her girl's hands had never been trained to Minerva's distaff') occurs again and again, be it in the young Catherine the Great who never cared to play with girlish dolls, or in Mrs Gandhi who employed her own dolls in creating Indian nationalist battles. The message put across is that an 'honorary boy' has been the father to the honorary man.

Fortunately adopting the role of the honorary male has not precluded the Warrior Queen from appealing at the same time to the chivalrous instincts of her compeers, the real males. Rather the reverse has been found to be the case, as the Warrior Queen, so clearly marked out by her femininity in a man's world, has employed another successful series of expedients based on this evidently singular fact. The use of masculine uniform or military accoutrements which set off rather than conceal her sex is one of them. The concept of chivalry due towards the tender woman is also responsible for the Shame Syndrome whereby the Warrior Queen is able to contrast her own willed courage with that lassitude of the supposedly courageous-by-nature males around her. Thus Queen Isabella's grandees were sufficiently 'mortified' at being outdone in zeal for the holy war by a woman to renew their energies.[18]

The Shame Syndrome can in turn lead on to the popular estimate of the Warrior Queen as being the 'Better-Man' (of the two: if a husband such as Frederick of Prussia and a wife such as Louise is involved). Or it can lead to the Warrior Queen's own protestations of being 'Only-a-Weak-Woman': 'just a lady and timid too' as the beautiful, bold Caterina Sforza declared herself, in order to show up her superior strategic skill. This pose of being 'Only-a-Weak-Woman' is of course also convenient when trouble looms: for the Warrior Queen can hope to avoid responsibility at the same time. Hence wily Zenobia was able to live on in her Roman villa, swift female dromedary forgotten, on the grounds that 'many persons', i.e. her male advisers, 'had seduced her as a simple woman' into mounting her campaigns.[19]

Since none of these poses, attitudes or expedients would be possible without the existence of the masculine audience at which they are aimed, all of them merely serve to emphasize the Appendage Syndrome. Very few outstanding women in history have achieved or been granted their place without the benefit of some kind of male-derived privilege, generally that of descent, whatever glorious destiny has ensued. This is certainly true of the Warrior Queens, up to the second half of the twentieth century.

Understandably, most Warrior Queens have underlined their claims as honorary males by emphasizing such connections. 'I am descended from mighty *men*!': Thus Boadicea boasted in her last speech, at least according to Tacitus.[20] It is a pattern – that of Elizabeth 1, 'Great Harry's daughter' still, to the end of her long reign – which has been pursued. For such emphasis, like the pose of being an honorary male, once again enables the Warrior Queen to preserve her place within the natural order. She must never forget that the original importance of the Amazon tribe to the Greeks was as a tribe of unnatural as well as belligerent females, unnatural because they were outside the control of men, and nobody's appendage.

It is however in the confrontation with the whole treacherous theme of motherhood and the unsuitability of the mother to do battle, that the wits of the Warrior Queen have had to be most subtly exercised. In this connection it is significant how many successful Warrior Queens – in the eyes of the world – have been seen to be acting on behalf of their children. Even Cleopatra drew about her the authority of co-rulership, according to Ptolemaic custom, with her infant son. This is one extension of the Appendage Syndrome which carries with it considerable allure. For there is nothing in the slightest bit unnatural about the mother's defence of her young, which can even be quite blatantly aggressive without incurring the taint of 'masculinity'. The rape of Boadicea's daughters, the imagined agonies of the mother as a result, provide after all the most sympathetic explanation for the atrocities which followed her uprising.

Otherwise a protective and appealing maternity casts a pleasant gloss on what might be the harsh picture of a Warrior Queen, as Maria Theresa realized when she sent a picture of herself with her son to General Khevenmüller with the poignant question: 'What do you think will become of this child?' No wonder the troops the next day at Linz, shown the picture and read the letter, roared their enthusiasm! The persistent legends concerning the Rani of Jhansi riding into battle with her adopted son Damodar on the horse behind her, and similar depictions, even if not accurate, belong to the same tradition as does the legend of her dying words 'Look after Damodar', spoken in a temple (although, as has been seen, a variety of independent witnesses confirm that she died in the heat of battle). In the nineteenth century Agnes Strickland summed up a widespread feeling of approval for the Mother–Warrior when she described Stephen's wife, 'good Queen Matilda', as avoiding 'all Amazonian display' by acting in the name of her son.[21]

There is another way of handling the whole matter of war and woman's maternal role in terms of war and that is – triumphantly ignoring the 'unnatural' taint – to make of it something boldly transcendent. It is this which accounts for the palpitating thrill which the idea of the Warrior Queen arouses, threat as she may be. The most successful Warrior Queens have always been those who pre-empted the obvious disadvantage of their sex in this field by turning it into an apparent advantage; and biological motherhood is after all the one role which is totally closed to man. Thus the role of the fighting mother in wartime can be put across as primordially patriotic, instead of primitively distasteful, that of Catherine the Great for example, being hailed by her troops as the 'Little Mother' of Russia. Soon the 'Mother of her Country' begins to be seen in a supernatural rather than an unnatural light: a goddess, a Mother–Goddess perhaps, and by extension a Goddess of War.

The supernatural aura of the Warrior Queen has the further effect of sanctifying the nation's struggle in its own eyes: and all through history it is always good for morale to be fighting a holy war. When Judith struck off the head of Holofernes, according to the tenth-century poem, she 'ascribed the glory of all that to the Lord of Hosts'. A kind of pious patriotism, like the stance of outraged motherhood, gives moral authority to many a Warrior Queen, enabling her to become a Holy Figurehead of her nation's aspirations, as the Arab Lady of Victory with her long hair and her lute in the forefront of the battle embodied an appeal to valour, honour and passion.[22] When the Warrior Queen is successful in her dominion, the way is paved for the idea of the golden age of the nation – especially golden since over it presides a goddess.

The type of goddess most usefully personified by a given Warrior Queen alters, of course, from country to country, age to age and civilization to civilization. If Boadicea represented some kind of Celtic war-goddess and Queen Jinga of Angola an ancient African mother–deity, then Isabella the Catholic was elevated as 'the new Eve', the madonna of her country. This is a conspiracy into which the male population enters willingly: given that circumstances have brought about some form of female rule in war, a supernatural woman leader is infinitely better than an unnatural one.

There is certainly a sexuality at the heart of this conspiracy, as the ancient goddesses, those creations of the universal subconscious, were generally creatures of human sexual feeling and appetite if of divine power and strength. Very few Warrior Queens, whatever the true facts of their lives, have been allowed to enjoy an ordinary female sexuality in terms of the propaganda spread about them. The Chaste Syndrome being marked, the

Warrior Queen has been depicted, where possible, as a virgin by her supporters (and sometimes where not possible, as in the case of Zenobia and Matilda of Tuscany): virginity too having its own connotations of sanctity. For Gibbon, for example, Zenobia's 'chastity' meant that her 'valour' surpassed that of Cleopatra: an interesting argument if not exactly a logical one. Conversely by the Voracity Syndrome, accusations of lust (so much more exciting in a queen regnant than in a king, where prodigious amours tend to be taken rather wearily for granted) are used to vicious political purpose, as in the case of Caterina Sforza, denounced by the same ruler – the Pope – who wanted her possessions for his son Cesare Borgia.[23] It was axiomatic to many of the nineteenth-century British that the Rani of Jhansi *must* be 'the Jezebel of India', just because she was an outstanding warrior leader: another interesting if once again illogical argument.

Yet the overriding impression of the personal lives of the Warrior Queens, if one may generalize for a moment, is of austerity, even puritanism, Tamara of Georgia, Isabella of Spain and the real Rani being far more typical in this respect than the admitted exceptions such as Caterina herself, Catherine the Great and Semiramis; details of the latter's life are however sufficiently veiled in time for it to be quite possible that she never actually possessed the rampant voracity which has enabled her legend to survive. That overriding impression may be put against another subtler one, to which it is most likely to be connected: there is no lack of personal ambition among these Warrior Queens, whatever the fluttering protestations which contemporary social standards may have called forth from some of them. And ambitious women have seldom so far had much time to spare to be *grandes amoureuses*, with so many more demanding problems to tax their time: preferring to bond men to them by a more ethereal kind of loyalty (in short, acting out their own version of the goddess).

Is it not just this appreciation of the Warrior Queen which continues to make her an inspiration to women as well as a source of threat and excitement to men? Whether or not woman's nature is in truth more pacific and more tender than that of the other sex, the Warrior Queen is secretly seen by women as one who has made a dazzling job of a position so seldom granted to one of her own sex. Boadicea *is* a heroine, cruel knives on her chariot notwithstanding: and it can be argued that women need heroines even more than men need heroes because their expectations of independence, fortitude and valour have generally speaking been so much lower.

So Queen Boadicea still towers above her reckless horses on the banks of the Thames. In her case the hand that once rocked the cradle now drives the chariot and shakes the spear and 'yet though overcome in hapless fight' she does so in manifest victory. Secure within her monument constructed equally of Thornycroft's bronze and history's myth, her conduct is no longer unnatural but triumphant. Her glory may be expected to endure.

Reference Notes

Bibliographical details of each book or article are given at its first point of entry (the place of publication is London unless otherwise stated). Thereafter, only a short entry is given, with a note indicating where the first full reference can be found in brackets, i.e. in Chapter Four, note 6, 'Tacitus (III–1), p. 265' refers back to Chapter Three, note 1, Tacitus, *The Annals of Imperial Rome*, translated and with an Introduction by Michael Grant (revised edn 1977 pbk).

Chapter 9: Matilda, Daughter of Peter

1 *The 'Epistolae Vagantes' of Pope Gregory VII*, edited and translated by H. E. J. Cowdrey (Oxford 1972), p. 13.

2 Dudley and Webster (1–3), p. 115.

3 Cit. Briey, Comte Renaud de, *Mathilde, Duchesse de Toscane, Comtesse de Briey, Fondatrice de l'Abbaye d'Orval (1046–1115): Une Jeanne d'Arc Italienne* (Brussels 1934), p. 50.

4 See Overmann, A., *Gräfin Mathilde von Tuscien* (Innsbruck 1895) for *Regesta* of her life pp. 123–90; also Tondelli, Leone, *Matilda di Canossa – profilo storico* (3rd edn Reggio 1969); Duff (1–21), for biographical details.

5 Vedriani and Paluda, cit. Duff (1–21), p. 77; Tondelli (IX–4), pp. 30–1.

6 Huddy (V–5), p. 104.

7 See Colucci, G., *Un nuovo poema latina dello IX secolo* (Rome 1895), pp. 132–3.

8 Villani, Giovanni, *Istorie Fiorentine*, Vol. 1 (Milan 1802), pp. 201f.

9 Tondelli (IX–4), pp. 5, 144–5; Schevill, Ferdinand, *History of Florence from the Founding of the City through the Renaissance* (New York 1961), p. 54.

10 Erra, C. A., *Memorie storico-critiche della gran contessa Matilda* (Rome

1768), p. xiii.

11   Dante, *De Monarchia*, translated by P. H. Wicksteed, Book III (1896), pp. 277–8.

12   Cit. Duff (1–21), p. 91.

13   Tondelli (IX–4), pp. 30–1.

14   Cit. Duff (1–21), p. 127.

15   Cit. Briey (IX–3), p. 53.

16   See Gregory VII, *Epistolae* (IX–1) *passim* and biographies of Matilda, esp. Briey (IX–3), Duff (1–21) and Tondelli (IX–4).

17   Briey (IX–3), p. 56.

18   Donizo's *Vita Comitissae Mathildis* – in two books of Latin verse – is the principal souce for events at Canossa (1734) BL: 12 f.6; see also the latest Italian translation by G. Marzi and V. Bellocchi (Modena 1970).

19   Gregory VII's letter in Duff (1–21), Appendix D pp. 290–1.

20   Donizo, 1, 2, v. 203 cit. Briey (IX–3), p. 127.

21   Cit. Briey (IX–3), p. 151.

22   Schenetti, Matteo, 'La vittoria de Matilde di Canossa su Arrigo IV', *Studi Matildici*, Reggio 7–9 ottobre 1972 (Modena 1978), pp. 238–9.

23   Cit. Duff (1–21), p. 204.

24   Schevill (IX–9), pp. 58f.

25   See Rough, Robert H., *The Reformist Illuminations in the Gospels of Matilda Countess of Tuscany: A Study in the Art of the Age of Gregory VII* (The Hague 1973).

26   Inscriptions given in Duff (1–21), pp. 275–6.

27   Cit. Stephan, Rt. Hon. Sir James, *Essays in Ecclesiastical Biography*, Vol. I (1907), pp. 35f.

28   *The Vision of Purgatory and Paradise* by Dante Alighieri, translated by Rev. H. F. Cary (1893), Cantos XXVIII, XIX, XXXI and XXXII, and p. 120 note 1. Tasso's *Jerusalem Delivered*, translated by Edward Fairfax, The Carisbrooke Library, Vol. VII (1890), Book XVII, p. 352.

29   Nencioni, G., *Matilde di Canossa* (Milan 1937), p. 190.

30   Tondelli (IX–4), Preface.

Chapter 10: England's Domina

1 For the Empress Maud see *Dictionary of National Biography* entry by Kate Norgate (1908–9); Onslow, the Earl of, *The Empress Maud* (1939) and Pain, Nesta, *Empress Matilda: Uncrowned Queen of England* (1978); for the period generally, Chibnall, Marjorie, *Anglo-Norman England, 1066–1166* (Oxford 1986) is the principal source.

2 *DNB* (x–1).

3 *The Works of Gildas, in Six Old English Chronicles*, edited by J. A. Giles (1878), p. 301.

4 See Dudley and Webster (1–3), p. 114.

5 Ruskin, *Mornings in Florence*, cit. Purdie, Edna, *The Story of Judith in German and English Literature* (Paris 1927).

6 *William of Malmesbury, The History of the Kings of England* . . ., Vol. III, Part 1 (The Church Historians of England 1854), p. 109.

7 *Judith*, edited by B. J. Timmer (1966), p. 7.

8 *Anglo-Saxon Poetry*, selected and translated by Professor R. K. Gordon (revised edn 1954), pp. 320–6.

9 See Chibnall (x–1), pp. 83–5.

10 Cit. Chibnall (x–1), p. 67 note 33.

11 *The Idea of a perfect Princesse, in The Life of St Margaret Queen of Scotland. With Elogiums on her children David and Mathilda Queen of England. Now englished* (Paris 1661).

12 Chibnall (x–1), p. 68.

13 *The Historia Novella by William of Malmesbury*, edited by K. R. Potter (1955), pp. 3–5.

14 See Gillingham, John, *The Angevin Empire* (1984 pbk), p. 9 for the view that Henry had Geoffrey in mind as his successor at the time of the betrothal; Chibnall (x–1), p. 85; 'no reliable evidence that he ever changed his mind about his heir'.

15 Cit. Strickland, Agnes, *Lives of the Queens of England*, Vol. 1 (reprint 1972), p. 203.

16 Gillingham (x–14), pp. 10–11.

17 *Gesta Stephani*, edited and translated from the Latin by K. R. Potter, with a new Introduction and Notes by R. H. C. Davis (Oxford 1976), p. 5; William of Malmesbury (x–6), III, Part 1, p. 389.

18 Fell, Christine, Clark, Cecily and Williams, Elizabeth, *Women in Anglo-Saxon England and the Impact of 1066* (1984), p. 170.

19 Strickland (x–15), p. 1 where the quotations are given in Latin, slightly mixed up.

20 Geoffrey of Monmouth, *Histories of the Kings of Britain*, translated by Sebastian Evans, introduction by Lucy Anne Paton (1934), p. 34.

21 See Reilly, Bernard F., *The Kingdom of León-Castilla under Queen Urraca 1109–1126* (Princeton, New Jersey 1982), especially Ch. 12, pp. 352f.

22 *DNB* (x–1); Chibnall (x–1), p. 94 note 103.

23 *Gesta Stephani* (x–17), pp. 179–84.

24 *The Anglo-Saxon Chronicle*, edited and translated by D. Whitelock, D. C. Douglas and S. I. Tucker (1961), p. 200.

25 Cit. *DNB* (x–1).

26 Strickland (x–15), p. 225 gives the various contemporary references; *Gesta Stephani* (x–17), pp. 94–5; William of Malmesbury (x–6), III, Part 1, pp. 421–2.

27 Onslow (x–1), p. 106; Pain (x–1), p. 102.

28 Cit. Pain (x–1), pp. 85, 91.

29 *Matthaei Parisiensis, Monachi Sancti Albani, Chronica Majora*, edited by H. R. Luard (part of *Rerum Britannicarum Medii Aevi Scriptores or, Chronicles and Memorials of Great Britain and Ireland During The Middle Ages*), Vol. II (1874), p. 324; *DNB* (x–1).

Chapter 11: Lion of the Caucasus

The principal sources for this chapter are W. E. D. Allen's *History of the Georgian People* (xi–3) and D. M. Lang's *The Georgians* (xi–7).

1 Professor Mariam Lordkipanidze, communication to the author; Kelly, Lawrence, *Lermontov: Tragedy in the Caucasus* (1983 pbk), p. 78.

2 'The Demon' translated by Robert Burness (Edinburgh 1918), cit. Kelly (xi–1), p. 79.

3 Thubron, Colin, *Among the Russians* (1985 pbk), p. 165; Allen, W. E. D., *A History of the Georgian People: From the Beginning down to the Russian Conquest in the Nineteenth Century* (1932), pp. 40, 103.

4 Allen (xi–3), p. 2.

5 Shota Rustaveli, *The Knight in Panther's Skin*, a free translation in prose by Katharine Vivian, Foreword by David Lang (1977), p. 39.

6 Allen (xi–3), pp. 39–40.

7 Cit. Lang, D. M., *The Georgians* (1966), pp. 112, 28.

8 Lang (xi–7), pp. 64f. gives a good summary.

9 Cit. Allen (xi–3), p. 107.

10 Cit. Maclean, Sir Fitzroy, *To Caucasus* (1976), p. 20.

11 Allen (XI–3), p. 102.

12 d'Auriac, Eugène, *Thamar Reine de Géorgie* (Paris 1892), p. 2.

13 Allen (XI–3), p. 103.

14 Lang (XI–7), p. 225.

15 Allen (XI–3), p. 106.

16 d'Auriac (XI–12), pp. 9, 12.

17 Cit. Katharine Vivian to author.

18 d'Auriac (XI–12), p. 12.

19 Allen (XI–3), p. 103.

20 *Titus Andronicus*, Act V, scene iii; *Georgian Shakespeariana*, III, edited and with a Foreword and notes by Nico Kiasashvili (seminar in Georgia to celebrate the 400th anniversary of Shakespeare's birth) (Tbilisi 1964), p. 336.

21 Rustaveli (XI–5), p. 9.

22 Rustaveli (XI–5), p. 11.

23 *The Georgian Chronicle*, cit. David Lang's Foreword to Rustaveli (XI–5), p. 18.

24 Urushadze, Venera, *Shota Rustaveli's The Knight in Panther's Skin*, translated from the Georgian, Introduction by David M. Lang (Tbilisi 1979), p. 11.

25 Bowra, C. M., *Inspiration and Poetry* (1955), pp. 45–67.

26 Allen (XI–3), p. 244: his own translation.

Chapter 12: Isabella with her Prayers

The principal modern sources consulted for this chapter are J. H. Elliot's *Imperial Spain 1469–1716* (XII–1), J. N. Hillgarth's *The Spanish Kingdoms 1250–1516* (XII–4) and F. Fernández-Armesto's joint biography of Ferdinand and Isabella (XII–2).

1 J. H. Elliott's *Imperial Spain 1469–1716* (1963), p. 65.

2 Cit. Fernández-Armesto, F., *Ferdinand and Isabella* (1975), p. 96.

3 Fernández-Armesto (XII–2), p. 149.

4 Bernáldez cit. Hillgarth, J. N., *The Spanish Kingdoms 1250–1516* (Oxford 1978), p. 451.

5 Hillgarth (XII–4), p. 483.

6 Cit. Fernández-Armesto (XII–2), p. 53.

7 See Elliott (XII–1), p. 11: 'a consideration lately gives her the benefit of the doubt'.

8 Elliott (XII–1), pp. 10, 66.

9 Walsh, W. T., *Isabella of Spain* (1931), p. 137.

10 Fernández-Armesto (XII–2), p. 83.

11 Fernández-Armesto (XII–2), p. 27.

12 Prescott, W. H., *History of the Reign of Ferdinand and Isabella the Catholic* (new and revised edition 1885), p. 592 note 3.

13 Fernández-Armesto (XII–2), p. 64.

14 Fernández-Armesto (XII–2), p. 41.

15 Prescott (XII–12), pp. 591f.; Fernández-Armesto (XII–2), pp. 106f.

16 Hillgarth (XII–4), p. 363; and see Walsh (XII–9), p. 616 note 2 writing in 1931: 'The canonization of Isabel as a saint has been urged strongly in Spain during the past year.'

17 Elliott (XII–1), p. 11.

18 Viaggio cit. Prescott (XII–12), p. 596.

19 Prescott (XII–12), p. 240.

20 Laffin, John, *Women in Battle* (1967), pp. 20–1.

21 Walsh (XII–9), p. 365.

22 Prescott (XII–12), p. 244.

23 Fernández-Armesto (XII–2), p. 90.

24 Elliott (XII–1), p. 20.

25 Prescott (XII–12), p. 240; Walsh (XII–9), p. 325.

26 Nervo, Baron de, *Isabella the Catholic: Queen of Spain. Her Life, Reign and Times 1451–1504* (1897), p. 203.

27 Nervo (XII–26), p. 195.

28 Fernández-Armesto (XII–2), p. 49; Walsh (XII–9), p. 22.

29 See Colby, Kenneth Mark, 'Gentlemen, the Queen', *Psychoanalytic Review*, Vol. 40 (1953), pp. 144–8.

30 Fernández-Armesto (XII–2), p. 136.

31 Ernst Breisach's biography of Caterina Sforza (1–21) is the basis of the ensuing pages; see also Kelly (1–7), pp. 31f.

32 See Breisach (1–21), p. 296 note 99 for sources of the various versions.

33 Fernández-Armesto (XII–2), p. 55.

34 Elliott (XII–1), p. 42; Walsh (XII–9), p. 605.

Chapter 13: Elizabetha Triumphans

1 *Harborowe* (III–9).

2 Knox (II–13), p. 12.

3 Knox (II–13), pp. 31f.

4 Knox, John, *History of the Church of Scotland*, cit. Knox (II–13), Appendix.

5 Abbott, *Aishah* (1–11), p. 176; see Phillips, James E., Jr, 'The Background of Spenser's Attitude Toward Women Rulers', *Huntington Library Quarterly* (1941–2), pp. 5f.

6 Knox (11–13), pp. xvii, 31.

7 Knox (11–13), Appendix; Phillips, (xiii–5), *passim*.

8 *Harborowe* (111–9), *passim*.

9 Ridley, Jasper, *Elizabeth I* (1987), pp. 25–6, 85.

10 Prescott, H. F. M., *Mary Tudor* (1953), p. 164.

11 Erickson, Carolly, *Bloody Mary* (1978), p. 56.

12 Waldman, Milton, *The Lady Mary: A Biography of Mary Tudor 1516–1558* (1972), p. 204.

13 Neale, J. E., *Queen Elizabeth I* (1960 pbk), p. 69.

14 Williams, Neville, *Elizabeth I: Queen of England* (1971 pbk), pp. 48, 70.

15 Fraser, Antonia, *Mary Queen of Scots* (1969), p. 163; *Jewels and Plate of Queen Elizabeth I: the Inventory of 1574*, edited by A. Jefferies Collins (1955), p. 112; Neale (xiii–13), p. 288.

16 Cit. Erickson (xiii–11), p. 388.

17 *The Works of Anne Bradstreet in Prose and Verse*, edited by John H. Ellis (Charlestown 1867), p. 361.

18 Heisch, Allison, 'Queen Elizabeth I and the Persistence of Patriarchy', *Feminist Review*, February 1980, pp. 45–55.

19 Longford, Elizabeth, *Victoria RI* (1964), p. 395.

20 Cit. Erickson (xiii–11), p. 390.

21 *The Memoirs of Sir James Melville of Halhill*, edited and with an Introduction by Gordon Donaldson (1969), p. 37.

22 Buchanan cit. Phillips, James E., Jr, 'The Woman Ruler in Spenser's *Faerie Queene*', *Huntington Library Quarterly* (1941–2), p. 220.

23 Strong, Roy, *The Cult of Elizabeth: Elizabethan Portraiture and Pageantry* (1977), p. 50.

24 Williams (xiii–14), p. 168.

25 Williams (xiii–14), p. 324.

26 Palliser, D. M., *The Age of Elizabeth: England under the Later Tudors 1547–1603* (1983), pp. 12, 107f.; Adams, Simon, 'The Queen Embattled: Elizabeth I and the Conduct of Foreign Policy' in *Queen Elizabeth I: Most Politick Princess*, edited by Simon Adams, *History Today* special issue (1984).

27 Cit. Fraser, *Mary* (xiii–15), p. 344; Palliser (xiii–26), p. 108.

28 Creighton, Rev. Mandell, *Queen Elizabeth* (1896), p. 179.

29 Nichols, John (ed.), *Bibliotheca Topographica Britannica*, 2 vols

(1780–90), Vol. 1, Appendix vii pp. 525–6.

30 Williams (XIII–14), p. 290.

31 Williams (XIII–14), pp. 279, 347.

32 See Strong, *Cult* (XIII–23), *passim*; most recently Strong, Roy, *Gloriana: The Portraits of Queen Elizabeth I* (1987).

33 Strong, *Cult* (XIII–23), p. 47.

34 *Jewels* (XIII–15), p. 112; Williams (XIII–14), pp. 350–1.

35 Dunlop, Ian, *Palaces and Progresses of Elizabeth I* (1962), p. 85; Williams (XIII–14), p. 250.

36 Chambers, Anne, *Granuaile: The Life and Times of Grace O'Malley, c. 1530–1603* (Dublin 1983 pbk), Ch. VI, pp. 127f.

37 Dunlop (XIII–35), p. 32; cit. Erickson (XIII–11), p. 276.

38 *Henry VI Part III*, Act I, scene iv.

39 Savile, Henry, *The Ende of Nero and the beginning of Galba. Fower bookes of the histories of Cornelius Tacitus. The life of Agricola* (1591), Preface.

40 Dudley and Webster (1–3), p. 115; *Polydore Vergil's English History*, Vol. 1, edited by Sir Henry Ellis (1846), pp. 17, 70–2.

41 *The Chronicles of Scotland*, compiled by Hector Boëce, translated into Scots by John Bellenden 1531, edited by R. W. Chambers and Edith Batho, Vol. 1 (Edinburgh 1938), pp. 141–5.

42 Holinshed (v–27), 1, pp. 43–8.

43 Ubaldini, *Donne* (1–5).

44 Ubaldini, 'Fatti' (1–5).

45 *Camden's Britannia*, Introduction by Stuart Piggott (1971 facsimile), pp. 311, 347, 366; Dudley and Webster (1–3), pp. 117, 156 note 10.

46 Spenser (11–5), Vol. 1, p. 297.

47 Spenser (11–5), Vol. 11, p. 199.

48 Williams (XIII–14), pp. 307, 311; Camden (XIII–45), p. 10.

49 'Elizabetha Triumphans' in Nichols, John, *The Progresses, and Public Processions, of Queen Elizabeth . . .*, Vol. 11 (1788), p. 22.

50 This account is based on Christy, Miller, 'Queen Elizabeth's Visit to Tilbury in 1588', *English Historical Review* (1919), pp. 43–61; Mattingly, Garrett, *The Defeat of the Spanish Armada* (1959), pp. 290–7; also *The Queenes visiting of the Campe at Tilburie with her entertainement there*, BL c. 18 l. 2 (64) (1588); 'Elizabetha Triumphans' (XIII–49); Ridley (XIII–9), p. 285 and note.

51 Calendar of State Papers Domestic 1581–90, p. 516; Neale (XIII–13), p. 301.

52 See Barker, Felix, 'If Parma had Landed', *History Today* (May 1988),

p. 40. Recent research dismisses Arden Hall as the Queen's residence.

53 Barker (XIII–52), p. 38 questions the text because Aske reports the speech differently; but Sharp would have been closer to the Queen than Aske and, as Leicester's chaplain, closer to court circles. Letter to *The Times*, 12 May 1988.

54 CSP Domestic (XIII–51), p. 514.

55 Hacker (1–10), p. 653.

Chapter 14: Jinga at the Gates

1 Oakley, Stewart, *The Story of Sweden* (1966), p. 82.

2 Kelly (1–7), p. 86.

3 Cit. Green (11–17), p. 187.

4 Swift, *Jack Frenchman's Lamentation*, cit. Green (11–17), pp. 191, 360 note 28.

5 Blake, Robert, *Disraeli* (1966), p. 637.

6 *Bonduca* (VII–11), Act III, scene i; Fletcher, John, *Bonduca* (Malone Society reprint Oxford 1951) suggests it is 'hardly open to doubt' that the play is 'substantially Fletcher's'.

7 *Bonduca or, The British Heroine*, A Tragedy Acted at the Theatre Royal by his Majesty's Servants (1696); Price, C. A., *Henry Purcell and the London Stage* (Cambridge 1984), pp. 97, 117–25.

8 Price (XIV–7), p. 117.

9 Piggott (IV–9), p. 81; Mossiker, Frances, *Pocahontas: The Life and the Legend* (1977), pp. 43, 157, 166.

10 Piggott (IV–9), p. 136; Heywood (11–12), p. 72.

11 Petition of Women, BL E551 (14) (1649); Shepherd, Simon, *Amazons and Warrior Women: Varities of Feminism in Seventeenth-Century Drama* (Brighton 1981), pp. 87f.

12 Sammes, Aylett, *Britannia Antiqua Illustrata, or, The Antiquities of Ancient Britain*, Vol. 1 (1676), pp. 223–9.

13 *The British Princes*, An Heroick Poem Written by the Honourable Edward Howard Esq. (1669).

14 Dudley and Webster (1–3), p. 125.

15 See Piggott, Stuart, *William Stukeley: An Eighteenth-Century Antiquary* (Oxford 1950), *passim*, especially pp. 54–5 and note 1: *Lincolnshire Notes – Queries*, MS in the possession of W. A. Cragg of Threckingham, Vol. 10 (1909), pp. 177–80.

16 Piggott, *Stukeley* (XIV–15), p. 56.

17 G. E. C. (Cokayne), *The Complete Peerage* (reprint 1981), XII/1, p. 81; *The Complete Poetical Works of James Thomson*, edited by J. Logie Robertson (1908), p. 413.

18 *The Works of William Cowper*, 8 vols (1853–5), Vol. v, pp. 265–6.

19 Information supplied to the author from resident in Angola in 1987.

20 Buttinger, Joseph, *Vietnam: A Dragon Embattled*, Vol. II: *Vietname at War* (New York 1970), pp. 54–6. Karnow, Stanley, *Vietnam: A History* (New York 1983), p. 100.

21 Ladner, Joyce A., 'Racism and Tradition: Black Womanhood in Perspective' in Carroll (11–7), pp. 179–93; Diner (11–6), pp. 221–7; Laffin (XII–20), pp. 47–51.

22 Diner (11–6), pp. 223; *Spectator* (London), 29 October 1987.

23 The main sources for the life of Queen Jinga are: Birmingham, David, *Trade and Conflict in Angola: The Mbundu and their Neighbours under the Influence of the Portuguese 1483–1790* (Oxford 1966); Boxer, C. R., *Race Relations in the Portuguese Colonial Empire 1415–1825* (Oxford 1963) and *Salvador de Sá and the Struggle for Brazil and Angola 1602–1686* (1952); Chilcote, B., *Portuguese Africa* (1967); Duffy, James, *Portuguese Africa* (1959).

24 Birmingham (XIV–23), pp. 92–5.

25 Boxer, *Salvador* (XIV–23), p. 243.

26 Boxer, *Race* (XIV–23), p. 25.

27 Ogilby (1–6), II, pp. 563–5.

28 Cit. Boxer, *Race* (XIV–23), p. 29.

29 Cit. Boxer, *Race* (XIV–23), p. 30.

30 Ogilby (1–6), II, p. 563.

31 Child, Mrs, *An Appeal in Favor of that Class of Americans called Africans* (Boston 1833), p. 161.

32 Birmingham (XIV–23), p. 125.

32 Child (XIV–31), p. 161.

Chapter 15: Queen versus Monster

1 Napoleon (11–14), p. 488.

2 Napoleon (11–14), p. 326; Gluck's *Armide*: libretto by Philippe Quenault, Act v, scene v.

3 Voss, Sophie Marie Countess von, *Sixty-Nine Years at the Court of Prussia: From the recollections of the Mistress of the Household*, 2 vols (1876), Vol. II, p. 42.

4 Burke, Edmund, *Reflections on the Revolution in France . . .*, edited and with an Introduction by Conor Cruise O'Brien (1969 pbk), p. 170; *Life of General Sir Robert Wilson*, edited by Rev. Herbert Randolph, Vol. II (1862), p. 53.

5 Wilson (xv–4), p. 53; Gibbon (1–9), I, p. 302.

6 Biographies consulted for Maria Theresa and Catherine respectively are: Crankshaw, Edward, *Maria Theresa* (1971 pbk); Cronin, Vincent, *Catherine Empress of all the Russias* (1978); Gooch, G. P., *Catherine the Great and Other Studies* (1954); Troyat, Henri, *Catherine the Great* (1–16).

7 *Saint Simon at Versailles*, selected and translated by Lucy Norton. With a preface by Nancy Mitford (1985 pbk edn), p. 241.

8 Cit. Crankshaw (xv–6), p. 59, 61; *The Love Letters of Thomas Carlyle and Jane Welsh*, edited by Alexander Carlyle, 2 vols (1909), Vol. I, p. 41.

9 Crankshaw (xv–6), p. 78.

10 Crankshaw (xv–6), pp. 308f.; *c* 1749 cit. *Maria Theresia's Politisches Testament*, edited by J. Kalbrunner and C. Biener (Vienna 1959).

11 Voltaire (III–4), IX, p. 32.

12 *Memoirs of Catherine the Great*, translated by Katharine Anthony (New York 1927), p. 15.

13 *Memoirs of the Princess Daschkaw [Dashkova], Lady of Honour to Catherine II, Empress of all the Russias, Written by Herself*, edited by Mrs W. Bradford, 2 vols (1840), Vol. I, pp. 78f.

14 Catherine's *Memoirs* (xv–12), p. 266.

15 Troyat (1–16), p. 187; Gooch (xv–6), p. 95.

16 Troyat (1–16), p. 270.

17 Gooch (xv–6), p. 18; Troyat (1–16), p. 166.

18 Voltaire (III–4), IX, p. 84.

19 Voltaire (III–4), IX, *passim*, esp. pp. 51, 68.

20 Voltaire (III–4), IX, p. 84.

21 Cronin (xv–6), p. 183.

22 Wright, Constance, *Louise, Queen of Prussia* (1970), p. 47.

23 Wright (xv–22), p. 18; *Memoirs of Madame Vigée Le Brun*, translated by Lionel Strachey, 2 vols (1904), Vol. II, p. 167.

24 *The Diaries and Letters of Sir George Jackson, KCH, from the Peace of Amiens to the Battle of Talavera*, edited by Lady Jackson, 2 vols (1872), vol. I, p. 126.

25 Voss (xv–3).

26 Taack, Merete von, *Königin Luise: Eine Biographie* (Tübigen 1978), pp. 226–7; Delbrück, Hans, 'Von der Königin Luise, dem Minister v. Stein und dem deutschen Nationalgedanken', *Preussische Jahrbücher*, Vol. 136 (1909), p. 452; Maass, Joachim, *Kleist: A Biographe* (1983), pp. 88, 122, 206.

27 Kleist, Henrich von, *Penthesilea: A Tragedy*, English version by Humphrey Trevelyan (1959), Act I, scene xv.

28 Vigée Le Brun (xv–23), II, pp. 168–9.

29 Jackson (xv–24), I, pp. 153, 241; Klett, Tessa, *Königin Luise von Preussen in der Zeit der Napoleonischen Kriege* (Berlin 1937), p. 131.

30 Voss (xv–3), II, pp. 29–30.

31 Voss (xv–3), II, p. 30.

32 Napoleon (II–14), p. 425.

33 Klett (xv–29), p. 72.

34 Wright (xv–22), p. 81.

35 Krieger, Bogdan, 'Russischer Besuch am preussischen Hof vor 100 Jahren', *Deutsche Revue*, Vol. 29 (1904), p. 348.

36 Aretz, Gertrude, *Queen Louise of Prussia 1776–1810* (New York 1929), p.144.

37 Wright (xv–22), p. 141.

38 Napoleon (II–14), p. 324; Delbrück (xv–26), p. 520.

39 Hardy, Thomas, *The Dynasts: An Epic Drama* (1920), p. 155.

40 Taack (xv–26), p. 371.

41 *Mémoires et lettres inédits du Chevalier de Gentz* (Stuttgart 1841), p. 296.

42 Napoleon (II–14), p. 363; Princess Louise of Prussia (Princess Anton Radziwill), *Forty-five Years of My Life 1770–1815* (1912), p. 228.

43 Taack (xv–26), p. 371; Bailleu, Paul, *Königin Luise: Ein Lebensbild* (Berlin and Leipzig 1908), p. 199.

44 Klett (xv–29), p. 145; Leveson-Gower, Lord Granville (First Earl Granville), *Private Correspondence 1781 to 1821*, edited by Castalia Countess Granville, 2 vols (1916), Vol. II, p. 265.

45 Napoleon (II–14), pp. 367–8.

46 Bailleu (xv–43), p. 210.

47 Taack (xv–26), p. 380.

48 *Memoirs of Prince Metternich (1773–1815)*, edited by Prince Richard Metternich, Vol. II (1880), p. 144.

49 Klett (xv–29), p. 154; Bailleu, Paul, 'Königin Luise in Tilsit', *Hohenzollern Jahrbuch*, 3 Jahrgang (1899), p. 224; Aretz (xv–36), p. 214.

50 Aretz (xv–36), p. 216; Granville (xv–44), II, p. 70; Jackson (xv–24), I, p. 163; Wilson (xv–4), p. 298.

51 Granville (xv–44), II, p. 271.

52 The best account in English is in Wright (xv–22), pp. 169–178, and in German in Taack (xv–26), pp. 398f.; see also Bailleu, 'Tilsit' (xv–49).

53 I.e. Taack (xv–26), p. 405; Palmer, Alan, *Alexander I: Tsar of War and Peace* (1974), p. 141.

54 Jackson (xv–24); Wilson (xv–4), p. 310.

55 Maass (xv–26), p. 111; Richardson, Mrs Charles, *Memoirs of the private life and opinions of Louise, Queen of Prussia* (1847), p. 193.

56 Richardson (xv–55), p. 263.

57 Moffat, Mary Maxwell, *Queen Louise of Prussia* (1906), p. 308.

58 Louise of Prussia (xv–42), p. 27; Richardson (xv–55), p. 1.

59 See Bellardi, Paul, *Königin Luise, ihr Leben und ihr Andenken in Berlin* (Berlin 1893), for a description of the many kinds of memorial to Queen Louise; Treitschke, Heinrich von, 'Königin Luise' in *Historische und Politische Aufsätze*, IV (Berlin 1897), pp. 310f.: Kelly, Rev. John, *Louise of Prussia and other sketches* (1888), p. 93.

60 Richardson (xv–55), p. 291.

Chapter 16: The Valiant Rani

1 Thornycroft, Elfrida, *Bronze and Steel: The Life of Thomas Thornycroft, Sculptor and Engineer* (Shipston-on-Stour 1932), pp. 51f.

2 Tennyson, Charles, *Alfred Tennyson* (1949), p. 323; Tennyson, Alfred, *Poetical Works Including the Plays* (1953), pp. 224–6.

3 *The Letters of Queen Victoria, 2nd Series, 1862–1878*, edited by G. E. Buckle, 2 vols, Vol. II (1926), p. 119.

4 Royal Archives, Windsor Castle, Vic. Add. EI/1048.

5 Tahmankar, D. V., *The Ranee of Jhansi* (1958), p. 19.

6 Tahmankar (xvi–5), pp. 13f.

7 See the most recent biography, Lebra-Chapman, Joyce, *The Rani of Jhansi: A Study in Female Heroism in India* (Honolulu 1986), pp. 15 and note 11, 168 for a discussion of the date, Indian sources mostly reporting 19 November 1835; also Tahmankar (xvi–5), p. 23: 'about 1827'; Smyth, Brigadier the Rt. Hon. Sir John, Bt. VC MC, *The Rebellious Rani* (1966), p. 11: 'about 1828'.

8 Shastiko, Pyotri, *Nana Sahib*, translated by Savitri Shahani (New Delhi 1980), p. 25.

9 See Agnew, Vijay, *Elite Women in Indian Politics* (New Delhi 1976), p. 3; Gaur, Albertine, *Women in India* (British Library Publications 1980), *passim*, esp. pp. 2–25; Gupta, A. R., *Women in Hindu Society: A Study in Tradition and Transition* (New Delhi 2nd edn 1980), pp. 6f.; Jacobson, Doranne and Wadley, Susan S., *Women in India: Two Perspectives* (New Delhi 1977), pp. 114f.

10 Royal Archives, Windsor Castle, RA Z502/49.

11 Allen, Charles, *A Glimpse of the Burning Plain: Leaves from the Indian Journals of Charlotte Canning* (1986), p. 149; Maclagan, Michael, *'Clemency Canning': Charles John, 1st Earl Canning. Governor General and Viceroy of India, 1856–1862* (1962), p. 287.

12 Low, Ursula, *Fifty Years with John Company, From the Letters of General Sir John Low of Clatto, Fife: 1822–1858* (1936), p. 176; Russell, W. H., *My Diary in India in the year 1858/9*, 2 vols (1860), Vol. II, p. 299.

13 Bryce, James, 'British Opinion and the Indian Revolt' in *Rebellion 1857* (XVI–65), p. 303.

14 Tahmankar (XVI–5), p. 28.

15 Maclagan (XVI–11), p. 32.

16 See Sinha, Shyam Narain, *Rani Lakshmi Bai of Jhansi*, with a Foreword by Bisheshwar Prasad (Allahabad 1980), pp. 13f. for a discussion of Hindu adoption law; Maclagan (XVI–11), p. 33 note A.

17 Kaye, J. W., *A History of the Sepoy War in India 1857–1858*, 3 vols (9th edn 1880), Vol. III, p. 360.

18 Maclagan (XVI–11), p. 316.

19 *Private Letters of the Marquess of Dalhousie*, edited by J. G. A. Baird (2nd imp. Edinburgh 1911), p. 33; Sen, Surendra Nath, *1857*, with a Foreword by Maulana Abul Kalam Azad (Calcutta 1958), p. xii.

20 Tahmankar (XVI–5), pp. 37–9.

21 Tahmankar (XVI–5), p. 39.

22 Kaye (XVI–17), III, p. 362.

23 Dalhousie (XVI–19), p. 427; Diver, Maud, *Honoria Lawrence: A Fragment of Indian History* (Boston and New York 1936), p. 371.

24 Maclagan (XVI–11), p. 21.

25 Surtees, Virginia, *Charlotte Canning, Lady-in-Waiting to Queen Victoria and Wife to the First Viceroy of India 1817–1861* (1975), p. 229; See Hibbert (V–5), pp. 59–60 and 404 note 5 for the evidence re the chupatties; *The Letters of Queen Victoria, 1837–1861*, edited by A. C. Benson and Viscount Esher, 3 vols (1907), Vol. II, p. 313.

26 Tahmankar (XVI–5), p. 54.

27 Tahmankar (XVI–5), p. 67.

28 See Sen (XVI–19), pp. 273–9 for the evidence and the pros and cons of the Rani's guilt/complicity; Rice Holmes, T., *A History of the Indian Mutiny* (5th edn 1898), pp. 491f., for a characteristically British view.

29 Tahmankar (XVI–5), pp. 70f.

30 Sen (XVI–19), pp. 276; Sinha (XVI–16), p. 55.

31 Cit. Tahmankar (XVI–5), pp. 73–5; Sen (XVI–19), p. 279.

32 Sen (XVI–19), Appendix pp. 297–306 for Erskine and the Rani's letters.

33 Sen (XVI–19), p. 301.

34 Lang Cit. Hibbert (V–5), p. 378.

35 Royal Archives, Windsor Castle, RA Z502/49; Hibbert (V–5), p. 378; Clayton (VIII–9), II, p. 180.

36 Royal Archives, Windsor Castle, RA Z502/49; Smyth (XVI–7), p. 195 note 2.

37 Tahmankar (XVI–5), pp. 84 note 1, 90f.

38 Gupta, Pratul Chandra. *Nana Sahib and the Rising at Cawnpore (Oxford 1963), pp. 7, 71;* Trevelyan, G. O., *Cawnpore* (1865) for details; Fitzmaurice, Lord Edmond, *The Life of Granville George Loveson Gower, Second Earl Granville 1815–1891*, 2 vols (1905), Vol. 1, p. 253.

39 Gupta (XVI–38), p. 116.

40 See Thompson, Edward, *The Other Side of the Medal* (1925), p. 83, where it is pointed out that Forrest (XVI–49) avoids any reference to British excesses in three volumes of 1,500 pages, while the *Oxford History of India* (1919) merely writes (p. 719): 'the justly infuriated troops took a terrible vengeance'; Sen (XVI–19), p. xvi for British atrocities 'glossed over'; Tahmankar (XVI–5) p. 69 for Prof. R. C. Majumdar's point: 'very few' outside historians have 'any knowledge' of the 'massacre in cold blood' of the Indians, including women and children.

41 Roberts cit. Smyth (XVI–7), p. 54; Hare, Augustus J. C., *The Story of Two Noble Lives, being memorials of Charlotte, Countess Canning and Louisa, Marchioness of Waterford*, 3 vols (1893), Vol. II, p. 256 note 1; Maclagan (XVI–11), p. 141; Trevelyan (XVI–38), p. 359.

42 Lowe, Thomas, *Central India during the rebellion of 1857 and 1858* (1860), pp. 236–7.

43 Tahmankar (XVI—5), p. 120.

44 Lowe (XVI—42), p. 250.

45 Lowe (XVI—42), p. 233.

46 Burne, Major-General Sir Owen Tudor KCS, *Clyde and Strathnairn*, Rulers of India series (Oxford 1895), p. 116.

47 Smyth (XVI—7), p. 11.

48 Kaye (XVI—17), III, p. 362; Ballhatchet, Kenneth, *Race, Sex and Class under the Raj: Imperial Attitudes and Policies and their Critics, 1793–1905* (1980), pp. 2–5.

49 Clayton (VIII—9), II, p. 180; Forrest, G. W., Ex-Director of Records, Government of India, *A History of the Indian Mutiny*, 3 vols (1912), Vol. I, p. 282.

50 Royal Archives, Windsor Castle, Vic. Add. E1/1048.

51 Tahmankar (XVI—5), p. 130; Smyth (XVI—7), p. 135.

52 Savarkar, Barrister, *Indian War of Independence* (Calcutta 2nd edn 1930), p. 94.

53 Tahmankar (XVI—5), pp. 132, 134; Lowe (XVI—42), p. 259.

54 Lowe (XVI—42), p. 263.

55 Smyth (XVI—7), p. 148.

56 Lowe (XVI—42), p. 301; Tahmankar (XVI—5), p. 140.

57 Savarkar (XVI—52), p. 104; Royal Archives, Windsor Castle, Vic. Add. E1/1048.

58 Smyth (XVI—7), pp. 193f. summarizes the theories concerning the Rani's death and the sources.

59 Lord Canning's Notebook cit. Maclagan (XVI—11), p. 220.

60 Royal Archives, Windsor Castle, Vic. Add. E1/1070.

61 Royal Archives, Windsor Castle, Vic. Add. E1/1070; Smyth (XVI—7), p. 11.

62 Malleson, Col. G. B., CSI, *History of the Indian Mutiny 1857–1858*, 3 vols (1896), Vol. III, p. 221.

63 See Gupta (XVI—38), for the subsequent career of Nana Sahib.

64 Sinha (XVI—16), p. 102 note 11.

65 See Joshi, P. C. (ed.), *Rebellion 1857* (New Delhi 1957) for P. C. Gupta, '1857 and Hindi Literature', pp. 225f.; P. C. Joshi, 'Folk Songs on 1857' in *Rebellion 1857*, pp. 271f.

66 Joshi, 'Folk Songs' in *Rebellion 1857* (XVI—65), p. 277.

Chapter 17: Iron Ladies

1 Colville, John, *The Fringes of Power: Downing Street Diaries 1939–1955*, Vol. 1 1939–41 (1986 pbk), p. 447, 20 April 1941.

2 Warner, Marina, *The Dragon Empress: Life and Times of Tz'u-Hsi, 1835–1908, Empress Dowager of China* (1972), p. 235.

3 Thornycroft (XVI–1), pp. 56–70.

4 Gleichen, Lord Edward, *London's Open-Air Statuary* (1928), p. 97.

5 See Warner, Marina, *Monuments and Maidens: The Allegory of the Female Form* (1985), pp. 49f.

6 Trevelyan, Marie, *Britain's Greatness Foretold: The Story of Boadicea, the British Warrior-Queen* (1900), pp. xi, lv, 369.

7 See Hamilton, Cicely, *A Pageant of Great Women* (1910); *Edy: Recollections of Edith Craig*, edited by Eleanor Adlard (1949), pp. 38–44; Holledge, Julie, *Innocent Flowers: Women in the Edwardian Theatre* (1981), pp. 69–71.

8 *The Dinner Party* (1979) Catalogue, Diehard Productions and Judy Chicago.

9 Grahn, Judy, 'The Queen of Bulldikery', *Chrysalis*, 1980.

10 Milton (IV–32), p. 60.

11 Piggott (IV–9), p. 136.

12 Cit. Grant (III–11), pp. 184–5.

13 Reynolds, Robert, *Boadicea: A Tragedy of War* (New York 1941), p. 201; Treece, Henry, *Red Queen, White Queen* (1958), p. 24; Warner, Marina, *Imaginary Women*, Channel Four Television, 13 July 1986.

14 De Gaulle (1–13), pp. 13–14; Kleist (XV–27), Act 1, scene xv.

15 Ferraro, Geraldine A. with Francke, Linda Bird, *My Story* (New York 1986), pp. 261f., 273, 314.

16 Seneviratne, Maureen, *Sirimavo Bandaranaike: The World's First Woman Prime Minister* (Colombo Sri Lanka 1975), p. 178.

17 Seneviratne (XVII–16), p. xiv.

18 Carras (1–21), p. 245; Moraes, Dom, *Mrs Gandhi* (1980), p. 123.

19 *Indira Gandhi, Letters to a Friend 1950–1984*, Correspondence with Dorothy Norman (1986), p. 12.

20 Shoksi, M., *India's Indira* (Bombay 1975), p. 20; Carras (1–21), pp. 47f.

21 Carras (1–21), p. 48; Shoksi (XVII–20), p. 113; Mann, Peggy, *Golda: The Life of Israel's Prime Minister* (1972); Raju, R. Sundra, *Indira Gandhi: A Short Biography* (New Delhi 1980), pp. 5, 96.

22 Moraes (XVII–18), p. 193; Norman (XVII–19), p. 20.

23 *Golda Meir Speaks Out*, edited by Marie Syrkin (1973), p. 73.

24 Mann (XVII–21), p. 231.

25 Meir, Golda, *My Life* (1976 pbk), pp. 321, 329.

26 Herzog, Major-General Chaim, *The War of Atonement October 1973* (Boston 1975), p. 282.

27 Herzog (XVII–26), p. 282.

28 Mann (XVII–21).

29 Fraser, *Cromwell* (VI–22), p. 607.

30 Mrs Thatcher's acute anxiety not to be seen to encroach upon the Queen's role has been confirmed to the author from a wide variety of sources.

31 *International Herald Tribune*, 5 November 1987.

32 *Observer*, 3 January 1988.

33 *Sunday Telegraph*, 27 July 1986; Young and Sloman (1–18), pp. 95, 52; Jardine (V–4), p. 233.

34 Cosgrave, Patrick, *Thatcher: The First Term* (1985), pp. 53, 57, 226 note 3; cartoon by Griffin, *Daily Express*, 24 June 1982.

35 Cosgrave (XVII–34), p. 226 note 3; Arnold, Bruce, *Margaret Thatcher: A Study in Power* (1984), p. 144.

36 Campbell, Beatrix, *The Iron Ladies: Why do Women Vote Tory?* (1987), p. 243.

37 Barnett, Anthony, *Iron Britannia: Why Parliament Waged its Falklands War* (1982 pbk), p. 19.

38 Barnett (XVII–37), p. 19; Cosgrave (XVII–34), pp. 209–10.

39 Wapshott and Brock (1–17), p. 251; Lord Lewis quoted in Young and Sloman (1–18), p. 119; author's conversation with John Keegan; *Sunday Telegraph*, 7 June 1987.

40 *Daily Mail*, 6 October 1987.

41 *Comus*, ll. 447–50, *The Poetical Works of John Milton*, edited by H. C. Beeching (new edn 1941), p. 60; Young and Sloman (1–18), p. 142.

42 Janet Watts quoting Julian Critchley, *Observer*, 24 April 1988; Cosgrave (XVII–34), p. 4.

43 Author's conversation with a former member of Mrs Thatcher's Cabinet.

44 Castle, Barbara, *The Castle Diaries 1974–76* (1980), pp. 518, 330; *The Times*, 27 January 1988; *Evening Standard Magazine*, 5 February 1988.

45 Cosgrave (XVII–34), p. 4; *Spare Rib*, August 1982.

46 Wapshott and Brock (1–17), illustration.

47 *The Times*, 12 June 1982.

48 Harris, Kenneth, 'Margaret Thatcher Talks to the *Observer*' (April 1979); *Daily Express*, 26 July 1982.

49 *New Statesman*, 28 May 1982; *Observer*, 23 May 1982; *Woman's Own* magazine, 15 June 1985.

Chapter 18: Unbecoming in a Woman?

1 Gildas (x–3), p. 301.

2 Camden (xiii–45), p. 117; Spenser (11–5), 1, p. 297.

3 *Bonduca* (vii–11), Act 1, scene i; Howard (xiv–13).

4 Thomson (xiv–17), pp. 375–6; Clark, J. E. D., *English Society 1688–1832: Ideology, Social Structure and Political Practice during the Ancien Régime* (Cambridge 1985), pp. 179–80.

5 Hall, Mrs Matthew, *The Queens Before the Conquest*, 2 vols (1854), Vol. 1, p. iv.

6 Doughty, Charles M., *The Dawn in Britain* (1943), pp. 9, 597, 346; Air Commodore Dame Felicity (Hanbury) Peake in conversation with the author, 1986.

7 Cit. Phillips, 'Woman Ruler' (xiii–22), p. 220.

8 Huston, Nancy, 'The Matrix of War: Mothers and Heroes' in *The Female Body in Western Culture: Contemporary Perspectives*, edited by Susan Rubin Suleiman (1986), pp. 119–38.

9 Mossiker (xiv–9), p. 225; Fuller Ossoli, Margaret, *Women in the Nineteenth Century*, edited by Arthur B. Fuller (Boston 1874), p. 307.

10 Deutsch, Helene, MD, *The Psychology of Women: A Psychoanalytic Interpretation*, 2 vols (New York 1944), Vol. 1, Ch. 8, pp. 279–324; see Foley, Helene B., 'The conception of women in Athenian drama' in Foley (111–5), p. 134.

11 Plutarch (111–20), p. 280.

12 Grant (111–11), p. 84.

13 Marshall, Catherine, Ogden, C. K. and Florence, Mary Sargent, *Militarism versus Feminism*, edited by Margaret Kamester and Jo Vellacott (1987 pbk reprint), pp. 40, 47, 96, 140.

14 Keegan, John, *The Mask of Command* (New York 1987), pp. 345–6, 351.

15 Segal, Lynne, *Is the Future Female? Troubled Thoughts on Contemporary Feminism* (1987 pbk), p. 198; Kelly, Petra, *Fighting for Hope* (1984), p. 104; Herodotus (111–3), p. 123; Boccaccio (1–19), p. 104.

16 Fuller Ossoli (xviii–9), p. 307; Gloria Steinem quoted in Attallah, Naim, *Women* (1987), p. 543.

17 Dinnerstein, Dorothy, *The Rocking of the Cradle and the Ruling of the World* (1987 pbk), p. 214, 191, 28, 164, 177.

18 Prescott (XII–12), p. 240.

19 Février (VIII–2), p. 36.

20 Tacitus (III–1), p. 330.

21 Lebra-Chapman (XVI–7), p. 128; Strickland (X–15), p. 204.

22 *Anglo-Saxon Poetry* (X–8), p. 326; Abbott, 'Women' (VIII–8), p. 262.

23 Gibbon (I–9), I, p. 302; Breisach (I–21), p. 130.

Index